THE PHARISEES

BY

R. TRAVERS HERFORD

Beacon Press   Boston

PREFACE

THE Introduction in Chapter I contains most of what would naturally be included in a preface.

The present book is in no sense merely a second edition of my early book, *Pharisaism, its Aim and its Method,* 1912, but a wholly new study on the same subject. Circumstances have led me to write it and publish it sooner than I might otherwise have done ; but, as the reasons are purely personal, I need not go into them. How far the book is an advance and an improvement on the former one, I leave to the reader to judge.

Of the many writers whose work has helped me in my studies of Pharisaism, I would mention two to whom I am especially indebted—Professor J. Z. Lauterbach, of Cincinnati, and Dr. Leo Baeck, of Berlin. Of the former I have written in the introductory chapter, and will here say only that without the help of his theory I could not have written the present book at all.

My debt to Dr. Baeck is no less great though not so clearly defined. I have read and re-read several times his profound work, *Das Wesen des Judentums,* in the enlarged second edition, 1922. If I have not directly quoted passages from it, I have learned very much from it, and its influence is to be felt in many pages of my book. To both these writers I tender my deepest gratitude.

CONTENTS

Foreword

by Nahum N. Glatzer

Robert Travers Herford (1860–1950) was motivated by a deep-seated sense of justice in his study of the religion of the Pharisees. He recognized that neither the early Christian references to the Pharisees, written in a spirit of polemics, nor the account of Flavius Josephus, written for Roman readers, provided the scholar with an objective view of the movement, and that the scholars who preceded him — Julius Wellhausen, Ferdinand Weber, Adolf V. Harnack, Emil Schürer, and others — overstressed the ritualistic and legal aspects of pharisaic religious thought, ignoring in the main its piety, loving concern, and humaneness. The realization prompted him to undertake a thorough reexamination of the talmudic and midrashic writings, the original sources of the period. He wished to reconstruct the faith of the Pharisees, their endeavor to understand God's will, their thinking on revelation, divine justice, and mercy, their ethics, prayers, and devotion to the study of Torah.

His works are not an apology for Pharisaism (he reveals much critical insight into the limitations of its doctrine) nor are they a historical investigation (his assertion on the origins of the movement is open to doubt); they are rather an honest presentation of the major themes of pharisaic beliefs, an attempt at a radical correction of the fateful misreading of Pharisaism as religious formalism and the identification of its adherents with hypocrites. In a lifelong dedication to this task, he demonstrated both the openmindedness of his scholarship and the liberalism of his Christianity.

Herford was born in Manchester, England, on March 13, 1860, to a family that had for generations cultivated the Unitarian interpretation of Christianity and the tradition of dissent.[1] He dated back the lineage of his nonconformism — spiritually, if not biologically — to Nicholas Hereford, the fourteenth-century translator of the Bible and friend of John Wiclif. His early interest in Hebrew he traced back to his fascination, when still a child, with

1

the Hebrew letters of the alphabet that he detected at the head of the twenty-two sections of Psalm 119 in an illustrated family Bible. At the age of thirteen he started to learn Hebrew. At Owens College, which he attended from 1877 to 1880, he studied Classics and Semitics; from 1880 to 1883 he continued his studies at Manchester College, London, especially under James Martineau; and from 1883 to 1885, as a Hibbert Scholar in Leiden, Holland, he studied under Professor Abraham Kuenen, outstanding Biblical scholar and exponent of the freethinking, scholarly motivated trend in Dutch Protestantism. He was twenty-five when called to the ministry at the Chapel in Stand, a small community in the vicinity of Manchester.

Simultaneously, he began to publish the results of his studies in post-Biblical Judaism. Among his first essays in this field was one on the Jerusalem Talmud (*Christian Reformer,* 1886), another, "The Prophecies of the Captivity" (London, 1890), and "A Unitarian Minister's View of the Talmudic Doctrine of God" (*Jewish Quarterly Review,* 1890). In 1903 appeared his first comprehensive contribution to the study of rabbinic literature: *Christianity in Talmud and Midrash* (London, 1903), "gratefully dedicated to the memory of Abraham Kuenen." The following years Herford devoted to the preparation of a major statement in his chosen field. Originally delivered as lectures in Manchester College, Oxford, in the autumn of 1911, that statement, somewhat expanded, appeared under the title *Pharisaism, its Aim and its Method.*[2]

Herford's key to the understanding of Pharisaism is its "theory of Torah," a term which throughout his books he gives in the original Hebrew. The translation of the term by the Greek *nomos,* Law, and its equivalents in other languages was the root of a misconception, since it narrowed down the idea of Torah to its legal — and legalistic — aspects. Herford attempted to restore the full sense of this basic term. In the pharisaic schools, he argued, Torah (literally, the teaching) was not only the record of the divine as such. It was designed to deepen spiritual life and to impart a strong sense of personal responsibility (p. 72). The full meaning of Pharisaism Herford found to be expressed in Psalm 119, the same Psalm whose Hebrew lettering attracted the boy. Stiff and mechanical in structure, almost monotonous in style, it yet conveys the delight and gratitude which the Pharisees inherited from the Psalmist "who is conscious of God in the immediate present, and of his close relation to Him" (p. 291). The Torah was the means by which that communion with God was realized (p. 293).

With the same scholarly objectivity he exercised in dealing with pharisaic piety, Herford approached the conflict between the Pharisees and Jesus as one "between two fundamentally different concepts of religion." In the teachings of Jesus, "the immediate intuition of God in the individual soul and conscience" stood against the concept of the supreme authority of Torah. The conflict developed gradually, Herford thought; but once the differences were established, they could not be reconciled (p. 144).

In his analysis of the two types of faith, Herford exercised remarkable subtlety. His boundless reverence for Jesus did not prejudice his profound undertaking of pharisaic piety. It is to be regretted, however, that he did not include in his deliberation a discussion of Messianism, a theme so pivotal to the grasping of early Christianity and its contemporary Judaism.

In 1914, Herford assumed the position of librarian of Dr. William's Library in London while continuing his ministerial work in small congregations in the area. His book on Pharisaism was followed by three shorter writings: "The Effect of the Fall of Jerusalem upon the Character of the Pharisees," originally a lecture at the London Society of Hebraic Studies, given in 1917;[3] "What the World Owes to the Pharisees," the Second A. Davis Lecture in London (1919); and "The Fundamentals of Religion as Interpreted by Christianity and Rabbinical Judaism."[4]

In the summer of 1923, Herford was invited by Dr. Stephen S. Wise to deliver a course of lectures on the "Sayings of the Fathers" (*Pirke Aboth*) at the Jewish Institute of Religion in New York. These maxims of the older teachers of Israel had for a long time attracted Herford's attention, and he had translated and annotated this treatise for R. H. Charles's *Apocrypha and Pseudepigrapha of the Old Testament,* published in 1913. In his elaboration of the New York lectures,[5] he treated the *Sayings* as "a document of Pharisaism" and defined the meaning of the study of Torah — the central theme of the *Sayings* — as the "closest approach to God; it might be called the pharisaic form of the Beatific Vision" (p. 15). With this central concept in mind, he

3

interpreted the various sayings in a popular commentary, which is followed by philological and historical notes intended for the scholarly reader.

Herford's definitive work on pharisaic Judaism is the present volume, which first appeared in 1924. In the twelve years that separate this work from *Pharisaism, its Aim and its Method*, Herford gathered additional knowledge of the original sources and deepened his insight into the crucial period of both Judaism and early Christianity. He singled out two scholars as exerting an influence on his own studies: Jacob Z. Lauterbach of Cincinnati and Leo Baeck of Berlin.

Lauterbach's comprehensive essay, "The Sadducees and Pharisees"[6] clarified the transition of Jewish religious leadership from the aristocratic and conservative priestly scribes, who based their authority on the written law, to the non-priestly, popular, teachers and wise men who arose in the third century B.C. The latter disputed the monopoly of the priests and liberally expanded the connotation of the term Torah, making it the basis for new decisions as required by the needs of life. The law of the priestly Sadducees class became more and more confined to the Temple and degenerated into mere formalism, while the Torah of the pharisaic lay teachers implied evolution and growth.

Das Wesen des Judentums[7] by the distinguished liberal rabbi Leo Baeck, the book to which Herford alludes, though it does not deal specifically with the historic phenomenon of Pharisaism, is nevertheless steeped in its religious philosophy. Baeck's own treatise on Pharisaism per se appeared a year after Herford's work.[8] In it, Baeck, like Lauterbach, spoke of the Pharisees as opposing the priestly class in the name of a universal and democratic priesthood of the people, and portrayed the Synagogue, with its service of prayer and study, as open to all and as supplanting the Temple in which the priests predominated. For the first time in history, he stated, a religious *community* was formed; not a state but a congregation of faith was the social structure of Pharisaism. Constituted as a community, Judaism could survive the fall of the state. Despite the different emphases in Herford's and Baeck's dissertations, the liberal minister and the liberal rabbi had much in common. Both strove to penetrate the surface of the subject in a search of what is essential.

4

Whatever Herford learned from other scholars, in his inquiry he went his own way. His work of 1924 improves upon the one of 1912 in many respects; the new effort is more comprehensive, more accurate, more mature. On one point Herford introduced a decisive qualification. In *Pharisaism* he spoke of the particularism of which, though they cherished a vision of universalism for the future, the Pharisees could not free themselves; this he contrasted with the all-embracing universalism of Paul's Gospel. In *The Pharisees* he realized that the Jewish conception of the fatherhood of God as a certitude that could be realized consciously only through entry into the comunity of Israel is paralleled by the Christian teaching that only through faith in Jesus could men effectively become children of God. Thus "Christianity only replaced one limitation by another"; unqualified universalism was "perhaps hardly conceivable" in the early centuries of the common era. Only in recent times have Judaism and Christianity taken the position that "all human beings are God's children, Torah or no Torah, Christ or no Christ" (p. 159).

In 1925, upon reaching the age of sixty-five, Herford retired from his position as librarian and concentrated on further research and writing. There appeared three essays, *The Truth About the Pharisees*,[9] "The Separation of Christianity from Judaism,"[10] "The Influence of Judaism Upon the Jews in the Period from Hillel to Mendelssohn,"[11] and the popular book, *Judaism in the New Testament Period*.[12] After restating the teachings of the Pharisees and surveying the sects and parties in the New Testament period, Herford resumed a theme that occupied his attention in his work of 1912 (*Pharisaism*): the conflict between Jesus and the Pharisees. Jesus is presented as having "repudiated the whole system of the Halachah" (rules of guidance based on the Torah), with the conflict being between "an Idea, viz. Torah, and a Person," Jesus (pp. 205 ff.). On the other hand, Jesus' preaching of the Kingdom of God did not refer to any of the Messianic expectations current at the time; the true understanding of Jesus' particular Messianic consciousness was beyond the grasp even of the immediate disciples. Keen is Herford's observation that neither side clearly understood the position of the other, that there was no attempt at mutual explanation. Thus it came to a tragic parting of the ways. The Church, a light to the Gentiles, marched to victory over the pagan world; Israel "went forward, through the mournful and cruel centuries, along the way appointed for her with a deeper conviction of the truth committed to her" (pp. 249 f.).

In the concluding passage of the present book, Herford faces the ultimate question about the relation between Judaism and Christianity. He sees them as the two great religions which throughout history are destined to accomplish "that for which God made them two and not one" and then to "join in this service, and side by side . . . inspire the lives of His children." In this faith Herford the Christian is joined by the Jewish thinker Franz Rosenzweig who, in his *Star of Redemption* (which appeared shortly before Herford's *The Pharisees*), spoke of the two religions as standing before God as equal partners in His truth.

Through the years, Herford remained active in the Unitarian movement. He was appointed Hon. Member of the General Assembly of the Unitarian and Free Christian Churches and served (1926–1928) as secretary of the National Conference. At the meeting of the General Assembly held in Manchester in 1929, he delivered the closing address on "The Idea of the Kingdom of God." In 1936 the aged scholar declined the nomination as president of the General Assembly. In recognition of his contribution to religious thought, the University of Amsterdam conferred upon him (1932) the degree of Doctor of Divinity, *honoris causa;* in 1941 an honorary degree of Doctor of Hebrew Letters was bestowed upon him *in absentia* by the Jewish Institute of Religion in New York.

His last major book, *Talmud and Apocrypha* (1933), Herford dedicated to the Rector and the Senate of the University of Amsterdam as a token of gratitude for the honor received. The work traces the thinking of the talmudic and apocryphal writings as the two main types of teaching, both being a natural development of the Old Testament Scriptures. But, Herford postulates, although the ethical element, common to both, suggests kinship and likeness, the differences between the two bodies of thought should be recognized. The talmudic (pharisaic, rabbinic) system was not mere ethical teaching but an ethical *discipline,* a guide to the application of ethics in active, private, and communal life, while the apocryphal books were books in the modern sense:

6

expressions of the thinking of solitary individuals. Also, most of the writings in the Apocrypha, and predominantly the apocalyptic visions, were composed against the background of national calamity and disappointment at the failure of the Messianic hopes to materialize. Their authors tried to "recapture the secret of the prophetic faith which had beheld that (Messianic) future" (p. 267). Yet that ancient faith was not recovered by these men who were inspired by anxiety and whose "hope was never far from despair" (p. 268). The ancient faith was maintained and strengthened by the Pharisees and the rabbis, who overcame the mood of catastrophe and concentrated on the will of God.

This line of argument led Herford to consider the apocryphal writings as inauthentic. Though "their authors were Jews and wrote as Jews," the books were "leading away from Judaism into something which was not Judaism" (p. 264). A critical student of history may agree with the sharp distinction drawn by Herford if reference is to classical Judaism after the fall of Jerusalem in 70 A.D. In the period preceding the fall, the existence of a greater diversity of religious and intellectual trends must be assumed. This became evident especially after the writings of the Qumran, or Dead Sea sect, became known, a discovery made shortly before Herford's death.

One of the highlights of the scholar's last years was a visit paid him in 1947 by the saintly scholar Leo Baeck after the latter's liberation from a German concentration camp. "He told me of his experiences without any bitterness and was very gentle and courteous in speech and manner," Herford wrote. Baeck repeated his visit in July, 1950. Possibly the last of Herford's publications was an article on "Divine Justice and Mercy" that appeared in March, 1950. He died on November 10, 1950.

Much scholarly attention has been devoted to various aspects of Pharisaism since Herford started to publish his findings. Max Weber interpreted sociologically the nature of the pharisaic order; [13] Louis Ginzberg has dealt with the conservative versus the progressive wings within Pharisaism; [14] the sociological background of both the Pharisees and Sadducees is the subject of the two-volume work, *The Pharisees,* [15] by Louis Finkelstein, who dealt also with the (indirect) influence of the pharisaic faith on Western religious thought. A strong Hellenistic influence on the pharisaic method of Scriptural exegesis has been shown by Elias Bickerman.[16] I. F. Baer has demonstrated some interesting parallels between the teachings of the "early pious men" (Hasidim), predecessors of the Pharisees in the pre-Hellenic period, and the social laws and political rules of late classical and early Hellenic Greece.[17] Pharisaic elements in the Gospels and in Paul have been studied by I. Abrahams,[18] W. D. Davies,[19] and David Daube.[20] All the material of the period pertinent to the issue has been examined and systematically presented in the works of Joseph Klausner,[21] and by George Foot Moore in his monumental *Judaism in the First Centuries of the Christian Era.*[22]

Yet, despite these and other efforts at an honest, unbiased, historical clarification of the entire issue, the old prejudices, or at least a onesided view, still prevail in the minds of many. As long as this is the case, Herford's noble endeavor to correct a fateful "misreading of history" deserves careful consideration.

NOTES

1. On Herford's life, *see* H. McLachlan, *R. T. Herford. A Brief Sketch of His Life and Work.* Printed for private circulation, n.d.

2. London, 1912. An American edition appeared the same year.

3. Reprinted in *Menorah Journal* XLVII, New York, 1960.

4. *Hibbert Journal,* 1923.

5. *Pirke Aboth. The Tractate Fathers from the Mishnah, commonly called Sayings of the Fathers.* New York, 1925. A revised edition appeared in 1944.

6. In *Studies in Jewish Literature, issued in honor of K. Kohler,* Berlin, 1913; reprinted in Lauterbach's *Rabbinic Essays,* Cincinnati, 1951.

7. Second, enlarged edition, Berlin 1922. An English translation (*The Essence of Judaism*) was published in New York, 1948, and a new, corrected edition in New York, 1961.

8. *Die Pharisäer,* Berlin, 1927; new edition, Berlin, 1934. An English version (*The Pharisees*) was published in New York, 1947.

9. Menorah Pamphlets, No. 3, New York, 1925.

10. In *Jewish Studies in Memory of Israel Abrahams,* New York, 1927.

11. In *The Legacy of Israel,* Oxford, 1927.

12. London, 1928.

13. Appendix to his *Religionssoziologie,* III, Tübingen, 1921; English version, *Ancient Judaism,* Glencoe, Ill., 1952.

14. "The Religion of the Pharisee," lecture at Harvard Divinity School, 1920: *Students, Scholars and Saints,* Philadelphia, 1929; "The Significance of the Halachah for Jewish History," in *On Jewish Law and Lore,* Philadelphia, 1955.

15. Philadelphia, 1938.

16. *Die Makkabäer,* Berlin, 1935.

17. In *Zion: A Quarterly for Research in Jewish History* XVII, 1-4 and XVIII, 3-4, Jerusalem, 1952 and 1953.

18. *Pharisaism and the Gospels,* First and Second Series, Cambridge, 1917 and 1924.

19. *Paul and Rabbinic Judaism,* 2nd ed., London, 1955.

20. *The New Testament and Rabbinic Judaism,* London, 1956.

21. *Jesus of Nazareth, His Life, Times and Teachings,* tr., Herbert Danby, New York, 1927; *From Jesus to Paul,* tr. by Wm. F. Stinespring, New York, 1945.

22. Cambridge, Mass., 1927.

THE PHARISEES

CHAPTER I

INTRODUCTION

It is only natural that such interest as is taken by the ordinary reader in the subject of the Pharisees and Pharisaism should be limited to their appearance in the period of history which includes the rise of Christianity. If they did not form part of the background of the Gospels, few would be at any pains to learn about them. It is not generally supposed that they had, or have, any importance on their own account, that their history began long before Christianity appeared and, in principle though not in name, is going on still. The Pharisees are commonly regarded as the opponents of Jesus, the men who had reduced Judaism to such a condition that Christianity was the reaction by which the free prophetic spirit was liberated from the bondage of the Law. Historical justice is thought to be satisfied by remembering against them the stinging gibe—" Scribes and Pharisees, hypocrites." Yet, however natural this view may be, it is obviously inadequate and superficial. It takes no account of the reasons why the Pharisees were what they were, nor of the process by which they became such, nor of the fact that being what they were they have continued to order their lives by the same principles of religion and morality down to the present day. Nor does it take account of the consideration that if the Pharisees had been in their real nature and characters such as they are usually depicted, and Pharisaism the organised hypocrisy commonly supposed, such continued existence and unfailing vitality would have been impossible.

Such limitation of view vitiates most of what has been written about the Pharisees by Christian scholars. Its effect is not merely to confine the study of Pharisaism to the period covered by Josephus, the New Testament and the Apocalyptic literature, but to lead to an estimate of its importance mainly dependent on its relation to Christianity. There is, indeed, a marked difference between the older writers, such as Lightfoot and Schœttgen, and modern scholars like Schürer [1] and Bousset, in their desire to be fair to the men of whom they were writing. The older writers frankly assumed that the Pharisees really were hypocrites, chargeable with all the enormities natural to enemies of Jesus. Lightfoot and Schœttgen knew their Talmud and Midrash far more thoroughly than Schürer and Bousset know it, and they were able to throw a great deal of light upon the thought and language of the New Testament. But they seldom lost an opportunity of contrasting the Law with the Gospel, to the dire discredit of the former. The modern writers, of whom those named are among the most distinguished, do honestly try to be just to the Pharisees ; and if they had such a mastery of the Rabbinical literature as their predecessors had acquired, they might have produced a far more adequate result than they have done. At least the older writers knew where to go for information about the Pharisees, though it had not dawned on them to inquire into the deeper meaning of what they found.

It is true that the modern writers have mostly been concerned with Pharisaism as one element in a larger and more complex whole, and might justly excuse themselves from a thorough investigation into the history and theory of Pharisaism. In a book dealing with the general subject of the Judaism of the New Testament

---

[1] For a devastating exposure of Schürer's acquaintance with the Rabbinical literature, see Chwolson, *Das letzte Passamahl Christi*, 1908, Beilage I, pp. 134–43.

period, an exhaustive treatment of the Pharisees would
be out of proportion with the rest. Nevertheless, the
preliminary work for such a general history ought to
have included an independent study of Pharisaism for
itself and by itself, in order that the summary to be
given in the larger work might contain only well-
ascertained truth, and facts on which sound conclusions
could be based. Weber did make such a thorough study
of Pharisaism, founded on a very wide reading in
the Rabbinical literature. But his book, *System der
Altsynagogalen Palestinischen Theologie*, shows not the
slightest comprehension of the real nature and intention
of Pharisaism ; and the abundant material he has collected, valuable as it is to those who know how to use
it, is presented in such a way as to make his picture
hardly more than a caricature. Weber is the guide of
most Christian writers who have no first-hand knowledge
of the Rabbinical literature ; and the result is what
follows when the blind lead the blind. Weber's standpoint is that of a Christian whose theology is arranged
on the lines of a creed, and he arranges his " system "
of Jewish theology on corresponding lines, regardless, or
ignorant, of the fact that Jewish theology was not a
system and never had a creed. Even if it had, it is a
pure assumption that it would have followed lines at all
corresponding to those of any Christian creed.

Neither Weber nor Schürer nor Bousset, nor Ewald
nor Hilgenfeld, nor Wellhausen,[1] nor any others of the
many non-Jewish scholars who have written about the
Pharisees, have, as it seems to me, been able to escape
the limitation of view referred to above. All seem to
have the contrast with Christianity more or less consciously present in their minds, not realising that two

[1] Wellhausen, a great authority in other fields, puts himself
out of court by the singular remark (*Phar. und Sadd.*, p. 123) that in
regard to Pharisaism it " hier eben möglich sei das Einzelne ohne
das Ganze zu verstehen." See on this, F. Perles, *Bousset's Religion
des Judentums . . . Kritisch untersucht*, 1903, p. 8. Also Chwolson,
Das letzte Passamahl Christi, 1908, p. 68.

things cannot be rightly compared until it has first been ascertained what each of them is in itself, apart from such comparison. The Pharisees may be intrinsically inferior to the type of character appropriate to the New Testament ; but to call the New Testament as the chief witness upon the question who the Pharisees really were, is false in logic and unsound in history.

It is not too much to say that little or nothing has been contributed by the Christian scholars named to the real understanding of Pharisaism. For the most part they have taken the material furnished by (*a*) the New Testament, which is strongly anti-Pharisaic, (*b*) Josephus, who wrote in the first instance for Roman readers ignorant of Judaism, and therefore unable to control his statements, and (*c*) the Apocalyptic literature, much of which is not Pharisaic at all. By the help of these materials they have drawn what can only be called a superficial sketch, honestly intended to represent Pharisaism, but seen at once to be wrong by those who know Pharisaism from the inside.[1] This result is due in part, and perhaps a large part, to the fact that the material referred to is easily accessible to every scholar who can read Greek, while the real and only true source of information as to the Pharisees, the Rabbinical literature, is not easily accessible even to those who can read their Hebrew Bible, and is a sealed book—in spite of Weber—to those who read only Greek or their mother-tongue.

The only real contributions made hitherto to the knowledge of the principles of Pharisaism have been made by Jewish scholars, for they alone have been able to make full use of the Rabbinical literature. For the further reason also, that they, by their ancestry and training, know what Pharisaism is like from the inside, even

---

[1] A remarkable illustration of this is seen in an article by Eerdmans, " Farizeen en Sadduceen." *Theol. Tijdschrift*, 1914 (Sonderabdruck, pp. 8–9). He there, by means of a re-translation of M. Jad. iv. 6, arrives at the astonishing conclusion that Johanan b. Zaccai sided with the Sadducees ! The translation of Jad. iv. 6 which he " corrects " is not quite literal, but it gives the true meaning.

though they may not have adhered in every respect to the traditional practices and ways of thought of the Pharisees. Jost, Grätz and especially Geiger have been pioneers in explaining Pharisaism. If Christian scholars have by this time recognised that the Pharisees were not a political party but represented the strongest religious element in Judaism, it is mainly due to Geiger.[1]

His chapter on the Sadducees and Pharisees was in its time by far the best that had been written on the subject, and contains much that is valuable even now. But he did not get to the heart of the matter by discovering the real ground of difference between the Pharisees and their opponents. He discussed the various points of difference alleged by Josephus, but did not perceive, any more than Josephus had done, that one of those points was far more important than all the rest.

The merit of that discovery is due to Lauterbach, who made it known in the brilliant essay[2] which he contributed to the *Kohler Festschrift*, 1913, pp. 177–98, Lauterbach finds the point of division between the Pharisees and the Sadducees in their respective attitude to the Oral Tradition in its application to the Torah. Josephus mentioned this but laid no stress on it, and combined it with other points of difference whose importance is that of description rather than definition. The difference in regard to Oral Tradition is fundamental and far-reaching.

It gives the clue to the real explanation of who the Pharisees were, what they did and why they did it. Pharisaism becomes no longer an isolated phenomenon in Judaism, emerging from an obscure past into a disagreeable present and passing into a merited oblivion ; on the contrary it is seen to be a natural and even necessary development from the principle laid down by Ezra,

---

[1] Geiger's theory is set forth in his *Urschrift und Uebersetzumgen der Bibel*, pp. 101–58.

[2] The essay is there stated to be part of a larger work which the author then had in preparation. I have not seen the larger work, if it has already been published.

and the Pharisees take their place in a consistent historical progression, having a strongly marked character
of their own and a very definite purpose. Lauterbach
naturally did not, in one short essay, cover the whole
ground so as to show how fruitful his theory was in its
application to Pharisaism in general. But beyond any
doubt he has spoken the master-word on the subject,
and all future treatment of Pharisaism must take account
of it.

In the following pages I have fully accepted and made
use of Lauterbach's theory, and I would here express
my deep obligation to him and my grateful acknowledg-
ment of the help that I have derived from his writings.
When I wrote my former book, *Pharisaism, its Aim and
its Method*, Lauterbach's essay was not published. The
fact that I have since read and studied it will account
for the main difference between the former book and the
present one. It has enabled me, I trust, to understand
Pharisaism more thoroughly than I did before ; and
while the main position taken up in the former book is
not modified, it is now presented in fuller detail. Many
points which were obscure to me have become clear, and
in particular the whole meaning of Pharisaism as a factor
in the religious development of the human race has dis-
closed itself to a degree of which I had no conception
when I wrote the former book. I do not now, any more
then formerly, offer an Apologia for the Pharisees, not
seeing, indeed, why any Apologia is needed. I have simply
tried to present what I believe to be the real truth about
them, as the result of a somewhat intimate acquaintance
with their literature. If what I offer is the truth, I am
not responsible for the conclusions which may follow
from it. If it is not the truth, I must be content to have
done my best, and to leave the work to abler hands
than mine.

The arrangement of the present book differs from that
of the former one. I have been able to include many
topics merely touched on or omitted in the former book,
and have been able to reduce into smaller compass some

features which were perhaps unduly prominent before. Twelve years of further study have, I trust, not been without effect in enabling me to offer something more adequate than my former attempt to solve the problems of Pharisaism.

CHAPTER II

HISTORICAL ACCOUNT OF PHARISAISM

THE starting-point of any history of Pharisaism must of necessity be the work of Ezra. He marks, in the long history of the Jewish people, the opening of a new period, a new stage of development, as important as the rise of prophecy, and only less important than the work of Moses. If Moses were the real founder of the Jewish religion, giving to it the power to rise above and draw away from the religions of "the peoples round about," Ezra stood forth at a most critical period to save the Jewish religion, and with it the national life, from relapsing into decay through contact with Gentile ideas and practices.

How great he deemed the danger to be may be judged from the severity of the measures which he took to counteract it. He found the small, weak community in and around Jerusalem like sheep in the midst of wolves, surrounded by jealous and unfriendly neighbours and, what was even more dangerous, exposed to temptations towards apostasy from their religion through want of any strong conviction, any definite principle in whose defence they might be rallied. The Temple was, of course, the central institution of the national religious life, and it is possible that even thus early there were already synagogues to maintain that religious life by simpler and more individual appeal. But there was no distinct sense of an object to live for, no opening of a prospect towards a higher ideal. The national vitality was apparently ebbing away, and what Ezra did was essentially to stop that fatal process and provide for the spiritual energy of his people, an object worthy to live for and, if need were, to die for. This is what he certainly did, whether or not he were himself fully aware of the significance of his work.

There is enough, even in the scanty information contained in the book which bears his name, to show that Ezra had two main ideas, both of which he succeeded to a great extent in carrying out in practice. One was to set up a barrier between Jew and Gentile, for the protection of the Jew in living the life that he ought to live in obedience to the will of God ; and the other was to proclaim in the Torah [1] the revelation of the divine will given to Israel, and the consequent duty of every faithful Jew to conform to it. The two ideas are closely related. The Jew had a religious life to live, else he would not be a Jew. The Torah was to be his guide in living that life ; but he could not follow its guidance unless he were shielded to some extent from contact with the Gentile world, with its many temptations to apostasy. There, in fewest words, is the explanation of the work of Ezra ; and, as I am not writing the history of Ezra and his times, I do not stay to enlarge on his activity. I have secured what is needed as the starting-point for the process which in course of time produced Pharisaism.

The period which followed the time of Ezra is wrapped in obscurity, and only a few dim rays of light penetrate here and there. Somewhere in that obscurity Pharisaism had its beginning and its early history, and all that can be done is to take the help of those few rays of light and try to make out what they disclose.

Of the two main ideas of Ezra just mentioned, the first was static, the second dynamic. The separation of the Jewish community from the Gentile world was the establishment of a state of things which might be main-

---

[1] For the full meaning and implications of the word Torah, which is intentionally left untranslated throughout this book, see Chapter III, " Torah and Tradition."

tained or might be abandoned, but which, while it lasted, remained as it was. It was the condition, or so Ezra thought, on which the vitality of the Jewish people depended ; but, in and by itself, it did not create or even increase that vitality. But the proclamation of the Torah as the guide of life for the Jew was a very different matter. A guide is useless unless its guidance is understood, unless those who would obey its directions are clearly aware of what those directions are, and unless they have some means of finding an answer if they are in doubt. From the time of Ezra, accordingly, there was need of those who should interpret the Torah, and provision was made to meet that need. Ezra himself was styled the Sōphĕr, the Scribe, and the period after him is known as the period of the Sōphĕrīm. What exactly the name Sopherim was intended to convey is not quite certain. Sopher meant more than a mere writer, even a writer of the sacred books. And it is hard to suppose that it was given merely to those who counted the letters in those books. No doubt the Sopherim were concerned with writing copies of the Scriptures ; and in their desire for accuracy they very likely did, on occasion, count the letters. But they were, first and foremost, " Men of the Book," and that Book was the Sepher Torah, which it was their duty to expound and teach. It is probably in this sense that the epithet Sopher was understood of Ezra. Now it is said of him (Ezra vii. 10) that " he had set his heart to ' seek ' the law of the Lord and to do it and to teach in Israel statutes and judgments." [1] The word ' seek ' does not represent what Ezra had set his heart to do. ' Darash ' in this connection, when its object is the Torah, is not to ' seek ' but to ' interpret,' and the result of so doing was ' Midrash.' The Chronicler, who is responsible for what is called in the Old Testament the Book of Ezra, lived in a time when the meaning of ' Midrash ' was quite well known, and he used the word himself (2 Chron. xxiv. 27).

[1] כי עזרא הכין לבבו לדרש את תורת יהוה ולעשות וללמד בישראל חק ומשפט:

Ezra was the first of those who made it their business to 'interpret' the Torah ; and he did so for the purpose of "teaching in Israel statutes and judgments." What he began the Sopherim continued, and presumably that is why they were called Sopherim.

It had been, from time immemorial, the function of the priests to give religious teaching to the people as occasion required. And doubtless many, perhaps most, of the early Sopherim were priests. Yet it is worthy of note that those who " caused the people to understand " the Torah, when Ezra read it (Neh. viii. 7), included Levites, even if those named were not themselves Levites. It should be noted, however, that although the term Sopherim, in its Greek equivalent γραμματεῖς, appears often in the New Testament, it has there a professional meaning somewhat different from its original one. Or, more exactly, while the name continued in use for certain purposes, the period of the Sopherim originally so-called was admitted to have come to an end long before the New Testament times. This clearly appears, if it be allowed that the Sopherim are identical with the persons called the "Men of the Great Synagogue." For it is stated in the Mishnah (Aboth i. 2) that Simeon the Just was " of the remnants of the Great Synagogue," i.e. he was one of the last who had belonged to that body. This Simeon, according to the more probable identification, died about 270 B.C. (see my *Pirkē Aboth, ad loc.*). The Great Synagogue, or the Sopherim, therefore, died out in or about 270 B.C.

The term " the Great Synagogue " does not necessarily imply a definitely organised assembly, such as the Sanhedrin of a later time. Kuenen's famous attempt to prove that there never was such an assembly is brilliant, but beside the mark. What is implied in the term is that there was some kind of teaching authority having a continuous existence ; and that requirement is met by the fact that the Sopherim were a teaching authority, and continued to exercise that authority for nearly two centuries. They were the only religious teachers of their time, and it is not to be supposed that they taught in entire independence of each other. Some amount of consultation and, where necessary, of agreed decision, was indispensable, if there was to be any teaching at all. Moreover, ancient tradition ascribed to the Sopherim and to the Great Synagogue certain acts, decisions and declarations which can only be understood as proceeding from a body of teachers and not from an individual. The three precepts recorded in Aboth i. 1 are clearly intended as the watchwords of a collective body, and would be presumptuous if uttered merely by a single teacher. Also, there is to be found in various places in the Rabbinic literature a list, more or less complete, of Scripture texts which were ' corrected ' by the Sopherim, תקוני סופרים . Amongst other places, this list is found in Tanhuma, Beshall.,[1] and after the last of the corrections the author of the Midrash goes on : " For the men of the Great Synagogue read these verses otherwise ; and they were called Sopherim because they counted all the letters in the Torah and interpreted it." [2]

The writer of these words identifies the men of the Great Synagogue with the Sopherim in the clearest manner ; and his identification is not affected by any later scruples about admitting that the Sopherim had corrected the sacred text.

From the time of Ezra, then, down to the year 270 B.C. or thereabouts, the work of interpreting and teaching the Torah was carried on by those who, as individuals, were called Sopherim, and collectively were styled the Great Synagogue. Their teaching was necessarily based on the Torah ; and their interpretation, Midrash, was presumably a simple explanation and application of the text to the case before them, whatever that might be.

The decline and disappearance of the Sopherim, or the

---

[1] It is contained in the Jelammedenu portion, and will not be found in the Tanhuma as edited by Buber. I have used the Tanhuma printed at Lublin, 1879. The passage there occurs p. 87[b].

[2] אלא שכינו פסוקי אלו אנשי כנסת הגדולה · ולכך נקראו סופרים שהיו סופרים כל אותיות שבתורה ודורשין אות

Great Synagogue, is certainly connected in some way with the change in the political condition of the people brought about by their transference from Persian to Greek rule. Under Persian kings the Jewish community was able to order its religious life with little or no interference from without. But when Judea came under the sway of a Greek sovereign, it began to feel that powerful and varied influence which is summed up under the name of Hellenism. It is easy to see how this new influence made the simple and peaceful practice of the religious life no longer possible for the Jew. But it is not clear why the Sopherim should have failed to deal with Hellenism, still less why, as an organised body of teachers, they totally disappeared. Simeon the Just would séem to have been the last representative of the old order, and to have left no successor. But why a man so eminent, and as his epithet shows, so highly respected, should have been unable to provide for the continuance of the teaching which till then had served the needs of the people, there is nothing to show. The religious history of the Jews is a blank from the death of Simeon for nearly a century. The last ray of light before the darkness closes down is the mention of Antigonos of Socho as having been a disciple of Simeon the Just (Aboth i. 3). Nothing is known of him except his saying recorded in Aboth (*ibid.*). His Greek name is noteworthy as an indication of the presence of the new influence of Hellenism. And, if there is anything of historic substance in the story about his two disciples, found in Aboth de Rabbi Nathan (A, § 5), it points to dissensions and doubts amongst those who were or who should have been the teachers of the people.

At the end of eighty years from the death of Simeon the Just, i.e. in or about the year 196 B.C., an important step was taken in the organisation of the religious, no less than of the political life of the Jewish people, by the establishment of a great council or senate, known, perhaps from the beginning, but certainly from an early date, as the Sanhedrin, a name which represents the

Greek συνέδριον. It is referred to, as the γερουσία, in the letter attributed to Antiochus III and recorded by Josephus, Ant. xii. 3, 3 (see Lauterbach, *Midrash and Mishnah*, pp. 48, ff.). This Senate was not composed exclusively of priests, which is only natural if it were the chief council of the community for all public affairs. But, however much it may have been concerned with political questions, the Senate or Sanhedrin was the supreme authority in religious matters ; and there is now for the first time a central religious authority of which some members were laymen.

The assertion that the Sanhedrin was established at or about the date above mentioned is confirmed in a remarkable way by the statement of the Zadokite Fragment, edited by Schechter and also by Charles in his Apocr. and Pseudepigrapha II. It is there said (i. 5) : "And in the period of the wrath three hundred and ninety years after He had given them into the hand of Nebuchadnezzar King of Babylon, He visited them, and He made to spring forth from Israel and Aaron a root of His planting to inherit His land." The deportation under Nebuchadnezzar took place in 586 B.C. Three hundred and ninety years from that date brings us down to 196 B.C., the very time in which the Sanhedrin was founded. A Sanhedrin is not expressly mentioned, but the phrase used : " A root from Israel and Aaron to inherit His land " may well denote such a body, especially if it represented Israel as well as Aaron, i.e. laymen as well as priests. If there be here nothing but mere coincidence of date, the coincidence is certainly striking.

The Zadokite Fragment seems to imply (*ibid.* v. 6) that after this body had been in existence twenty years the group of dissentients whose views are set forth in the Fragment dissociated themselves from the Sanhedrin and withdrew to Damascus. This would be in 176 B.C. We may suppose, therefore, that during this period the deliberations of the Sanhedrin reflected the opinions of various groups or parties not entirely in accord with each other. Although we have no precise information as to these parties, we are not left wholly in the dark. There certainly must have been amongst its members a number who were more or less favourable to Hellenism ; and it is no less certain that there were those also who were opponents of Hellenism and defenders of what may be called the religion of Torah. The Maccabean Revolt, which broke out only a few years later, 167 B.C., affords clear proof that the conflicting opinions must have been gathering strength for many years, and they could not fail to be represented in the Sanhedrin, the chief council of the nation.

But it is possible to get a little nearer to the facts. The Mishnah, Peah ii. 6, mentions the Zūgōth, Pairs, and M. Hagg. ii. 2 gives their names, representing them to have been respectively President (Nasi) and Vice-President (Ab-beth-din) of the Sanhedrin. This they almost certainly were not, for all the evidence goes to show that the High Priest always presided in the Sanhedrin. But this fact does not deprive the statement in the Mishnah of all its value. As there was certainly from the beginning a party in the Sanhedrin opposed to Hellenism and zealous for the Torah, it goes without saying that the members of this party must have been able to consult together with a view to common action. Whether or not they organised themselves under a chosen leader, a leader or leaders there must have been ; and it lies ready to hand to connect the appearance of the Zugoth with the earliest years of the Sanhedrin. The names of the first pair were Josē ben Joēzer of Zerēdah, and Josē ben Johanan of Jerusalem. Now Jose ben Joezer was certainly living at the time of the Maccabean Revolt, and there is good reason for believing that he was one of the sixty who were treacherously murdered by Alkimus (1 Macc. vii. 10–16, Ber. R. lxv. 22, and see Grätz, G.d.J. ii. 367, 369). This took place in 162 B.C. Jose ben Joezer was, it is said (Ber. R., *ibid.*) uncle of Alkimus, and presumably an old man at the time of his death. Moreover, those who came to Alkimus are called "a company of Scribes," which in this connection certainly

means teachers and exponents of Torah. It is reasonable
therefore to suppose that Jose ben Joezer and Jose ben
Joḥanan were leaders, in the Sanhedrin, of the party
who upheld the Torah.[1]

---

[1] Jose ben Joezer was called (M. Peah ii. 7) חסיד שבכהונה
which shows that he was a Ḥasid and also a priest. It is recorded
in a Baraitha (b. Shabb. 14[b]) that יוסי בן יועזר איש צרדה ויוסי בן
'יוהנן איש ירושלים גזרו טומאה על ארץ העמים ועל כלי זכוכית וגו
Two points in connection with this statement are worth attention. The object of the decree that the land of Gentiles was unclean
was presumably to deter Jews from living there. Now the Zadokite
Fragment states that after twenty years from the foundation of
the Sanhedrin (if this be the correct interpretation), and in any
case in or about the year 176 B.C., the dissentient party of Zadokites
receded to Damascus, which was certainly in a Gentile land. Was
the decree of the two Joses (presumably a decision of the Torah
party, if not a decree of the Sanhedrin) aimed at the dissentient
Zadokites, either before or after their session ? The conjecture
seems plausible. The Baraitha above quoted is made the subject
of a discussion in the Talmud (*ibid.* 15*a*), because it conflicts with
another and somewhat precise chronological statement. When
R. Ishmael b. Josē (b. Ḥalaphta) was on his deathbed, Rabbi sent
to him the request that he would relate two or three of the things
which he had heard from his father. He stated the following :
ק"פ שנה עד שלא חרב הבית פשטה מלכות הרשעה על ישראל פ' שנה
'עד שלא חרב הבית גזרו טומאה על ארץ העמים ועל כלי זכוכית וגו
Now if the decrees here mentioned were made eighty years before
the destruction of the Temple, i.e. 10 B.C., they could not have been
made by the two Joses. The Talmud does not, so far as I can
see, solve the difficulty, and in what it does say it uses a phrase
which seems to have led Grätz astray. It says that the decrees
were made by the רבנן דשמונים שנה. Grätz, G.d.J. iii. 484,
takes this to indicate a Beth Din not otherwise known by that
name, and he identifies it with the disciples of Hillel and Shammai.
But in that case why were they not called the Beth Hillel and Beth
Shammai, as in every other case ? I take the eighty years to be
merely borrowed from the declaration of R. Ishmael ben Jose.
They are the Rabbis (whoever they may have been) who, according
to him, made their decree eighty years before the destruction of
the Temple. This leaves the original difficulty unsolved. There
seems to be something wrong with R. Ishmael's chronology, and
I suggest an emendation of it. Whatever may be referred to in
the first statement, " one hundred and eighty years before the
Temple was destroyed," that at least gives a date, viz. 110 B.C.
I suggest that the eighty years next mentioned were reckoned not

The history of the Maccabean Revolt shows further that among the defenders of the Torah there was an extreme and also a moderate party. The former were called by a special name, Ḥasidim, 'Ασσιδαῖοι. The latter had no distinctive name, as they were the majority. The Ḥasidim had no other interest in the Revolt beyond the desire to practise the religion of Torah unhindered. They only joined the forces of Judas Maccabæus when they saw that the religion of Torah could not be defended except by war. And they were the first to make overtures for peace, after the earlier victories. All who joined Judas were zealous for the Torah, beyond a doubt; but the Revolt was an attempt to secure political as well as religious freedom, as became apparent in the rise of the Maccabean chiefs to sovereignty.

We shall therefore be not far from the truth if we represent the Sanhedrin, in the years from its foundation down to the outbreak of the Maccabean Revolt, as an Assembly of priests and laymen, some of whom inclined to Hellenism while others opposed it out of loyalty to the Torah; and if we further assume that of the defenders of the Torah some were more strict than others in their view of what was required for its fulfilment. That the Sanhedrin must have claimed and exercised supreme authority in deciding religious questions goes without saying; but it is only reasonable to suppose that the upholders of Torah, who included teachers amongst their number, had their own means of defining and teaching their opinions upon matters of religious practice.

When the Maccabean Revolt had resulted in victory,

prior to the destruction of the Temple, but prior to the date just given. This would give the date 190 B.C., which brings it within the time of Jose ben Joezer, though somewhat earlier than the date arrived at above. The change in the text would be that instead of פ״שנה עד שלא חרב הבית we should read פ״שנה עד שלא פשטה מלכות וגו׳ which is easily explained from the occurrence of חרב הבית in the previous line. I know of no MS. authority for this emendation; but at least it makes the statement of R. Ishmael intelligible, and brings it into remarkable conformity with the Baraitha.

one of its most important consequences was the rise of
the leading family to sovereign power. Simeon (142–
135 B.C.) the brother of Judas and of Jonathan (162–
142 B.C.) secured the political independence of the Jewish
people, and was virtually king though he exercised his
authority only as High Priest. He was succeeded by his
son, known as John Hyrkanus (135–105 B.C.), or John
the High Priest. He also did not assume the title of
king, though in all other respects he was king. As
Schürer points out (G.d.J.V.[I] i. 213), he was the first to
put his name on the coins, a sign of the growing tendency
of the Ḥasmonean House towards kingship. These facts
are of importance for the religious no less than for the
political history of the time. For it was pointed out
above that amongst the Torah party were those, the
Ḥasidim, who had no sympathy with the political aspect
of the Maccabean Revolt, and who withdrew from all
share in its later developments so soon as religious freedom had been won. Now the name Ḥasidim, as
denoting a party, does not appear again after the Maccabean period. And of course Hellenism, after the successful defiance of Antiochus Epiphanes, was no longer
the enemy to be fought. But the former aversion to
the mingling of political ambition with maintenance of the
religion of Torah revived again as the heads of the
Ḥasmonean House tended more and more to become
princes, and were no longer content to be High Priests.
Again, therefore, there appeared a divergence between
two groups or parties in the Sanhedrin, and amongst the
people. All were now upholders of Torah ; and so long
as the Hasmonean House held the sovereign power there
was no question of disowning it. But the party most
closely associated with the government, i.e. the priestly
families and the nobility, were of necessity concerned
with political questions and were not inclined to let
their devotion to Torah restrict their freedom to work
for the political interests of what was now the kingdom.
They were unwilling to allow the claims of the Torah to
be extended beyond the written word of the Pentateuch.

They took their stand on the text of the Torah as Ezra had read it, and as the heads of the people had pledged their countrymen to obey it. They would not allow the validity of the Oral Tradition as an interpretation of the Torah whereby its authority could be extended indefinitely into every department of life. (See the fuller treatment of this view and of the opposite one in the chapter on Torah and Tradition.)

On the other hand, those who were not associated with the government, and who were in close touch with the rank and file of the people, were chiefly concerned to uphold the Torah in its purity, and to guard it from the intrusion of worldly considerations. They held that it was a divine revelation, intended for the guidance of Israel in every act of life, and claiming the obedience of every member of the nation. Moreover, they held that it was given to all Israel, and that the duty of teaching and interpreting it was the privilege not of the priests alone, but of every one, priest or layman, who had the necessary knowledge. For them, Torah took precedence of everything else, and Torah not merely as the written text of the Pentateuch, but as the divine teaching contained in the Oral Tradition and finding there its only true interpretation.

The foregoing discussion has brought us to the time of the Ḥasmonean princes ; and it was during the reign of one of these, John Hyrkanus (135–105 B.C.) that the name Pharisee almost certainly made its first appearance. Those who came to be called by that name had held the principles already set forth in regard to the Torah for some considerable time ; but in the reign of Hyrkanus they took a step which, amongst other things, led to the common use of the name Pharisee as their distinctive epithet. The full significance of this fact, or rather of the evidence upon which the statement is based, has not hitherto, so far as I know, been clearly brought out.

Hyrkanus, as High Priest and virtual king, was concerned, not merely for the extension of his power by the defeat of his enemies, but also for the internal affairs,

and especially the religious affairs of the Jewish people.
There are indications to show that he took measures to
reform the abuses which had crept in during the time
since the Maccabean Revolt, in regard to the observance
of the Torah. Josephus does not mention this in his
account of the reign of Hyrkanus; but there are some
brief references in the Talmud of whose historical worth
I know no reason to doubt. A passage (b. Kidd, 66ᵃ.)
will be given below, in connection with the rupture between
the Pharisees and the Sadducees, which shows that even
in the fourth century c.e. the Rabbis had good information
in regard to the reign of Hyrkanus.

The particular reform which concerns us at present
had reference to the payment of tithes of the produce of
the soil, as required by the Torah. Hyrkanus sent out
a sort of commission of inquiry through the country,
which found that all the farmers offered the ' terumah,'
but that in regard to the tithe and the second tithe some
gave it and others did not.[1] Hyrkanus therefore ordered
that the farmer should only make the required declaration
that he had separated the ' terumah,' and he abolished
the declaration that he had also separated the tithes
(ביטל הוידוי); at the same time he threw the responsibility of separating the tithe upon the person who bought
the produce from the farmer, which was to be considered
as דמאי open to doubt as regards tithe (גזר על הדמאי).

The object of this regulation was to provide for the
proper separation of the tithes required by the Torah, by
no means to annul it. But Hyrkanus did not leave the

---

[1] T. Sot., xiii. 10 : אף הוא גזר על הוידוי וביטל את הדמאי לפי
שֶׁשָׁלח בכל עיירות ישר' וראה שלא היו מפרישין אלא תרומה גדולה
בלבד מעשר ראשון ומעשר שני מקצתן מעשרין ומקצתן אין מעשרין אמר
תרומה עון מיתה ותרומת מעשר עון טבל והיה אדם קורא שם
לתרומה ולמעשר ונותן לכהן ומעשר שיני מחולל על המעות והשאר
מעשר ומעשר עני המוציא מחבירו עליו הראיה וגו':
I have given the text according to the Vienna MS. and the printed
editions as found in Zuckermandel. The Erfurt MS. ascribes the
above to Johanan b. Zaccai, which is absurd. The Vienna MS.
reads " Johanan the High Priest," and this is confirmed by j. Sot.
ix. 11 ; cp., j. Ma. Sh. v. 9.

matter here. He appointed inspectors to see that the tithes were properly separated ; [1] and, whether he himself took the initiative or only gave his approval to the action of others, there was formed a voluntary association of those who definitely pledged themselves to separate their tithes in accordance with Torah. It is not, so far as I know, expressly stated that this institution was founded in the reign of Hyrkanus ; but it certainly was not later, and there is no reason to place it earlier. If it had been earlier, then there would have been no need for the reforms of Hyrkanus. Why it cannot have been later will be seen presently. The members of this association called themselves חברים, ḥabērim, companions, and they pledged themselves not merely in regard to tithes but in general to maintain in their own practice the laws of clean and unclean laid down in the Torah. There were four grades of חברים, ranged one above the other in accordance with the increasing strictness of their practice. These grades are enumerated in M. Hagg. ii. 7.[2] The passage runs as follows : The garments of the " people of the land, Am-ha-aretz, are a source of uncleanness to the Pherushim ; those of the Pherushim to the eaters of ' terumah ' ; those of the eaters of terumah to the eaters of what is sacred ; those of the eaters of what is sacred

---

[1] j. Sot. ix. 11. וכימיו אין צריך לשאול על דמאי שהעמיד זוגות וגו' The word זוגות is not one which would be naturally used to describe inspectors, and the question suggests itself whether there is any connection between these זוגות and the famous pairs of teachers already mentioned (see above, p. 25 and M. Peah ii. 6). It has been thought that these latter were instituted by Hyrkanus ; which is clearly impossible, because Jose b. Joezer, one of the first pair, was murdered in the Maccabean Revolt, thirty years before the reign of Hyrkanus began. It is possible that Hyrkanus made the זוגות of his own time and later responsible for the oversight of the tithes ; but in that case we should expect to find הזוגות. It seems to me more likely that Hyrkanus appointed inspectors to act two together in each district, which would be a much more effectual precaution.

[2] בגדי עם הארץ מדרס לפרושין · בגדי פרושין מדרס לאוכלי תרומה בגדי אוכלי תרומה מדרס לקודש · בגדי קודש מדרס לחטאת · יוסף ב יועזר היה חסיד שבכהונה והיתה משפחתו מדרס לקודש וגו':

to those who use [the water of sprinkling] the sin offering. Joseph b. Joezer was a ḥasid of the priesthood, and his kerchief was a source of uncleanness to the eaters of what is sacred." This passage is full of technical terms which would need much explanation ; but what is of importance for the present purpose is that the members of the first class are called Pherushim, i.e. Pharisees.[1] The word means " separated," and the separation is obviously that between the members of the association חברים on the one hand, and the Am-ha-aretz, the people of the land, on the other. The higher grades of חברים were all within the association, marked off from each other, but all alike separated from the Am-ha-aretz.

The Pherushim as a class marked the actual line of separation, and that is clearly what their name implies. As the lowest order of חברים they would be the most numerous, because the severer tests of the higher grades would be satisfied only by a smaller and smaller number of men. The passage under consideration mentions that Jose b. Joezer, a saint, ḥasid, of the priesthood, was only in the second grade. This is the same Jose b. Joezer

---

[1] Pherushim, פרושים, is the Hebrew form. The name Pharisee has passed into the English language through the Greek φαρισαῖος or perhaps the Latin of the Vulgate, Pharisæus, which represents פרישיא Pharishaia. This is the Aramaic plural form, which would be naturally used in the common speech of the people. ' Pherushim ' presumably remained as the name used by the Pharisees themselves, when they had occasion to use it, and by them more often as signifying an abstainer than as denoting one holding the principles of Pharisaism. The original name by which the Pharisees designated themselves seems to have been חכמי ישראל, the Wise of Israel, as in the passage presently to be given from b. Kidd. 66ᵃ. That does not mean that they claimed to be the only wise members of the nation. It is used, as opposed to חכמי כהנים the wise among the priests, to indicate those who were wise, i.e. competent to interpret Torah, not being priests but laymen. The name embodies their challenge of the exclusive right of the priests to interpret Torah (see Lauterbach, *Sadducees and Pharisees*, pp. 190 et *seq*.). When the Pharisees were left as the only interpreters and teachers of Torah, they dropped the distinctive word Israel and called themselves החכמים the Wise, as may be seen on wellnigh every page of the Mishnah.

who has been mentioned above, p. 25, as one of the first pair of teachers, and leader of the Torah party in the early Sanhedrin. The mention of him in this connection does not necessarily imply that the association existed in his time, but only that he would, if he were living, be in the second grade. At the same time it is possible that something of the kind did exist in his time, on a small scale and as a private society, and that in the reign of Hyrkanus the idea of such an association was taken up and made general. But, however this may be, the point at present is, that the association is most probably to be connected with the reform of Hyrkanus. Its purpose, as already stated, was to maintain in practice the laws of clean and unclean, as well as the due payment of tithes and the like, and it stands to reason that its members would be just those who were most zealous for the Torah. Therefore, those whose principles in regard to the Torah have already been explained, the descendants of the Sopherim and the Ḥasidim would be the most eager to join the association and become חברים. They must of necessity begin with the first grade, whatever rank they might reach afterwards; and thus they all became Pherushim, Pharisees. That was the primarily distinctive name which applied to them all, and the only one of general importance. And that remained their name as distinguishing them from the Sadducees; because the latter, while quite as eager for the maintenance of levitical purity, etc., differed from those who had come to be called Pharisees in respect of their views upon the interpretation of Torah.[1]

So it came about that the Pharisees, who were chiefly important in history from their attitude towards Torah, got their name from a particular phase of their practice,

---

[1] The name Pharisee is sometimes thought to be derived from פרש meaning to interpret, but in that case their name ought to have been מפרשים, which is never specially applied to them. Moreover, this particular meaning of פרש rests on the idea of 'separating,' and thus we are led back to the explanation adopted in the text.

which marked them off, not from the Sadducees, but from
the Am-ha-aretz. And this will explain why the name
Pharisee, pharūsh, is used in a two-fold sense, either as
denoting those who held a particular theory of the interpretation of Torah, or as denoting those who practised
certain forms of abstinence in regard to food and the
like. The word פרישות, pherishuth, is regularly used in
the philosophical Hebrew of the Middle Ages to denote
abstinence, and not the general principles of the Pharisees.
(See Baḥya, Ḥoboth-ha-lebaboth, where a whole chapter
is devoted to pherishuth.) This also perhaps explains
why the Pharisees, as religious teachers, did not often
use the name in referring to themselves. True, they
were ' pherushim ' in the strict sense ; but that name
only indicated one department of their practice, and not
the broad principle which led to that practice and to
much else besides.

It was said above that the institution of the association,
of which the first grade of its members was that of the
' pherushim,' was not earlier than the reign of Hyrkanus,
and could not have been later. The reason why it could
not have been later is simply that the name ' pherushim '
is used to denote the opponents of the Sadducees in the
story of the rupture between them which will be dealt
with below. Otherwise, it might be argued that since
the statement about the four grades is found only in
the Mishnah it might be as late as the second, or even
the third, century C.E. But both Josephus and the New
Testament are evidence of the common use of the name
Pharisee at a much earlier date ; and also Rashi, in his
commentary on the passage in the Mishnah, Ḥagg. 18[b],
says that all these grades were instituted by the
Sopherim.

Finally, the explanation here given is in accordance
with the statement of Josephus (Ant. xvii. 2, 4) that in
his time the Pharisees numbered above six thousand
men. These are the actual members of the association.
The great majority of the people, who willingly recognised
their authority as religious teachers and followed their

lead, were not themselves Pharisees. Strictly speaking, in relation to the Pharisees, the majority of the people were of the Am-ha-aretz class ; but in that class there must have been all types of Jews, from those who were just not Pharisees to those who wholly disregarded the injunctions of the Torah.

Such, I believe, to have been the way in which the name Pharisee came to be attached to those religious leaders and teachers who developed the theory of the interpretation of Torah mentioned above. Their interpretation went beyond the written word of the Torah, and called in the aid of the unwritten tradition. This was the fundamental ground of difference between them and their opponents, to whom the name Sadducee was applied. But while the appearance of the name Pharisee can be dated with approximate certainty as shown above, the principles of the men who came to bear that name had been developed through a long period of time, being the result of the labours of the earlier Sopherim. And, in like manner, the name Sadducee may have been first brought into use at some definite date, perhaps much about the same time as the name Pharisee ; but the principles represented by the bearers of the name Sadducee were much older, dating from the time when conscious opposition began to be felt and expressed towards the Oral Tradition appealed to in support of the interpretation of Torah.

It will be seen, therefore, that there was no sudden divergence between the two parties, no moment at which they definitely came into being. They represent two conflicting views, slowly developed into increasing clearness, of the true meaning of Torah and of its bearing upon the national life, and they probably found some expression, even in the very early days of the Sanhedrin. The Pharisees did not revive the name of the Ḥasidim, and probably did not themselves choose the name Pharisee ; possibly they modified some of their practices, but in essentials they were the Ḥasidim over again. The Sadducees, on the other hand, were by no means a revival of the Hellenists,[1] either in fact or in principle. Yet the Sadducees were only new in so far as their policy was shaped by the successful issue of the Maccabean Revolt. If the prophets of old had denounced the rulers of their time for intriguing with foreign powers (e.g. Isa. xxxi), those rulers judged of the needs of the kingdom from the worldly, not the prophetic point of view, and no doubt had strong reasons for what they did. The Hellenists had done the same in their time, not *quâ* Hellenists, but as believing that the friendship of the Greek kings was in the best interests of the Jewish people. Similarly the Ḥasmonean rulers, and the party most closely associated with them, sought to promote the interests of the kingdom by political as well as religious methods ; and the party in question did this not *quâ* Sadducees but *quâ* rulers and associates of rulers. The two names, Pharisee and Sadducee, whatever their origin may have been, were attached to two parties whose principles were much older, and only modified in their expression by the particular circumstances of the time.

But while it is impossible to point to an exact date at which the Sadducees and the Pharisees began, except in name, to exist as distinct parties, it is possible to determine (at least with much probability) the time when the difference between them led to an open and declared separation. Both in Josephus and the Talmud an incident is described which can hardly be other than the occasion of the final breach between the Sadducees and the Pharisees. Josephus (Ant. xiii. 10, 5–6) has the following : " This prosperous state of affairs moved the Jews to envy Hyrkanus [i.e. John Hyrkanus, the High Priest] ; but they that were the worst disposed to him were the Pharisees, who are one of the sects of the Jews, as we have informed you already. These have so great

---

[1] Halevy, in his *Doroth Harishonim*, maintains that the Sadducees were identical with the Hellenists, and pours scorn, after his manner, upon Weiss, Grätz and Schürer for not sharing that opinion. See the whole section of his book which treats of the Sadducees, etc., Ic. pp. 359–502.

power over the multitude that when they say anything against the King or against the High Priest, they are presently believed. Now Hyrkanus was a disciple of theirs, and greatly beloved by them. And when he once invited them to a feast, and entertained them very kindly, when he saw them in a good humour, he began to say to them that they knew he was desirous to be a righteous man and to do all things whereby he might please God, which was the profession of the Pharisees also. However, he desired that if any observed him offending in any point and going out of the right way they would call him back and correct him. On which occasion they testified to his being entirely virtuous ; with which commendation he was well pleased ; but still there was one of his guests there, whose name was Eleazar, a man of an ill temper, and delighting in seditious practices. This man said : 'Since thou desirest to know the truth, if thou wilt be righteous in earnest, lay down the high priesthood and content thyself with the civil government of the people.' And when he [Hyrkanus] inquired why he should lay down the high priesthood, 'Because,' said he [Eleazar] 'we have heard from our elders that thy mother had been a captive in the reign of Antiochus Epiphanes.' The statement was false, and Hyrkanus was furious with him, and all the Pharisees were deeply hurt. 6. Now there was one, Jonathan, a very great friend of Hyrkanus, but of the sect of the Sadducees, whose principles are the opposite to those of the Pharisees. He said that Eleazar had, in casting that reproach against him, uttered the sentiments of all the Pharisees, and that this would become apparent if he asked them what punishment the offender deserved. So when Hyrkanus asked the Pharisees what punishment they thought he deserved (for he was sure that the insult had not been approved by them if they gave sentence according to the justice of the case) they said, ' Stripes and fetters, but that it did not seem right to inflict death for speaking evil ' ; the fact being that the Pharisees are inclined to mild punishments. Hyrkanus was very angry at this, and concluded that the man had insulted him with their approval. Jonathan especially urged him on, and so influenced him as to attach himself to the party of the Sadducees and oppose that of the Pharisees, and to annul all the decrees they had imposed on the people and to punish those who observed them. From this source arose the hatred which he and his sons met with from the people."

That is the account given by Josephus, and I have given it in full for the sake of its importance and also for the purpose of comparison with the Talmudic account. This I now give [1] from b. Kidd, 66[a]. " An incident relating to King Jannai, who went to Kochlith in the desert and captured there sixty fortresses. And on his return he made great rejoicing, and he called to all the Wise of Israel and said to them, ' Our fathers used to eat salted (herbs ?) while they were engaged in building the Temple. Let us also eat salted herbs in memory of our fathers.' And they served salted herbs upon golden tables, and they did eat. There was one there, a man of mockery, of a bad heart, a vile fellow, by name Eleazar ben Poïrah. And Eleazar ben Poïrah said to King

מעשה בינאי המלך שהלך לכוחלית שבמדבר וכיבם שם ששים כרכים [1]
ובחזרתו היה שמח שמחה גדולה וקרא לכל הכמי ישראל אמר להם
אבותינו היו אוכלים מלוחים בזמן שהיו עסוקים בבנין בית המקדש אף
אנו נאכל מלוחים זכר לאבותינו והעלו מלוחים על שולחנות של זהב
ואכלו והיה שם אחד איש לץ לב רע ובליעל ואלעזר בן פועירא שמו
ויאמר אלעזר בן פועירה לינאי המלך ינאי המלך לבם של פרושים עליך
ומה אעשה הקם להם בציץ שבין עיניך הקים להם בציע שבין עיניו היה
שם זקן אחד ויהודה בן גדידיה שמו ויאמר יהודה בן גדידיה לינאי המלך
ינאי המלך רב לך כתר מלכות הנח כתר כהונה לזרעו של אהרן שהיו
אומרים אמו נשבית במודועים ויבוקש הדבר ולא נמצא ויבדלו חכמי
ישראל בזעם ויאמר אלעזר בן פועירה לינאי המלך ינאי המלך הדיוט
שבישראל כך הוא דינו ואתה מלך וכהן גדול כך הוא דינך ומה אעשה
אם אתה שומע לעצתי רומסם ותורה מה תהא עליה הרי כרוכה ומונחת
בקרן זוית כל הרוצה ללמוד יבא וילמוד אמר רב נחמן בר יצחק מיד
נזרקה בו אפיקורסות דהוה ליה למימר תינח תורה שבכתב תורה שבעל
פה מאי מיד ותוצץ הרעה על ידי אלעזר בן פועירה ויהרגו כל חכמי
ישראל והיה העולם משתומם עד שבא שמעון ב' שטח והחזיר את
התורה ליושנה :

Jannai, 'King Jannai, the heart of the Pharisees is against thee.' 'And what shall I do?' 'Prove them by means of the gold plate which is between thine eyes.' And he proved them by means of the gold plate which was between his eyes. There was there an old man, by name Jehudah ben Gedidiah. And Jehudah ben Gedidiah said to King Jannai, 'King Jannai, enough for thee the crown of royalty; leave the crown of priesthood to the seed of Aaron.' For people said that his mother had been a captive in Modiim. And inquiry was made but no truth was found [in the report]. And the Wise of Israel withdrew in anger. And Eleazar ben Poïrah said to King Jannai, 'King Jannai, such is the treatment of a private man of Israel, and such is the treatment of thee though thou art King and High Priest.' 'And what shall I do?' 'If thou wilt hearken to my counsel, crush them.' 'And the Torah, what will become of that?' 'Lo, it is rolled up and left in a corner. Whoso wishes to learn let him come and learn.' [Rab Nahman b. Itzḥak said, 'Straightway unbelief was injected in him; for he ought to have said, 'There is no need to fear for the Written Torah; what will become of the Unwritten Torah?] [1] And straightway the evil sprouted through the act of Eleazar ben Poïrah, and they slew all the Wise of Israel and the world was desolate until Simeon ben Shetah came and restored the Torah to its former state."

There can be no doubt that the same event is referred to in both these narratives, in spite of the difference in their details. Thus there is an Eleazar in both, and he is the mischief-maker in both. Josephus says that he was one of the guests, and thus by implication a Pharisee; the Talmud does not call him a Sadducee but represents him as the adviser of the King against the Pharisees. Jonathan does not appear in the Talmud

[1] The clause in brackets is part of the text as it appears in the Talmud. It is a note by an Amora upon the story, which is resumed at the words " and the evil, etc." The difference of language in the original shows this clearly.

version ; and the part he played in persuading the King
to join the Sadducees is ascribed to Eleazar. Clearly,
therefore, the two narratives cannot be brought into
exact harmony.[1] But the question which of the two is
the more credible cannot be disposed of by giving at
once the preference to Josephus on the ground that he
is much earlier in time and by so much the nearer to
the event described. It is true that the story is cited
in the Talmud by Abaji, who lived in the fourth century
(d. c.e. 338). But, in the first place, he cited it as a
Baraitha, which means that it is not later than the
Mishnah. And, in the second place, the very remarkable
style of the Hebrew shows that it is much earlier than
the Mishnah, for its Hebrew is almost purely Biblical
and not that of the Mishnah at all.[2] It is therefore
highly probable that our passage was written within no
long time after the event which it describes.[3] How it
came to be written, whether it is a fragment of some

[1] Kohler, in *J.E.*, art. " Pharisees," says that this story is un-
historical, but he gives no reasons for his view. Whatever may
be the truth in regard to minor details, the main outlines of the
story are surely historical.

[2] In the few lines of the passage there are seven instances of the
Vav consecutive with the imperfect, a grammatical form which
does not appear in the Mishnah, but is still found in the Hebrew
text of Ben Sira (Ecclesiasticus) l. 11, 12, 16, 18, 19, 21. It is
not used consistently either in Ben Sira or in the Talmud passage,
but it is used. If the author had been a late imitator of Biblical
Hebrew, he would have been careful to make frequent use of an
idiom so characteristic of classical Hebrew. See, e.g. the version
of this same story in Jos. ben Gorion, iv. 6. The story about
Simeon the Just and Alexander in b. Joma, 69a, also does not contain an instance of Vav consecutive.

[3] As Simeon b. Shetah is mentioned, the story was written after
the recovery of the Pharisees from the persecution to which they
had been exposed as the result of the breach with the king. But
the story confuses John Hyrkanus with his son and successor,
Alexander Jannæus. This is shown partly by the fact that the
King is called Jannai, and partly by the fact that the massacre of
Pharisees, ויהרגו, was the act of Jannæus and not of Hyrkanus.
The latter is said to have contented himself with annulling the
ordinances of the Pharisees.

historical work of which all else is lost, there is nothing
to show. But there it is, bearing the marks of its
antiquity on its face.

It is equally uncertain what was the source from which
Josephus derived his version of the story. Schürer
holds that it was merely founded on popular tradition,
and not on any written authority. If this be so, then
the version in Josephus is less reliable than the Talmudic
version, on the assumption of its early date as suggested
above. All that can safely be said is that we have here
two versions of the same incident, not very far removed
in time from the date when the incident took place.
Josephus has taken the substance of the story and told
it in his own way. The author of the Baraitha com-
pressed the story into such small compass that it is only
interpreted with difficulty.

Josephus uses the name Pharisee freely throughout
the story, and evidently has no doubt that that name
is correctly applied to the party which opposed the king ;
yet he does not make any of the speakers use the name.
In the Talmud version it is used once, but then only by
Eleazar, the enemy of the Pharisees. The Talmudic
version is, of course, a Pharisaic document, and its name
for the king's opponents is חכמי ישראל, the Wise of Israel.
It is thus conceivable that the name Pharisee had not
come into general use at the time of the incident, and
that it was first applied as a nickname by the opponents
of the party. Lauterbach suggests (" Sadducees and Pharisees " in *Kohler Festschrift*, p. 196) that Eleazar may
have used another name, for which פרושים, Pharisees,
was afterwards substituted. But he inclines to think
that פרושים is right, and he finds the explanation of the
name in the separation which took place, and as merely
a synonym of נבדלים. But this can hardly be correct,
for Eleazar used the name פרושים before the separation
took place. It was only after the quarrel that they
departed, separated themselves, ויבדלו. Moreover, if
the name נבדלים was in use there was no reason for
inventing another name of precisely the same meaning.

I hold that the name Pharisee was in existence before the quarrel, presumably as that of the ḥaberim already mentioned, and that it was now applied as a term of abuse or mockery on the part of their opponents. And while it is no doubt true that the name Pharisee was thenceforth accepted in common usage as the distinctive name of the party, as is evident from the Gospels, it is remarkable that the members of that party very seldom used it when speaking of themselves.[1]

Both versions agree in making the cause of offence a challenge to the king that he should lay down the High Priesthood and content himself with the royal office. According to Josephus, the Pharisees disowned the man who had given the challenge, but secretly approved his action, and for this reason they appointed only a comparatively light punishment for him. According to the Talmud, it was one of the Pharisees themselves who gave the challenge, viz. Jehudah ben Gedidiah, who is not blamed, although his action led to the separation. But, again according to the Talmud, it was the king who had provoked the challenge, and that of set purpose. The extreme compression of the Talmud story needs some expansion if it is to be understood. The king was told by Eleazar that the hearts of the Pharisees were against him. He asked what he should do in order to obtain proof of this. Eleazar advised him to put them to the test by wearing the special mark of his office as High Priest, to see what they would say. This is curious; because it might be expected that the Pharisees would accept him as High Priest, but would object to his assumption of royalty. And perhaps that was what the king expected. The objection made, however, was to his being High Priest, on the ground that his mother had been a captive in Modiim, and that he himself was under suspicion of illegitimacy. The objection seems a weak one, and indeed proved to be unfounded. The punishment of the offender is not mentioned in the Talmud,

[1] The clearest instance I know is M. Jad. iv. 6, where Johanan b. Zaccai uses the name when speaking on behalf of his own party.

but is clearly implied, and presumably was that indicated in Josephus, viz. stripes and fetters. Punishment, deemed to be inadequate, is implied in the Talmud story, for Eleazar contrasts the condition of the private citizen so lightly punished with that of the king so grossly insulted. This was said after the Pharisees had departed in anger (or perhaps with gloomy looks, see Levy, N.H.W. s.v. זעם) ; and it is not explained why they departed, nor why they were disturbed in mind. The king, after they were gone, and when Eleazar had pointed the lesson of what had just taken place, asked him what he should do next. Eleazar advised him to crush his opponents. And what will become of the Torah, in that case ? was the king's question. A remark which shows how the position of the Pharisees as teachers of Torah was admitted. If they were crushed, who was going to carry on their work of teaching the people ? Eleazar gave a thoroughly Sadducean answer : The Torah is safely put away ; anyone who wishes to learn let him come and learn. In other words, let him come and ask the priests as had been the ancient custom, and not expect to have it brought to him according to the newer fashion of the Pharisees. The reference to the Torah is not found in the Josephus version of the story ; and whether or not the king actually alluded to it, the story as told from the Pharisaic side naturally emphasises the importance of the Torah as a factor in the case. The Amora, R. Nahman b. Itzhak, whose comment interrupts the story, noticed this. He pointed out that the real danger was in regard to the Unwritten Torah, which was the especial concern of the Pharisees. As to the Written Torah, that was in no danger ; the Sadducees, no less than the Pharisees, accepted it.

The story then concludes by saying that this was the beginning of unbelief [1] in the king, i.e. of his rejection

---

[1] The word used is אפיקורסות, the regular term in the Talmudic literature for unbelief. If אפיקורוס, " unbeliever," is not derived from ' Epicurus,' there was certainly an allusion to that name. Since Epicurus held that Gods took no heed of human ills, it was not unnatural for the Jew to apply the name Epicurus to one for whom, in practice, the divine reality did not exist.

of the Pharisaic system of Oral Tradition, that he slew all the Pharisaic teachers, and that there was no place for them and their teaching until Simeon ben Shetaḥ came and restored the Torah, i.e. the Unwritten Torah, to its old place of honour.

Finally, the date of the separation between the Pharisees and the Sadducees must, on the evidence of the story which has been examined, be placed near the end of the reign of John Hyrkanus, i.e. somewhat before 105 B.C.E.

Before tracing further the history of the Pharisees as a party, it will be well to consider the meaning of the separation between them and the Sadducees. The unity of the people which had made possible the success of the Maccabean Revolt was now definitely at an end. That unity had only been possible on the common ground of defence of the Torah as the charter of the national religion. In that defence were associated those whose chief, or indeed only, desire was for liberty to live according to the Torah, and those whose desire was as much and perhaps even more for freedom from the rule of a non-Jewish sovereign. Both desires were fulfilled, and for some years there was no divergence between their adherents. But neither party ceased to exist ; and, as the political aims of the Ḥasmonean princes became more evident with the increase of their power, the non-political, purely religious aims of the Pharisees also became more evident, supported as they were by the great majority of the people. John Hyrkanus, when he broke with the Pharisees, can have been under no misapprehension as to what he was risking ; and that may have been the reason why he delayed the rupture so long. He knew that he would no longer have the people behind him ; and though they might be of little account in his political schemes, he knew by the experience of his house what their stubborn devotion to the Torah could mean. If now the nation fell asunder again, there would be no more unity, unless by some such desperate means as had brought the people to the side of Judas Maccabæus. And another revolt would necessarily involve the ruin of the Ḥasmonean House. In point of fact there was no unity any more. Even in the war against the Romans, when Jerusalem fell, there were divided counsels amongst the leaders, though all were fighting for their lives ; and in the last desperate struggle under Bar Cocheba, though so great a man as R. Akiba espoused his cause, there were yet many who stood aloof.

From the time of the breach between the Pharisees and the Sadducees there were in the nation a non-political party whose chief concern was for religion, and a party which, while by no means indifferent to religion, combined with it the conduct of political affairs. This distinction is of importance, especially in regard to the Pharisees. They remained, so far as possible, a non-political party, standing aloof from the strife which shattered the Ḥasmonean House under the sons of Jannæus. But it would not be correct to identify the Sadducees with the political party. With the intervention of the Romans, and also through the long reign of Herod, other groups and parties formed, all more or less involved in the politics of the time, and representing often non-Jewish ideas which would be as repugnant to the Sadducees as to the Pharisees. For, after all, the Sadducees were Jews, and from their own point of view most loyal Jews. Herod the Idumean was detested by both, and the Sadducees suffered from his cruelty no less than the Pharisees. But the separation between them in the reign of John Hyrkanus was the sign that the process had already begun, of which the end could only be the final ruin of the Jewish state. It was the trial of strength between the purely religious and the political theory of Jewish national life ; and, though the political catastrophe was complete and overwhelming, the religious vitality of the nation was uninjured, as its results in later centuries abundantly show.

After what has been said it will not be necessary to describe in detail the history of the Pharisees as a separate party. The full story of the last two centuries of the

Jewish state can be read best of all in Schürer's great work. But it will be well to indicate briefly the part which the Pharisees played in those centuries.

When John Hyrkanus turned against them and allied himself with the Sadducees, he did no more, according to Josephus, than annul the ordinances that they had made for the religious conduct of life, thereby hoping to win the favour of the people through their release from irksome restrictions. But the people sided with the Pharisees, and hated their would-be deliverer,[1] and his descendants after him. Real persecution began with his son, Jannæus who made no pretence of any love for the Pharisees. Owing to his violence, many of the leaders of the Pharisees fled for safety out of the country ; and even Simeon ben Shetaḥ, the chief of them, who was brother of the queen, probably owed his life only to her secret protection. Jannæus might make overtures of reconciliation to the Pharisees, but they hated and feared him too much for that to be possible. Even apart from his cruel treatment of themselves, they could not but be offended to see a man such as he, a rough soldier and man of the world, wearing the robes and performing the duties of High Priest, as by hereditary right he continued to do. It is true that when he died they gave him a magnificent funeral. But this was at the entreaty of the queen, who had always been their friend. And it is possible to imagine a certain satisfaction in giving a pompous funeral to a man who could now do them no more harm.

If, as Josephus relates, he advised the queen Alexandra (Salome [2]) to seek the support of the Pharisees, it was

[1] See the conclusion of the passage quoted from Josephus above, p. 38.

[2] The real name of the queen was Salampsio. See Derenbourg *Essai*, p. 102 *n.* 2, where the different forms of her name are given, שלמתן, שלמינון, שלמצה, "et par erreur, שלצינן, et en deux mots, של ציון." The " erreur " is the nearest approach to the true form of all the names in the list. The name is clearly שלמצינן, a form from which all the others can easily be explained, and without which they are unintelligible. As one of Herod's daughters

advice which she was most willing to follow. During
the nine years of her reign (78–69 B.C.), the Pharisees had
the control of the government, and Simeon ben Shetah,
her brother, was, so to speak, Prime Minister. This is
not a contradiction of what was said above of the Pharisees as a non-political party ; for their influence during
the reign of Alexandra was exerted mainly on the side
of the religious life of the people, partly by strengthening
their own position as opposed to the Sadducees, and partly
by reintroducing the ordinances which John Hyrkanus
had annulled and which Jannæus had kept in abeyance.
It is said in the passage from the Talmud translated
above, that Simeon ben Shetah restored the old order ;
and that means, among other things, that he filled the
Sanhedrin with Pharisaic supporters, that the exclusive
jurisdiction of the Sadducees in criminal and civil law
was abolished, and that the Sadducean High Priests
were compelled to follow the Pharisaic views in the performance of the ritual of the Temple. It is not distinctly
said that this control of the Temple ritual was acquired
by the Pharisees in the reign of queen Alexandra ; but
there does not seem to be any later period to which its
origin can be reasonably assigned. It must be remembered that the Temple ritual, at all events at the great
festivals, was performed in the sight of vast crowds of
people, who, according to Josephus (Ant. xiii. 13, 5 and
cp. b. Succah, 48[b]) were quite ready to resent any departure
from what they believed to be the only right way of performing the ceremonies. They looked to the Pharisees as
their leaders and teachers, and would have the service
performed according to the Pharisaic order. And the

---

was afterwards called Salampsio, Σαλαμψιώ, the existence of the
name in the Ḥasmonean family is probable enough. Why Derenbourg should have been at the trouble to prove that Salampsio
is practically the same as Salome, by inserting a ' p ' before ' sio '
when he does not account for the ' sio,' is not apparent. Klausner,
ישו הנוצרי, 1922, p. 130 and note, adopts the form שלום ציון without hesitation. Chwolson (Das letzte Passamahl Christi, 1908, p. 14
n. 3) took the same view many years earlier.

Pharisees had enjoyed, during the nine years of queen Alexandra's reign, an opportunity, which they assuredly did not neglect, of enforcing their own ideas upon the priests responsible for the Temple service. It would be difficult, and perhaps even dangerous, for any High Priest to attempt a return to the older order after the Pharisees had once shown the people what they accepted as the right way.[1]

After the death of queen Alexandra, the Pharisees never again exercised so great an influence in public affairs; as they never again had so devoted a friend on the throne. The Sadducees regained some of their former power, while the Pharisees resumed their old attitude of distrust towards the reigning house and abstention from affairs of state. The quarrel between Hyrkanus and Aristobulus, the sons of Alexandra, ending in the triumph of the latter, only so far concerned them that it marked a further departure from their ideal of the national life; and its most important consequence was the intervention of the Romans, on the appeal of the disputants to Pompey (63 B.C.). It is highly significant that, besides the two rivals, there was a third party who joined in the appeal, representatives of the people who besought the Roman general to abolish the office of King and restore the ancient form of government under the High Priest (Jos. Ant. xiv. 3, 2).

The Pharisees are not named in this connection, but there can be no doubt that this last appeal was their work. It is entirely in keeping with their principles, and they were the only leaders who could possibly represent the people at large. If Simeon ben Shetah were still alive he must certainly have been concerned in this attempt to abolish the kingship, in which case he would be opposing the claims of two rivals who were both his own nephews. Pompey did not take the bold course suggested to him, a course which might have saved the

---

[1] For the unwilling compliance of the priests with the requirements of the Pharisees, see the very candid explanation given by a priest to his son, T. Joma, i. 8.

Romans a vast amount of trouble in later years. The quarrel was not settled, for Aristobulus was by no means inclined to submit to the authority of Pompey, and his rashness led to the capture of Jerusalem by the Romans after a three months' siege. The reign of Aristobulus was ended, but much more was ended by the intervention of Pompey. While he restored, at the petition of the people, the High Priesthood of Hyrkanus, he gave him no supreme power. The holder of the highest place among the Jews, whether he were the High Priest or the titular king, was henceforth a vassal of Rome, willing or unwilling. Even Herod, the ablest of all who mounted the Jewish throne in the last years of its existence, only held his position by favour of the Roman power. The independence of the Jewish state, which had lasted nearly a century, was gone for ever ; and even the Pharisees, who would feel the least regret at that loss, could hardly fail to observe that they had not got the form of government for which they had hoped, and that bad as the rule of the Hasmoneans had become, that of Herod was worse, and behind all was the possibility of far greater ills in the oncoming might of Rome.

The reign of Herod (37–4 B.C.), though of the greatest importance in the general history of the Jewish people, offers but little which specially concerns the Pharisees. Herod would have been quite capable of repeating the attempt of Antiochus Epiphanes to replace Judaism by Hellenism ; for he was no Jew, and all his inclination was towards the ways of the Roman world and its Greek culture. But he was not disposed to provoke another Maccabean Revolt, and he could see that the materials for it lay ready to hand in the power of the Pharisees over the mass of the people. He avoided an open defiance of the Pharisees, and even made a considerable show of deference to their views in such matters as the rebuilding of the Temple, which was done by priests only, in the avoidance of placing his own image on the coins and the like. Moreover, he showed favour to the leaders of the Pharisees, whose names are given by Josephus

(Ant. xv. 10. 4) as Pollio and Sameas, the Abtalion and Shemaiah (or possibly Shammai [1]) of the Mishnah.

For their sake, apparently, he refrained from punishing the Pharisees who refused to take the oath of fidelity to himself, which he required of them. But these marks of deference could not lessen the intense hatred and loathing felt towards Herod by the Pharisees and their supporters among the people. They, too, remembered what had made their fathers rise up against Antiochus, and only the fear of the heavy hand of Herod restrained them from doing the same. In the last days of the king, when his death, eagerly awaited, was known to be near, two men [2] whom Josephus (Ant. xvii. 6. 2) describes as two of the most eloquent men among the Jews, most celebrated interpreters of the Torah and men well beloved among the people, led a sedition directed to pulling down the buildings which Herod had erected contrary to the law of their fathers. The attempt failed, and the two leaders were burnt alive. This incident is significant, not only as an indication of the popular feeling towards Herod, but as marking the appearance of what afterwards became the party of the Zealots.

Hitherto it has been possible to regard the Pharisees and the Sadducees as the two main groups opposed to each other, the former having the support of the common people as a whole, the latter associating themselves with the ruling powers. The reign of Herod introduced complications unknown before, if only because he himself was not a Jew and those who supported him, whether Jews or not, had no direct concern with Judaism as such. Probably many, perhaps most, of those who called themselves Herodians were not Jews at all.

[1] For the identification of the names, see my *Pirkē Aboth*, on I. 10, 11.

[2] The two men, Judah son of Sariphæus, and Matthias son of Margaluth, are not known in the Rabbinic tradition. In Wars. i. 33. 2, the former is called " son of Sepphoræus," which no doubt means that he was a native of Sepphoris. It is remarkable that the Meg. Taanith, which notes the day of Herod's death, says nothing about the two fanatics.

But the Pharisees can no longer be treated as a strictly homogeneous party. The cruelties of Herod and his open disregard, in spite of occasional lip service, for the Torah and the religion founded on it, caused many of its defenders to question whether the peace policy, which the Pharisees had always pursued, could or ought to be maintained. The main body of the Pharisees remained firmly attached to that policy, even down to the last war. But alongside of the Pharisees, from the time of Herod onwards, two other parties come into view, each representing an extreme position as compared with the moderation of the Pharisees. On the one hand, the Essenes solved the practical problem of living under the Torah by withdrawal from the world and forming a community of their own. They practised an asceticism which was never adopted or even approved by the Pharisees, but which, after all, was only the logical development of Pharisaism. The Essenes are, so far as I know, not named in the Rabbinical literature and, as a community, had little or no direct influence upon the development of Pharisaism. But it is quite probable that individual Pharisees owed a good deal to their teaching and example. When the Talmud speaks of the ' Early Ḥasidim,' החסידים הראשונים it describes persons who seem to have had something of the Essene about them.[1]

Of far greater direct importance were the Zealots. They were in full accord with the Pharisees in their devotion to Torah, but they could no longer be satisfied to defend it by merely peaceful means. Cruelty and oppression awakened the desire to rebel, and rebellion meant the defence of Torah against those who flouted it. In the early days of the movement there was probably no clearly marked division between the Zealots and the Pharisees, and it is significant that the two men who preached sedition in the last days of Herod were said to have been known and admired as teachers. But later, when the

---

[1] But see Büchler, *Some Types of Jewish Palestinian Piety*, 1922, where the distinction between the Ḥasidim and the Essenes is clearly drawn, and abundantly illustrated.

war against Rome broke out, which ended with the fall of Jerusalem, the Zealots were wild fanatics with whom the Pharisees had little, if anything, in common. And again, in the War of Bar Cocheba, the Pharisees as a whole stood aloof, the most notable exception being R. Akiba. The Zealots, like other revolutionaries, started a movement which passed out of their control ; and what had begun as an attempt to realise certain ends in accordance with a definite policy became a mere orgy of fanatical passion.

The Zealots remained, the wild men of the Pharisees, down to the last war ; and while the Pharisees continued to hold their ascendancy over the people, and steadily maintained their peace policy as long as they could, yet their authority was diminished, and in the two great periods of war was reduced almost to nothing. The history of the Pharisees, therefore, from the time of Herod, must describe them as being much less prominent in the national affairs than they had been. Powerful they always were ; but in this period they were obliged to contend against increasing difficulties, and when the storm broke, they could only wait till it had spent its fury and save what they could out of the wreck.

It is therefore needless to attempt to describe in detail the history of the Pharisees down to the defeat of Bar Cocheba. The story is to be found in the history books, and the Pharisees are only one element, and that by no means the most conspicuous, in the confusion and tumult which was crushed into stillness by the heavy hand of Rome.

When the storm died away, the Pharisees alone survived. The Sadducees, as a body, disappeared when the Temple fell. The Zealots ended their career when Bar Cocheba was captured in Bethar. The Pharisees were the only guides and teachers who had a word for the people ; and they, and none others, saved from the ruin of the Jewish nation all that could be saved, and spoke to the stricken hearts of their countrymen the words of comfort and hope. The Judaism which has come down through the centuries is essentially Pharisaism.

CHAPTER III

TORAH AND TRADITION

In the previous chapter I have traced the history of the Pharisees, as an element in the Jewish people, from their origin down to the time when they were left the sole survivors after the War of Bar Cocheba. It was impossible to avoid some reference to their distinctive principles, and more especially their attitude towards the Torah, because there was no other means of identifying them in the period before the name Pharisee came into use. In the present chapter I shall deal at length with the fundamental principles upon which their whole conception of religion and life was founded, and by reason of which they were distinguished from Sadducees, Essenes, Am-ha-aretz, and whatever other types of Judaism may have borne a special name.

The key to the understanding of the ground principles of Pharisaism is found in the two words which stand as the title of this chapter, Torah and Tradition. It is, of course, true that there was Torah long before there were Pharisees, that Torah was recognised as the supreme authority by the Sadducees no less than by the Pharisees, and that Tradition did not begin with Ezra and the Sopherim. But Torah and Tradition meant more to the Pharisees than to the Sadducees; and not only so, but it was the peculiar combination of Torah with Tradition, effected by the Pharisees, which especially called forth the opposition of the Sadducees, which indeed gave to the Judaism of the Pharisees the distinctive character that it has retained down to the present day. To the

examination, therefore, of these two fundamental conceptions I now proceed.

Torah means Teaching : it does not mean Law. Unless
that elementary fact be clearly grasped and constantly
borne in mind, there is no possibility of understanding
Pharisaism. There were reasons, no doubt, why the
LXX always rendered תורה by νόμος, as there were
reasons why Paul, who ought to have known better,
perpetuated the same mischievous error. But the fact
remains that the word Law does not and cannot represent
what the Jews in general and the Pharisees in particular
meant by Torah ; and for this reason the word Torah is
left untranslated throughout this book as a technical
term having its own special meaning.

Torah is, of course, in itself a common Hebrew word,
and denotes teaching—any kind of teaching given by one
person to another. But long before the time of Ezra
the word acquired also a religious meaning, and denoted
teaching given by or on behalf of Yahveh, the communication of his will or of whatever else he would make known
to his people. This usage can be traced in the Old Testament as early as the date of the composite document
JE, i.e. approximately 750 B.C., and in fact was probably
much older. In Exodus xviii. 20, which is assigned to
JE, it is said : [1] " And thou (Moses) shalt make clear
to them the statutes and the ' toroth,' and make known
to them the way wherein they should walk and the thing
which they should do." The evidence of the Pentateuch
is confirmed by the independent witness of Amos and
Hosea. In Amos ii. 4 it is said: " Because they have
rejected the ' torah ' of Yahveh, and have not kept his
statutes." Hosea iv. 6 : " Because thou hast rejected
knowledge, I will also reject thee, so that thou be no
priest to me ; and thou hast forgotten the ' torah ' of
thy God, I also will forget thee and thy sons."
Hosea viii. 1 : " They have transgressed my covenant and
trespassed against my ' torah.' " Hosea viii. 12 : "Though
I should write for him myriads of my ' torah,' they are

[1] See Lauterbach, *Sadducees and Pharisees*, p. 186 and note.

counted as a strange thing." These passages show that
the close connection of Torah with religion was familiar
both to prophets and their hearers as early as the eighth
century ; and not only that but also such characteristic
ideas as " walking in his ways," and the association
of ' torah ' with statutes. These ideas became much more
prominent in later times, but they were no invention of
Ezra. They are found more abundantly in the Priestly
Code and the allied portions of the Pentateuch, as may
be seen in any Concordance or even by a glance at the
pages of the Pentateuch ; and, whatever part Ezra may
have taken in publishing the collected Torah, he was
certainly not the author of it. What he did was to proclaim in the hearing of the people the full and complete
Torah, the teaching which Yahveh had given through
Moses for the guidance and instruction of Israel. The
association of Torah with Moses may well have come
down from the time of Moses himself, though it will be
observed that he is not named in the passages cited above
from the two prophets. After the time of Ezra, the association of Torah with Moses was a matter of course, and
the name was applied to the five books forming the
Pentateuch. Strictly speaking, the Torah of Moses meant
the teaching given by and through Moses and contained
in those five books. Ezra, of course, knew nothing of
the modern theory which unfolds the gradual growth of
the Pentateuch ; but if he had known how it was the
outcome of the labours of many generations of prophets
and priests, embodying ancient traditions and later ordinances, he would only have said that all these did
but develop the original teaching which Moses had given.
The critical theory of the Pentateuch almost necessarily
implies such a view on the part of those who accepted
Deuteronomy in addition to the older Code, and those
later who accepted the Priestly Code and finally the entire
Pentateuch as the Torah of Moses. They did not feel
that they were asked to accept something entirely new,
although they had not heard it or read it before. It was
but the fuller and more explicit presentation of what had

been known to their fathers from time immemorial. If they had thought that they were bidden to make a complete breach with their past they would never have accepted either Deuteronomy or the Priestly Code, and Ezra would have been the last man to lead them away from Moses.

The conception of the " Torah of Moses " was accordingly of unknown antiquity in the time of Ezra, and he only made known the full and complete written record of it. Full and complete, that is, as a written record embodying all that was in his time regarded as being Torah of Moses.[1] Moreover, even if it were established that the book which Ezra proclaimed was only the Priestly Code, without the earlier portions of the Pentateuch, the reform of religion which placed the Torah in the position of supreme authority was based on the Pentateuch substantially complete, including all those earlier portions. If Ezra had confined himself merely to the Priestly Code, the results which actually did follow from his labours would not necessarily have followed, perhaps would not even probably have followed. It has often been held that Ezra's chief aim was to establish and strengthen the priestly system, which centred in the Temple and became articulate in the ceremonial law. Of course, it would be foolish to deny that his activity as a reformer was much concerned with the Temple and its services, as the visible embodiment of the nation's worship, or that his sympathies were entirely with an administration on priestly lines. But, judging from the results of his work, it seems to me clear that his real aims were more inclusive and far-reaching, and that what he set himself to do was to make the Torah of Moses the dominating factor in the national life to a degree and in a manner till then unknown. The Torah was to become the supreme authority

---

[1] It is, of course, true that additions were made after the time of Ezra ; but my present argument does not turn on the question whether the Pentateuch as Ezra proclaimed it was actually the Pentateuch as we have it now. Substantially it was ; and in any case he dealt with what was to him the whole Torah of Moses.

of the nation, the guide of its actions, the source of its knowledge of the divine will; and this, not only for the community as a whole but for each individual member of that community. The people were to become the People of the Torah, so that their whole life in its every detail would bear more or less clear witness to the influence of Torah and their acceptance of its teaching.

If this were what Ezra consciously aimed at (and it is certainly the result which eventually followed), then it is obvious that success was more easy to reach in some directions than in others. To elaborate the Temple services, to exalt the priestly organisation and enforce the laws of ceremonial purity was the easiest part of his task, as well as the most conspicuous, the most readily observed. It is this, accordingly, which has been most usually noticed and described, as if it were the chief or even the only object of Ezra's reforming zeal. If it had been, then the other results which did follow would not have followed, simply because there was no reason why they should follow. There was nothing in a mere elaboration of a sacerdotal system to make them follow. But if, on the other hand, Ezra made it his supreme object to constitute the Torah the governing factor in the whole national life, then those other results would naturally follow, as, in fact, they did; and the elaboration of the Temple ritual, etc. was only one of those results. Certainly the Torah contained a great number of laws bearing upon the ritual and the priesthood and kindred matters, and Ezra laid the greatest stress upon the most scrupulously exact observance of these. But their real and only claim to observance at all was that they were enjoined in the Torah; and apart from that fact he would have had no special reason for setting up an elaborate hierarchy. In what he did as touching the Temple services he was applying his general principle to the object which lay nearest to hand, by no means to the only object within his view. For the Torah was not the concern of the priests alone, either to observe or to administer; it was not even for the whole community as such. It was for each individual Jew, being a member of the community, to take its teaching to heart as it might concern him, and each one must learn that he was responsible for obedience to the Torah in his own case. Ezra was but following the lead of Ezekiel in thus individualising religion, and he was enabled to enforce the lesson at the time when it was most needed. To live *for* the Torah, *by* the Torah and *with* the Torah was the ideal which Ezra cherished for the national life ; that was what the Jew must strive for, work for, and to that he must give the devotion of his whole life—a devotion without qualification or reserve, a whole-hearted allegiance to the will of God set forth in the Torah. I cannot, indeed, directly prove that these ideas were in the mind of Ezra, still less can I quote reputed words of his which express them ; but there is no question that a great movement did begin about a century after the return from the Exile, a movement whose significance and intention are truly described in such terms as I have used. There must have been a great personality to start such a movement ; and since Ezra was there, and was in later times [1] regarded as the man who re-founded the religion of Israel and who actually founded Judaism, we cannot be far wrong in ascribing to him the more or less conscious possession of the idea which inspired the whole.

We have, then, as the outstanding result of Ezra's work, the establishment of the Torah of Moses as the

[1] For Ezra as the restorer of the Torah, see b. Succ. 20[a]. This is the Talmudic way of saying that he was the founder of the Judaism specifically based on Torah. In j. Meg. 75[a], and more fully in b. B.K. 82[ab]., a list is given of ten ordinances made by Ezra, Whether these were really due to him is open to question ; but they show what the later teachers regarded as attributable to him, and it is noteworthy that not a single one of them has any reference to the Temple ritual. Some of them are quite trivial ; the two most important being that the Torah should be read in the villages on the second and fifth day of each week, in addition to the Sabbath, and that the local tribunal, Beth Din, should also sit on those same two week-days. All the ordinances were concerned with the daily life of the members of the community.

dominating factor in the life of the Jewish people. He laid, as it were, one of the foundation stones upon which the structure of all subsequent Judaism was built, and that foundation stone has never been removed or undermined from the time of Ezra to the present day. It was shown in the previous chapter that the divergence of the Pharisees from the Sadducees was due to a difference in their respective estimate of the true nature and significance of the Torah, the former finding in it a far greater and loftier meaning than the latter would admit. I do not know of any evidence to show what Ezra himself thought, or whether the diverging lines were already recognised in his time. It would certainly be rash and unwarranted to ascribe to him such a view of the meaning of Torah as was afterwards held by the Pharisees, and I think it probable that such ideas never came within the range of his thought. At all events, I shall not assume that he had any knowledge of them. It is sufficient that he left as his great legacy to his people the Torah as their supreme authority and the interpretation of it their greatest need. The need arose from the fact that the guidance to be found in the Torah could only be made effective if it could be brought to bear upon problems not expressly dealt with in its written words. For the Torah was instruction, intended to be learned and, where action was called for, to be obeyed. The whole point would be missed, the whole effect would be lost unless there were, on the part of those who, by their representatives, had pledged themselves to accept the Torah and abide by it (Neh. x. 29), a practical response and not a merely theoretical aquiescence. This is fundamental for Judaism, not merely in the times of Ezra and the Sopherim but in all subsequent periods of Jewish history.

It was therefore the task of the Sopherim to teach and interpret the Torah, applying that teaching as occasion might require by such simple interpretation as would meet the case. More than this, it is not safe to assume : less than this there could hardly be if there were to be any teaching at all. Merely to teach the written word without explanation would obviously be useless when the case to be decided was not expressly mentioned in the written text. If we ask the question, What principle guided the Sopherim in giving the required interpretation in such a case ? there is no first-hand evidence on which to base the answer. But it seems natural to suppose that they would consider what was the existing practice, if any such existed, and what, according to their own judgment, seemed to be the right course to follow, the right teaching to give. Some innovation, some addition of what was new, in form if not in substance, there must necessarily have been. But it must not be forgotten that the Sopherim had the past behind them, and though they were shaping the future they did so only out of their sense of what that past required. Ezra was a great innovator, and the Sopherim who carried on his work were laying down lines of progress which were to stretch far down the centuries ; but neither he nor they were making a completely new beginning, nor ever supposed that they were. If they started a tradition they also inherited a tradition, and the one helped to determine the form and the contents of the other. The importance of this will be seen more clearly when we come to the fully developed Pharisaic conception of Torah.

The process of applying the teaching contained in the Torah involved of necessity the statement of precepts not explicitly taught before, directions for religious action not expressly contained in the written text of the Torah. The question could not and did not fail to arise, sooner or later, By what authority those new precepts were enjoined ? What was their rightful claim to obedience and acceptance ? What was their relation to the written text of the Torah, whose authority was undisputed ? The raising of that question was the beginning of the divergence between the Pharisees and the Sadducees, and it would be very interesting if we could point to the exact date at which it was first raised or name the man who raised it. But we can get no further than the fact that it was raised, at some point of time between Ezra and the breach between the Pharisees and the Sadducees. The question was answered in two ways. It was held by one party or school of thought that the Torah was the written text alone of the Pentateuch, containing such-and-such precise statements, so many definite precepts and no more ; and that the pledge of obedience taken by the representatives of the people committed them only to the observance of what was in so many words enjoined in the written Torah. When directions were needed, in regard to cases not expressly provided for in the written Torah, it was the right and duty of the priests, as the guardians and teachers of Torah from ancient times, to make such ordinances as they judged necessary and adequate. These ordinances, Gezērōth, גזרות,[1] were not part of the Torah, and did not claim to be ; they were the injunctions of a purely human authority, whose members acted, no doubt, in accordance with the divine will, and exercised a privilege expressly conferred upon them in the Torah itself (Deut. xvii. 9–11). " And thou shalt come to the priests and Levites and the judge which shall be in those days, and thou shalt inquire, and they shall declare to thee the word of judgment. And thou shalt do according to the word which they shall declare to thee from that place which Yahveh shall choose, and thou shalt observe to do according to all which they shall teach thee. According to the Torah which they shall teach thee, and the judgment which they shall say to thee thou shalt do ; thou shalt not turn aside from the word which they shall declare to thee to the right hand or to the left."

Lauterbach has pointed out (*Sadducees and Pharisees*, p. 185) that this means that the priests gave to the inquirer their own opinion and not what was set down in the Torah, because that was already provided for. Whether or not this was the intention of the authors of Deuteronomy may be left an open question ; but it was certainly the construction put upon the passage by the priests and

[1] On the Gezeroth, see Lauterbach, *Sadducees and Pharisees*, p. 186 and note *ibid.*

rulers who administered the Torah after Ezra had made it supreme. They claimed the right to direct the people what they should do, and not merely to recite the words of the Torah to them, but to make ordinances which were not Torah. This must have been the line taken in regard to Torah from the earliest times after Ezra, simply because there was then no reason to take any other line; the priests were there, the Torah gave them authority to direct the people, and they used that authority.[1]

But in course of time the consequence of this policy began to appear, and gradually suggested another answer to the question as to the authority of the 'ordinances.' When every fresh case where guidance was needed and where no explicit direction was given in the Torah was dealt with by an ordinance, there was a gradual but inevitable tendency for the Torah to become obsolete, even in time a mere archaic relic, having no longer any relation to the life and thought of the later age. The ancient words were there, and were still binding, because these were what the people had pledged themselves to obey; but the occasions on which they could be practically observed became fewer and fewer as the number of 'ordinances' became greater and greater. Accordingly, an opposite view began to be held and advocated. The 'ordinances,' if they were to be admitted as binding the people, could only do so if what they enjoined was itself Torah or in harmony with Torah. The people had pledged themselves to obey the Torah and not anything outside it. Therefore all the religious duty of the people must have the sanction of Torah and not merely the legislative authority of priests and rulers. To ascertain whether that sanction was really given was a matter of interpretation; and the answer was to be found by all who could rightly interpret the Torah, not merely by the bare authority of the priests. Moreover,

---

[1] It should be remembered that most of the early Sopherim were priests, as Ezra himself had been. There were probably some Levites, but not at first any laymen.

the Torah had been given to all Israel, and not to the priests alone. If, therefore, there were those who not being priests were yet competent to interpret Torah, then they had an inherent right to do so. And they exercised that right by establishing the sanction of Torah for what had previously been merely ordained by the independent authority of the priests. The means by which they did this is indicated by the one word, Tradition.

It has been pointed out above that the ' ordinances ' of the priests were to some extent based on existing custom, and the effect of an ' ordinance ' would be to give validity and binding force to some practice which was either already customary or generally in accordance with custom. It is scarcely probable that the priests would introduce and enjoin a practice entirely unknown till then, and having no relation to previous practice. Now those who took the second line, in regard to the binding authority of the ordinances, maintained that what was enjoined by the ordinances was right to be done only if or because it had the sanction of Torah behind it. They did not dispute that action so enjoined was a religious duty. They were as insistent as the priests in requiring the performance of such actions. But they held that since these actions were based on tradition, the tradition which made them valid was a tradition of the interpretation of Torah, that there had been handed down along with the written Torah an unwritten explanation of it which gave as its result the precepts embodied in the ordinances. The holders of this view therefore introduced the conception of the unwritten Torah, תורה: שבעל. פת alongside of and supplementary to the written Torah, תורה שבכתב or rather they enlarged the whole conception of Torah so as to include both the written and the unwritten, the Text and the Tradition. The Sadducees adhered to the written text alone and rejected the unwritten, traditional Torah. Those who opposed them and maintained the Torah written and unwritten, the Torah interpreted by Tradition, were the Pharisees ; and this conception of Torah is fundamental in the whole

of their religious thought and practice, and the literature
which expresses their ideas. This is the real point of
cleavage between Sadducees and Pharisees ; the differences usually mentioned and taken from Josephus (chiefly,
Wars. ii. 8, 14) are of secondary importance only, inci-
dental results partly of their main theory and partly
of their social and political position. Josephus himself
(Ant. xiii. 10, 6) gives the true ground of difference
without apparently realising its importance.

At what precise date this enlarged conception of Torah
began to be present to the minds of some of its interpreters there is no evidence to show.   But, as it is fundamental in Pharisaism, and as the Pharisees broke with
the Sadducees in the reign of John Hyrkanus, and as the
Sadducean view is the one which would naturally be held
at the beginning, when the written Torah was still able
to meet the demands made on it, we are warranted in
placing the first appearance of the enlarged conception
of Torah in the long interval between Ezra and Hyrkanus,
but at what precise date we cannot tell. There is no
certain trace of it in the Chronicler, though he makes
frequent reference to the Torah of Moses, and to the
duty of observing what is written therein.   The Chronicler,
however, was, if not a priest himself (and he may quite
well have been), entirely devoted to the priestly conception of religion, and would not be likely to mention or
countenance a view of Torah so directly in conflict with
that of the Priests.   Sirach also does not mention it,
though he does refer to the Torah.   But it is quite possible that he knew about it and did not approve of it ;
and this may be the reason why he left Ezra without a
word in his enumeration of famous men (Ecclus. xlix.
12, 13).   For, whether or not Ezra himself originated
this view of Torah, the Pharisees who maintained it
took Ezra, so to speak, as their patron saint.   Yet there
is clear evidence, even in the Old Testament, of their
new view of Torah, the specifically Pharisaic conception
of its true significance.   Psalm xix and Psalm cxix are
entirely without meaning unless read in the light of this

Pharisaic conception of Torah. Psalm xix may, perhaps, be taken as the first literary proclamation of it, called forth as a protest against the older and narrower conception, and as a vehement assertion of the new. The two halves of that Psalm are often thought to have no connection with each other, and the Revisers have so far yielded to this view as to leave a space between the one portion and the other. But the connection is really extremely close. The whole point of the author of the Psalm is that what the sun is in the heavens the Torah is in the soul. And for him, the Torah is no longer the mere written text of an ancient book, becoming year by year more archaic and useless, but a living word from God, a revelation not confined to the written text, an inexhaustible treasure of divine teaching. That is why he bursts out, in triumphant assertion : " The Torah of the Lord is perfect, restoring the soul," etc., and follows it up with a series of declarations in terms which became the familiar watchwords of the religion of Torah as the Pharisees held it.

Similarly, Psalm cxix is one long joyous hymn of praise, in glorification of Torah and of God who gave it. And, if anyone desires to know what a Pharisee meant by Torah, and even more, what Torah meant to a Pharisee, let him study this Psalm, in its length and breadth and depth and height. The somewhat artificial form is a mere detail ; if the author chose that form for his hymn, that was his own affair. What matters is the rapture which he could, and most certainly did, express under the conditions of style which he imposed on himself. Whether this Psalm were written before the rupture between Sadducees and Pharisees took place cannot be determined ; but the presence in the mind of the Pharisees of such ideas as are found in Psalm xix and Psalm cxix would fully account for their opposition to the views of the Sadducees.

For the Pharisaic view, their enlarged conception of Torah, was of the utmost importance, and had the most powerful influence upon the subsequent development of Judaism. In a single sentence the effect was this : To break the fetters which were cramping the religious life of the people, and to set its spirit free to receive fresh inspiration from God. As shown above, the old Sadducean view tended to make the Torah an archaic relic, a sacred text venerable indeed from its age, but whose teaching had an ever-decreasing relation to the religious needs of the time, and even whose very meaning became, with every generation, less intelligible. If this process had gone on unchecked, the Jewish religion would have become a mere ceremonial performance, a dead ritual with no breath of divine life in it, nothing to help the worshipper to realise his communion with the living God or even to suppose that such a communion was still possible. It was from this danger that the religious life of the Jewish people was saved; and it was saved by the exaltation of the Torah from being a closed revelation to an open one, from a dead letter to a letter made alive again, from a text long ago set and hardened, whose meaning could never change and which could say nothing new, to a text whose meaning was plastic because freshly interpreted in the light of the growing moral discernment of religious teachers, age after age. This is the real significance of the unwritten Torah, and of its introduction beside the written text. In form it was an appeal to tradition; in effect it was a declaration that what God intended to teach his people was something greater and higher and holier than the mere written word by itself would indicate. Of course the Sadducees were right, from the point of view of grammar and exegesis, in saying that the words of the text did not mean what the Pharisees said they meant; and from their own standpoint they were justified in rejecting the Pharisaic interpretation, those traditions which the Pharisees placed beside or above the written word. But it is no less certain that the Pharisees were right and the Sadducees were wrong, the one in insisting on the need for a living revelation and the others in blindly opposing it.

A modern student will ask the question, Why did the Pharisees not openly say that they discarded the mere letter and that they put in place of it the higher teaching which their own spiritual and moral discernment approved ? This is a very delicate and searching question, and I answer it with some hesitation. I may be wrong, and I only give what seems to me to be the true answer. I believe that the Pharisees, that is the accredited teachers among them, in effect really did discard the mere letter and put in place of it the higher teaching which their own spiritual and moral discernment approved ; but that they, perhaps necessarily, conceived of this process under the form of an interpretation of the written word. They used the vehicle of Tradition in all good faith, as a means by which to give the interpretation they desired, not because in every case they definitely knew that there was an explicit tradition to the effect that such and such was the real meaning of a particular text or precept, but because in this way, and apparently in this way alone, they could bring their new teaching within the scope of Torah, under the ægis of its divine authority. Whatever is possible now, it certainly was not possible then, to throw over the Torah and put any other teaching in its place. No Pharisee would have dreamed of any such thing ; and when Jesus did precisely this, in his later if not in his earlier teaching, the inevitable result was his rejection by the Pharisees and the general body of the people who sided with them. In the early days of the Pharisees there could be and there was no idea of superseding the Torah ; and what they did was to take the only means then open to them of providing for the religious wants of the people, the continuance of their divine guidance, the refreshing of the dry courses of their soul's life by the constant renewal of communion with God. They worked, in their time, with such ideas and instruments as their time afforded ; and no one who knows their work and can read their minds will deny that the blessing of God was upon them and upon those to whom, century after century, they have made known the Torah, the divine teaching entrusted to their care.

The exaltation of Torah indicated above is the great

achievement of the Pharisees, their chief contribution
to the religious ideas of the human race. Whether the
human race has paid much attention to it, or even been
aware of its existence, is another matter. But it was by
means of this exalted conception of Torah that the Jewish
religion was saved from decay and extinction in the days
of the Sadducees; and it was this same conception of
Torah which enabled the Jewish people to endure through
the centuries of persecution and the world's ill-will down
to the present day, enabled them to do for the human
race great and substantial services, seldom recognised
indeed, but of which the want would have been felt in
all the higher regions of thought.[1] The divine Torah,
so conceived, is the watchword of all the later Judaism
which found expression in the Talmud and the Midrash
and the Jewish literature generally; and when the non-
Jewish student comes across some passage in the Rabbinical
writings in which Torah is apostrophised in what seem
to him extravagant terms, and holds it up to ridicule,
he is only exposing his own failure to understand. For
no superlative of word or of idea can be too great for
what is regarded as the supreme gift of God to man, his
inexhaustible revelation of divine truth, the unfading
radiance of the heavenly light shining in the souls of
mortal men.

It was to this great spiritual conception that the Pharisees made their way. This was what they got to when,
in protest against the narrow literalism of the Sadducees,
they introduced the unwritten interpretation beside
the written text—combined Torah with Tradition. And
for the right understanding of Pharisaism, it is necessary
to bear constantly in mind that the inspiration of the
whole is this supreme conception of Torah. It is this
which combines in one consistent whole its numberless
minute details, often in themselves apparently trivial,
sometimes actually trivial, but which, though trivial,

[1] For a fuller development of this thought see my essay on
"What the World owes to the Pharisees," the second Arthur
Davis Lecture, 1919.

would not have been there at all unless there had been the compelling force of a great principle beneath them. A river will carry on its surface sticks and straws and the refuse from its banks ; but it is the river which matters, and without it the trifles it carries down would never have been noticed. The bearing of which remark is this, that the Pharisaic theory of Torah, of which the supreme development has been indicated above, involved consequences of thought and act which have given to Judaism a peculiar character shared by no other religion, and which have drawn down upon the Jews the hostile or scornful comment of their Gentile neighbours through twenty centuries. I go on to discuss the practical development of Torah in the hands of the Pharisees, and their application of it to the problems of religious life.

I take up the subject at the point where the Pharisees began to put in practice their new principle of interpreting Torah by the help of Tradition, the principle of the unwritten Torah. Their object in interpreting the Torah at all was essentially practical, viz. to make the divine teaching given to Israel such that Israel could assimilate it. Those to whom it was given must be able to understand the meaning of what was taught them ; if it were precept, they must know what was enjoined on them, and what they must do in order to fulfil the precept ; if it was instruction about God and his ways, they must be able to comprehend what was told them ; if it was ethical counsel, they must be able to apply the lesson to themselves and acknowledge the rightness of it ; if it was the illustration of human nature as shown in the lives of men of old recorded in the Scriptures, they must be in a position to compare such teaching with their own experience. The Torah, as teaching, included all these different types of lesson ; and the task of the interpreter was to draw forth all these from the Torah as written. This theory of interpretation began with the Pharisees, and it has continued down to the present day. The aim of the teachers in any given age has been to give to those whom they taught what the Torah had to teach to the people of that age, so far as the teachers were able to discern it, by their own insight aided, and indeed strongly influenced, by the gathered treasure of experience and wisdom handed down from earlier times.

In the beginning, the interpretation of Torah was a simple matter. It was called Midrash Torah, מדרש תורה an ancient name still found and used in much later times.[1] This is the generic term which covers all interpretation of Torah, for whatever purpose. In common usage it is shortened to Midrash, to denote the homiletic exposition either of Scripture in general or Torah in particular. The collections of such expositions, formed in the early centuries of the common era and containing material some of which goes back to the Sopherim, are called Midrashim, with various distinctive epithets, e.g. Midrash Rabbah, Midrash Tanḥuma and others. The form of exposition common to all these is that the text to be interpreted is given along with the interpretation, the teaching derived from it, or based upon it, or associated with it. This is known as the Midrash form, to distinguish it from the Mishnah form in which the result of interpretation is given without the text to which it refers. The Mishnah form, however, is, I think, exclusively confined to interpretation which has for its subject-matter the preceptive side of Torah. The Midrash form was older than the Mishnah form.[2] To teach in the Midrash form was called teaching " after the manner of Moses " (b. Temur, 15[b]).

I have been careful to remind the reader that the contents of Torah were of several kinds and the consequent interpretation of Torah of several types, in order to prepare the way for the study of the two main heads under which the results of the interpretation of Torah are classified. When interpretation dealt with the preceptive portion of Torah, the result deduced was called Halāchāh, הלכה ; when it dealt with the non-preceptive portion, for the

[1] b. Kidd, 49[b].
[2] See on the whole subject the most illuminating essay of Lauterbach, *Midrash and Mishnah.*

purpose of edification, the result was called Haggādah חגדה. Both of these famous terms belong to the very essence of the Pharisaic Midrash ; and it will be necessary to study each of them with care, in order to understand what the Pharisees aimed at in their teaching, and how far they attained their object. The term Haggadah is probably of earlier origin than the other, as will be shown below ; but it will be more convenient to treat first of Halachah.

The Torah, as written, contains a large number of precepts—positive and negative commands—enjoined upon Israel. These are, *ex hypothesi*, directions divinely revealed for the guidance of those to whom the Torah was given. They were intimations of the will of God, and they carried with them the demand for obedience. When the Torah was raised to the position of being the supreme authority for the life of the Jewish people, and when the people pledged themselves to accept it as such, they pledged themselves to do what the Torah told them to do. It was, as we have seen, one of the main characteristics of the reform instituted by Ezra that he insisted on the individual duty and responsibility of each member of the community to obey the commands contained in the Torah. Therein was declared the will of God, as it concerned each individual Jew, and he could only discharge that responsibility by obedience complete and unhesitating. Not to do so would be to disown his fellowship in the community of Israel, and with it his loyalty to God.

Now the Torah, as written, left the Jew at many points without specific directions, gave him no clear intimation, or no intimation at all, as to what the divine will was in such-and-such a case. Therefore the Torah needed an interpreter who should be able to deduce from what it did say in one case what it would say in another case if it had expressly dealt with that other case. The germ of the Pharisaic interpretation is to be found, I believe, in the passage already cited, Exodus xviii. 20, where it is said : " And thou shalt make clear to them the statutes

and the toroth, and make known to them the way wherein
they should walk and the thing which they should do."
This exactly indicates the object constantly kept in view
in the Pharisaic interpretation of the preceptive portion
of the Torah. That object was attained when some
religious duty was defined by competent authority in a
clear statement which served to guide the person concerned
in the way that he should go. Such a statement, containing
a rule of right conduct, was called a ' halachah.' [1]

[1] The word הלכה is derived from הלך to walk, to go. It is
a Hebrew word, not found in the Old Testament, but belonging
to the New Hebrew of the Mishnah, and of quite regular formation.
There is no sufficient reason to regard it as a translation from the
Aramaic, and good reason against so doing. For it was always
a term of the schools, meaning by the schools the assemblies of the
accredited teachers who interpreted the Torah on Pharisaic lines.
And it is not in the least likely that those teachers would go
outside the range of the sacred language to borrow a word whereby
to designate a conception derived immediately from the Torah,
and suggested by, though not contained in, the actual text. The
word is formed from הלך in the same way as יבמה, הויה, חזרה,
דרשה, חזקה from their respective roots. The idea denoted by
this word must have been known at a very early stage in the Pharisaic
interpretation of Torah ; but it is curious that there is no trace
of the first beginnings of its use. When we first meet with it in the
Mishnah it is used as a technical term apparently quite familiar,
and with nothing to make it likely that it was then of recent
origin. The earliest instance that I have so far been able to find is
M. Peah ii. 6 where, in reference to a doubtful case brought before
Rn. Gamliel I, it is said : " They went up to the Lishkath-ha-gazith
and asked there. Nahum the writer (libellarius) said: I have
received from R. Measha, who received from his father, who received
from the Zūgoth, who received from the Prophets, (it is) a halachah of Moses from Sinai, that," etc. This refers to a time before
the fall of Jerusalem but after the beginning of the common era.
הלכה למשה מסיני is itself a technical term, whose origin is far earlier
than this use of it. The word הלכה occurs in the story about
Jehudah b. Tabbai and Simeon b. Shetaḥ, b. Ḥagg. 16[b,] which would
bring it to eighty years B.C. But it is not there represented that
J. b. T. himself used the word. If the story in b. Pes. 66[a] is to be
relied on (and it is a Baraitha, i.e. contemporary with the Mishnah),
Hillel used the word, " הלכה זו שמעתי I have heard this halachah " ; and here also it is presumed to be quite familiar to the
hearers and not of recent origin. Hillel was probably earlier by

I believe that this is the original application of the
term. It denoted a statement as to conduct applicable to
such-and-such a particular case. Only when the number
of separate halachoth, הלכות had become very great,
making it necessary to classify and co-ordinate them,
did the term acquire the generic meaning of the whole
defined meaning of the Torah on its preceptive side.
In that sense it is correct to speak of the Halachah much
as one speaks of the Law as distinguished from particular
Laws. It is known that R. Akiba (d. 135 C.E.) laid the
foundations of the great organised collection of halachoth,
which afterwards became the Mishnah ; and I think it
probable that he did so because he had arrived at the
conception of the Halachah as an organic whole, no
longer a mere collection of separate items.

A halachah, according to the Pharisaic theory of the
Torah already explained, was a specific declaration of
the divine will applicable to a given case ; and, as such,
it was binding on all who accepted the Torah as their
supreme authority, and professed to ' walk ' in the way
which it indicated. Obviously, the task of defining the
halachah was one of extreme importance, because it
meant legislating for all who accepted the Pharisaic

a whole generation than the Nahum mentioned above. I have not
met with any attempt to trace the origin and history of the word
הלכה, and I have given only the scanty result of my own inquiry.

Neither have I found any precise and complete explanation of
the reason why that particular word was used or coined in order
to denote that particular idea. Jewish writers, as is only natural,
usually take for granted that their readers understand what is
meant, and perhaps would not be interested in the etymological
problem. The Aruch comes nearest to such an explanation when
it says : פירוש הלכתא דבר שהולך ובא מקודם ועד סוף׳ או שישראל
מתהלכין בו: (Aruch. s.v. הלך). Levy's *Wörterbuch* gives no help,
nor does Frankel, *Darkē ha-Mishnah*, nor Weiss, *Dōr Dōr*, valuable
as these works are in other respects. The fullest account of
Halachah which I know is contained in an essay, " Zur Einleitung
in die Halacha," by M. Guttmann, published in the *Jahresbericht
der Landes-Rabbinerschule* in Budapest, 1909 and 1913. I am
indebted for the opportunity of reading this to my friend Dr.
Marmorstein, of the Jews' College, London.

principle. It could not be, and it certainly was not, left to any individual teacher, still less to any individual Jew, to determine the halachah according to his own private judgment. It was always defined after consultation amongst the accredited teachers at any period of history, the supreme religious legislative body whatever it might be, whether the great Beth-Din in Jerusalem or, after the fall of Jerusalem, the Assembly of the Rabbis at Jabneh or Usha or Tiberias. The decision was based on a most careful and thorough study of the Torah, both written and unwritten, and the result was finally determined by the vote of a majority. A halachah so defined was thenceforth binding on all Jews, at least on all who followed the Pharisees ; and it could not be repealed or annulled except by the majority vote of another Assembly which excelled the earlier one in wisdom and number (M. Edu. i. 5). On the other hand, no Beth-Din could impose a law upon the community (apparently even though it was theoretically a halachah) unless the majority of the community were able to bear it (b. A. Zar. 36ª, B. Bathr. 60ᵇ). The dispersion of the Jewish people which took place, to some extent after the fall of Jerusalem, and to a much larger extent after the war of Bar Cocheba, prevented the growth of a uniform Halachah binding on all Jews, because there was no longer one central authority competent to legislate. But, for Jews in any one locality, the Halachah was decided by the authority of that place in the manner described above ; and for the understanding of the practical effect and working of Halachah this is all that is of importance.[1]

For the individual Pharisee the Halachah furnished the answer to the perpetually recurring question, What was the divine will concerning him in this or that or the other specific case ? What did God command him to do in such-and-such circumstances ? And, regarding as he did the Torah as God's especial revelation given to

[1] The student who wishes to pursue the subject will find a mass of detail, well arranged and admirably handled, in Guttmann's essay already referred to, " Zur Einleitung in die Halachah."

Israel, His choicest blessing bestowed on His people, the Pharisee rejoiced when he learned the halachah which he needed. Everything which was then enjoined, whether to do or to refrain from doing, was a command, mitzvah, מצוה, and every mitzvah was an opportunity of serving God by doing His will. To do the will of God, as completely and as exactly as he could, was the aim and end of the Pharisee so far as the religion of Torah related to conduct ; and, if the mitzvoth were many and minute, the knowledge of the divine will and the opportunity for exact performance of it were by so much the more made accessible to him. Therefore, the attitude of the Pharisee towards the mitzvoth and the Halachah which interpreted them and enlarged their scope was that of willing and joyful acceptance, because he felt that the goodness of God was bestowed on him in that special way. Christians, who have learned, chiefly from Paul, to talk about the ' burden of the Law ' and the ' bondage ' in which it holds those who live under it, are seldom aware of the point of view of those who have had experience of it during the whole of their lives, and who have not broken away from it as Paul did. I shall attempt in a later chapter to estimate the effect of the Halachah and the mitzvoth upon the mental and spiritual development of the Pharisee. At present I will point out one or two facts which need to be considered in this connection.

The Halachah was intended to cover the whole of practical life, not merely for the individual but for the community, and to do that by bringing to bear upon every question the specific teaching of the Torah. Therefore the Halachah had to fulfil, amongst other functions, that of a body of civil and criminal law, such as every community needs. Of course, the Jew living under the Roman Government, or the later Persian or French or Spanish or British or what not, was bound by the law of the country in which he lived, as was expressed in the famous dictum of Samuel, the great Babylonian teacher of the third century, " the law of the Government

is law," דינא דמלכותא דינא (b. B.K. 113ᵃ). But the
Jew needed a code of law, civil and criminal, based on the
Torah, since that was the supreme authority for the whole
of his life, individual and social. Now in every nation
which has a code of civil and criminal law, the individual
citizen seldom feels the constraint of more than a small
part of its provisions ; so under the Halachah, the individual Pharisee in his practical life would have no concern
with a large number of the separate halachoth, and whatever burden they might impose he would not feel it.
On the other hand, it is true that the Halachah, besides
regulating the social conduct of the Pharisee on the lines
of civil and criminal law, prescribed with great minuteness
very many actions of his private life. Whether in this
respect the Halachah was felt to be a burden is a question
which will be answered in very different ways according
as the Halachah is regarded as the ascertained and declared
will of God, or as the decree of an external and irresponsible
authority exercised by merely human agents with no
divine guidance behind them. I am not attempting to
estimate the absolute worth of the system, or comparing
its standard with that of other systems ; I am simply
trying to present, as clearly as I can, and without prejudice in favour of some other system, the Halachah as
the Pharisee understood it and lived under it.

The essence of the Halachah was the doing of an action
exactly in the appointed way, because that was what
God commanded. Obviously, therefore, the question
did not arise for the Pharisee whether the prescribed
action in a given case was trivial or important. That was
no concern of his, though he was perfectly well aware
that merely considered by themselves some were trivial
and some important. So, also, the Pharisee was quite
aware that the doing of an action in *this* way rather than
in *that* did not really matter so far as the mere doing of
the action was concerned. What did matter, the only
thing that gave religious meaning to the action and made
the doing of it a religious duty, was the belief that it was
the express will of God that it should be done *so* and not

otherwise.[1] The action by itself, without the conscious
intention of serving God by the doing of it, was worthless.

Now wherever a Jew lived in the same locality with
Gentiles, his observance of the Halachah would at once
draw attention to him. The Gentile would notice that
the Jew did many special acts as a religious duty,
that he made a point of doing many things, in
themselves apparently trivial, in a particular way, and
that he refrained from doing other things which to the
Gentile seemed harmless or indifferent. The Jew, in
these matters, was evidently bound by a law, and that
a very strict one. Whether the Gentile ever sought to
know the reason why the Jew acted as he did, or would have
understood if the reason had been explained to him, is
not now the question. The point is that his obedience
to the Halachah was the only side which the Gentile
could in general observe of the religious life of the Jew ;
it was that side where his religion found its most characteristic expression in action. Not, indeed, its only expression in action, because the Jew, as a humane and philan-
thropic man, did not wait for the directions of the Halachah to prescribe all his acts of kindness or to define
the limits of his sympathy. It was certainly a mitzvah
to help the poor and relieve the oppressed. But the
kind heart and the generous hand could find their own
way of fulfilling that mitzvah. But, apart from these,
the fact remains that on the whole that side of the life
of the Jew which chiefly came under the notice of Gentile
neighbours and marked him off as different from them
was the side which was concerned with the Halachah.
And, as the Halachah was the Torah on its preceptive
side, made definite and explicit, I believe that here is to
be found the reason why Torah was always rendered in
Greek by νόμος, and why in all languages it is rendered
by the equivalent of Law. Few Gentiles were or are in
a position to know that Halachah was only one element
in Torah, not the whole of it, as will be shown when we

[1] See this very clearly stated by Joḥanan b. Zaccai, Pesikta
R.K., 40[b].

come to consider the Haggadah. Paul, who as a former Jew did not know what else there was in Torah besides Halachah, has inflicted upon the Jews an injury without excuse by steadily ignoring that other element, in order to build upon that omission his argument for the superiority of the Gospel over the Law.[1]

I go on now[2] to examine that other constituent element in the Torah, the Haggadah, having, I trust, given a sufficient explanation of the theory of the Halachah. A detailed survey of the Halachah in all its ramifications is utterly beyond my power, as it is far too great in mass of material to be included in a single book. Maimonides took fourteen books, now printed in four folio volumes, in which to expound it ; and he was not a spendthrift of words. But it is enough for the present purpose if the reader understand what the Halachah was, and in what way it regulated the religious life of the Pharisaic Jew on its practical side.

The term Haggadah, הגדה [3] denotes the interpretation

[1] See also below, in the chapter on the Pharisees in the New Testament.

[2] In my earlier book, *Pharisaism*, I separated Halachah from Haggadah, dealing with the former in Chapter II, with the latter not till Chapter V. This was necessary because the limit of time imposed by a series of lectures made it impossible to deal with both in a single lecture. As I am at present under no such restriction of time or space, I include Haggadah where it properly belongs, in the chapter which deals with Torah and Tradition.

[3] The best explanation that I know of the origin and meaning of the word הגדה is that given by Bacher, in the *J.Q.R.*, 1892, pp. 406 ff. He points to the very frequent use of the phrase הגיד or מגיד in the older Tannaitic Midrash, especially of the school of R. Ishmael. The subject of this verb is הכתוב, expressed or understood. The phrase is used to introduce an explanation of some text under consideration, or to develop something contained or hinted in it. Literally it means : " The Scripture declares or teaches " such-and-such a lesson. From this use of the verb was formed the noun הגדה to denote the lesson so taught, and originally the word was applicable to all the results of the interpretation of Scripture ; but when the Halachah began to be recognised and studied as a special department of Torah, and as the result of a special branch of inter-pretation, then the name Haggadah, which had been of general

of Scripture in general or of the Torah in particular, for edification and not directly for the regulation of conduct. The process was based on the axiom that the Torah contained the whole revelation which God had given to Israel ; and the interpretation whose result was Hagga- dah was the process of drawing forth all else that the Torah contained, other than precept, for the purpose of making clear the religious and moral lessons to be found there. The subject-matter of the Haggadah included, therefore, all that in other religions is covered by the term Doctrinal Theology, it also included what would be assigned to ethics, psychology and metaphysics. Not, indeed, that there was any systematic study of philosophy in the interpretation of Torah, but that the problems of thought and experience which provide the main themes of philosophy were, so far as they came within the range of Jewish thought in Talmudic times, dealt with on the lines of Haggadah. That is, the interpretation of Torah was made the means of finding answers to such questions as came before the minds of the Jewish teachers con- cerning God, his works and ways and attributes, the nature and origin and destiny of man, his relation to God, the mystery of evil and many other kindred topics. It was self-evident that if there was anything to be learned on these subjects it must be learned from the Torah, and what the Torah declared, ' higgid,' when rightly interpreted, was what God had revealed in the Torah. Any explicit statement of the teaching so declared in a single passage of Torah was a ' haggadah ' ; and the sum total of such teaching came to be called by

application, came to be reserved for such results of interpretation of Toiah as were not concerned with its preceptive portion. This is, in fact, what Haggadah does mean ; and all the descriptions given by way of indicating the nature of Haggadah, e.g. tale, legend, fanciful narrative, etc., are good enough as showing some of the forms which the Haggadah took, but they do not explain why it took those forms. The form אגדה, often found, especially in the Palestinian Talmud, is only a New Hebrew variant, not an Aramaic form. Agada is the form generally used by German and other Continental writers, Haggadah by English ones.

the generic term the Haggadah. Thus, Halachah and Haggadah between them divided the whole contents of Torah ; they were each in their way the explicit statement of what was implicit in the Torah, the unfolding of its hidden meaning so that it could be received and apprehended in human minds.

It is easy to see that the Haggadah allowed of much greater variety of treatment than Halachah. As the object in view was not the definition of a strict rule of conduct, but the building up of character and the quickening of spiritual and moral life, the teacher was free to use other means than those of severe logic and strict attention to precedent. Haggadah was largely the result of allowing imagination to play round and over the contents of the Scripture, the imagination of men whose purpose was to teach religion, yet at the same time the imagination of men quick-witted and discerning, who had a deep if not a wide knowledge of human nature, and who were accustomed to meditate on the problems of religion and religious experience. Haggadah was the field where thought found free outlet ; for whereas the Halachah was only defined and settled by the vote of a majority after careful deliberation, the Haggadah was under no such restriction. Probably no one except an accredited teacher would be in a position to declare and teach Haggadah at all ; but I believe it is true to say that any such teacher was free to teach Haggadah if he had any to teach, if he had so studied and meditated upon Torah that he could bring forth the fruits of his meditation in some form that proved helpful to those who heard it. There were great masters of Haggadah among the Talmudic Rabbis who devoted themselves to this form of study and teaching ; but so far as I know there was nothing to prevent less eminent men from trying to do the same thing. If they succeeded, in however small a degree, they added something to the treasure of religious thought and instruction which was the inheritance of the Jewish community, enlarged and enriched with each generation. If they did not succeed there was nothing lost, since they had had nothing to give. But they were not fettered by any requirement of doctrinal uniformity, for no one was obliged to assent to any haggadah which was told him, as if it were an article in a creed. It was no argument against a haggadah that it differed from, or even contradicted, another haggadah on the same subject. There were, on the Rabbinical theory, many meanings in the Torah, even in a single sentence of the Torah. God could say many things in one utterance ; and the more of these could be unfolded and declared and learned, so much the more was God's purpose fulfilled in giving the Torah (see Yalk. Shimoni. on Ps. lxii. 11, § 783).

Haggadah, therefore, in the practice of those who expounded it, took such forms as stories founded on the lives of persons mentioned in Scripture, parables to illustrate types of character in which some virtue or vice was conspicuous, plays of fancy based on some slight hint hidden in a Scripture phrase, arbitrary changes in the wording of a text for the sake of pointing a moral or deducing a religious lesson, even sometimes mere freaks of wit and grotesque fancy, intended, we may suppose, to arrest the attention of a drowsy audience. Almost everything that imagination could do is represented in the Haggadah. Almost, but not everything. The Haggadists never so far lost sight of their true function as religious teachers that they would allow their imagination to descend to coarse and unclean jesting. There is much plain speaking in the Rabbinical literature upon sexual matters ; but I do not believe that there is a single story in the whole of the Haggadah which was told with a prurient purpose, or a play of wit in which the point depends on its obscenity. The absence of such features may by some be deemed a defect ; but, whether defective or not, the Haggadah is, so far as I have studied it, entirely free from that kind of literary embellishment.

As for the profanity which is sometimes charged against the Haggadah, there is some apparent ground for the charge ; for the imagination of the Haggadist did sometimes allow him to take considerable liberties with the thought of God and His dealings with mankind. Haggadoth could be quoted which on the face of them cer-tainly do seem to be highly irreverent in expression. Yet the intention was certainly not irreverent ; and the reader, at all events the Gentile reader, needs to be very cautious in taking a piece of Haggadah at its face value. Gentiles usually are not aware of this.

Haggadah, as already explained, is largely a work of imagination, a free creation of motive and incident for the purpose of teaching a religious or moral lesson. Statements of such a character are obviously of no value as evidence for the alleged historical events to which they purport to refer. Both the Haggadists and their hearers were quite aware of this, or would have been if they had thought about it, for such a question would probably seldom if ever arise. But a Haggadist was in no way debarred from referring to persons and incidents within his own immediate knowledge, such as the inci-dents of the war against Vespasian and Titus, or those of the three years' Terror which followed the defeat of Bar Cocheba. The Haggadah includes all that the teachers who lived through those terrible times had to say about them ; but the mistake of rejecting it all as unreliable invention is only committed by those who have but a slight and general acquaintance with Hag-gadah, and is readily avoided by those who have the patience to consider such statements each on its own merits. So studied, the Haggadah is an indispensable help in reconstructing the history of the times when its exponents lived. The foregoing account may serve to indicate the nature and intention of the Haggadah as the other element along with the Halachah of the defined contents of the Torah. I shall now, in the remainder of this chapter, deal with their respective relation to Tradition.

It has already been shown that the conception of the unwritten Torah was arrived at by combining Torah with Tradition, the unwritten Torah being regarded as teaching

which had been handed down along with the written
Torah as its true interpretation. To those who first
made use of the conception of the unwritten Torah, i.e. the
earliest Pharisaic teachers properly so called, the Tradition
to which they appealed must necessarily have been indefi-
nite in form though sufficient in substance. In other
words, they could appeal to the general fact, or at all
events presumption, that what they taught as their
interpretation of Torah rested on Tradition ; but they
could seldom if ever point to a precise authority for that
interpretation in the words of some older teacher. But
the case was different when, as time went on, a definite
halachah was taught upon this or that particular case,
or when some teacher of eminence gave his opinion that
the halachah was so and so. By the accumulation of
such decisions and opinions a quite definite Tradition
was gradually formed, resting for the most part upon
the authority of teachers whose names were known, at
all events at first, though forgotten later The development of Halachah was, as already shown, of vital importance in the religious and moral life of the Pharisees,
and it would have been folly and contempt of the divine
teaching to have allowed those earlier results of the
interpretation of Torah to be forgotten almost as soon as
uttered. It is true that even the marvellous Jewish
memory could not carry it all ; but it was always made
a part of the strict discipline connected with the study
of Torah to learn and to hand down from teacher to
pupil the results already defined in the field of Halachah.
Each generation added its own contribution to what it
had received from the past ; and this lengthening chain
of transmitted teaching, of which the several halachoth
were the separate links, is what is known (at all events
in the New Testament) as the Tradition of the Elders.[1]

[1] In the New Testament παράδοσις τῶν πρεσβυτέρων, Mark vii. 5
and elsewhere. It is curious that the phrase, in this form, does not
seem to occur in the Rabbinical literature. מסורת was, of course, in
common use, meaning tradition, but not combined with הזקנים, the
Elders. Usually it appears in the form מסורת היא בידינו מאבותינו,

At any given date at which the Tradition is examined, it is found (or would be if the material were completely preserved) to consist of a smaller or greater number of halachoth relating to a great variety of cases. The necessity made itself felt, as time went on, of reducing to some kind of order the ever-growing collection of halachoth ; and possibly Hillel, but more probably R. Akiba, made the first attempt at a classified arrangement of them. R. Akiba's death in the War of Bar Cocheba prevented his completion of the work. What he began was taken up and carried further by his greatest disciple, R. Meir, until in the next generation the work was completed, substantially at all events, in the Mishnah of Rabbi, Judah the Prince. The Mishnah was accepted as the authoritative statement of the Halachah, and such it has ever since remained. But not on that account did the chain of Tradition cease from lengthening, for the Mishnah in its turn became the subject of study and explanation in the schools of Palestine and Babylonia. The main object of such study was to verify the Halachah by establishing its connection with Torah, elucidating its meaning, and, in fact though not in so many words, bringing it up to date by showing how it was to be applied to the circumstances of the time. The result of such study of the Mishnah was called Gemara ; and the Mishnah, together with its Gemara, makes up the Talmud. There is only one Mishnah, but there are two Talmuds, known as the Palestinian or Jerusalem and the Babylonian respectively, from the countries where the Gemara was developed. For details on all this, see articles in the *Jewish Encyclopædia*.

The Tradition of the Elders represents the development of the Halachah. Historically it was made up of decisions and opinions formulated in each successive

---

"we have this tradition from our fathers," as in j. Shek. 48[d], though this instance refers to a family tradition and not to the main tradition of the Halachah. Of the fact implied in *Tradition of the Elders*, though not of the precise phrase, the classical illustration is M. Aboth i. 1, משה קיבל תורה מסיני ומסרה ליהושע:

generation and handed on to the next. The Rabbis
were perfectly aware of this; and besides recording the
names (when known) of those teachers whose definition
of this or that halachah had been adopted and confirmed,
they were often able to say that such-and-such a halachah
had been established in such-and-such an Assembly.
Many halachoth were of unknown origin, and of these
some were attributed in general terms to the Sopherim,
and some few were expressly described as " halachah
(imparted) to Moses from Sinai," חלכה למשה מסיני.[1]
There was some uncertainty as to which halachoth ought
to be described by that term; in some cases a halachah
so described was shown to have been defined by some
well-known teacher. But the phrase always served as a
reminder, if reminder were needed, that the tradition of
Halachah began with Moses. And the Pharisaic theory
is elucidated by the answer given to R. Akiba by some
of his disciples, which implies that the whole Torah is
Halachah of Moses from Sinai (b. Nidd 45[a]). For the
Pharisaic theory was this, that the whole Torah, as it
existed in the mind of God was imparted to Moses, not
explicitly but implicitly, and that the whole process of
interpretation consisted in rendering explicit what up till
then had been implicit, drawing forth some meaning or
lesson unknown till then, but which had been in the Torah
all the time. The divine revelation could never be
exhausted, and therefore every fresh interpretation,
though in appearance it were new, was really old—a
thought in the divine mind for the first time apprehended
by the human mind. And this is what is meant when
it was said (j. Peah 17[a]): " Whatever an acute disciple
shall hereafter teach in the presence of his Rabbi has
already been said to Moses on Sinai." [2] That dictum of
R. Joshua b. Levi, which on the face of it appears
to be and is sometimes hastily taken to be a mere

[1] See *Kohler Festschrift*, pp. 56–70, Bacher's article on " Satzung
von Sinai."

[2] See the whole passage j. Peah ii. 5, which contains some very
instructive remarks on the Pharisaic theory of tradition.

absurdity of exaggeration, sums up in a sentence the
Pharisaic theory of the definition and transmission of
Halachah.

It was only in the department of Halachah that the
idea of Tradition was worked out to its fullest extent,
because, as already shown, the results obtained by the
interpretation of Torah on its Halachic side were binding
and regulative in a way that the Haggadah was not.
Yet the results of Haggadic interpretation of Torah
were also valuable as being the fruits of the wisdom and
piety of the great " Masters in Israel " ; and it was an
obvious duty to gather up those fruits for future use.
There was no Haggadic Tradition of the Elders, but
there was an immense amount of Haggadah taught and
handed down and finally collected for the instruction of
later generations. Some of this material found a place
in the Talmud, but the great mass of it is now to be read
in the Midrashim. Excluding those known by the titles
of Mechilta, Siphra and Siphre, which are mainly halachic, there are a great number of haggadic midrashim,
large and small, from the Midrash Rabbah at the one
extreme to the smallest piece edited by Jellinek or
Eisenstein at the other. These are all traditional in the
sense that they contain the teaching handed down from
earlier times, sometimes centuries earlier than the date
when the collection was made. But there was not such
a progressive development of Haggadah as there was of
Halachah. It is accurate to distinguish between the
older Halachah and the younger, between the Halachah
as it was in the time of Hillel, and the Halachah as it
was in the time of Akiba or of Rabbi. But it would not
be accurate to distinguish, unless in a very general way,
between an older and a younger Haggadah. For the
Haggadah was the result of continual meditation upon
the sacred themes contained in the Torah and presenting
themselves to the mind ; and those sacred themes
remained for the most part unchanged, while men with
different gifts of thought and imagination, different
degrees of spiritual insight, and different occasions to

draw forth their powers, brought forth the fruit of their meditation in endless variety.

Such then, finally, was the Pharisaic conception of Torah, the divine revelation given to Israel through Moses, God's teaching to His people, instructing them what it was his will that they should do, the way in which they should walk—Halachah ; and imparting to them the lessons of truth and wisdom whereby they could become what His children should be—Haggadah. So regarded, it was only natural, as it was entirely right, for the Pharisaic teachers whose thoughts are enshrined in the Talmud and the Midrash, to exalt the Torah to the utmost height that speech could attain, as the supreme gift which the divine goodness had bestowed on the people whom He had chosen. They would have been unworthy of that gift if they had neglected to preserve, from age to age, the words in which its meaning was unfolded, and its hidden treasures gradually brought to light, or if they had ceased in their age-long search to know ever yet more of the deep things of God. According to the light vouchsafed to them and the way pointed out to them, the Pharisees and their successors, through all the Christian centuries, have been faithful, and have endured the scorn and reviling of men because they trusted in God and were not ashamed.

CHAPTER IV

THE PHARISEES AND THE SYNAGOGUE

FOR the sake of greater clearness of presentation of the whole subject, I reserve for separate treatment in this chapter a topic which is closely related both to the history of the Pharisees as described in Chapter II and their theory of Torah and Tradition explained in Chapter III. I refer to the Synagogue, which was preeminently a Pharisaic institution, and one without which the maintenance and development of their religious and moral life, whether communal or individual, are scarcely conceivable. When I say that the Synagogue was preeminently a Pharisaic institution, I do not mean that the Pharisees created it, for its origin dates, in all probability, from a time before the Pharisees had appeared. I mean that the Pharisees, when they did appear, found in the Synagogue an institution with whose purpose they were in the closest sympathy and whose influence they did their utmost to strengthen and extend. They controlled the ritual of the Temple by imposing their will upon the Sadducean priests, as shown above (p. 47) ; but they were at home in the Synagogue, and developed its two functions of worship and instruction without external constraint. If it had been otherwise, if the Pharisees had been obliged to capture the Synagogue as they captured the Temple, it is hard to see how they could have won the devoted adherence of the majority of the people, as it is common knowledge that they did. For the Synagogue was in every village, while the Temple was only in Jerusalem ; and while it is of course perfectly true that the Temple so long as it stood was the visible expression of the religion of the whole people, collectively, yet the Synagogue was the expression of their religion day by day and week by week, for Jews, not collectively as a nation, but as friends and neighbours, dwellers in the same village, inhabiting the same countryside. The Temple was the altar, the Synagogue was the hearth, and the sacred fire burned on each of them. With the fall of the Temple the fire was quenched on the altar, stamped out under the brutal heel of the conqueror ; but it still glowed on the hearth, and the Synagogue survived to shelter and preserve from that day to this the religion of the Pharisees.

It will therefore be no digression from the main subject if I stop to dwell on the history and function of the Synagogue and upon its close association with the Pharisees. The actual beginning of the Synagogue is unknown, and the first certain mention of it occurs at a date which must be far later than the institution itself. But it is generally agreed that the period of the Captivity presents the conditions under which the rise of the Synagogue can be most naturally explained. Among the many hardships and privations inflicted on those who were carried away to Babylon by Nebuchadnezzar not the least would be the loss of the Temple and the impossibility of joining in the worship there. It is true that for the individual member of the nation the opportunity of actually attending the Temple service was only enjoyed a few times in the year, and we do not know whether any regular provision was made for the ministration of religion at other times and places. But, in any case, while the Temple stood, the Jew, wherever he lived, knew that the worship of the God of Israel was being offered in the ancient Sanctuary, on behalf and in the name of all the people. With the Exile that assurance came to an end. There was no Temple any more ; the captives were deprived of what had been the chief external support of their religion. The question could not fail to present itself to the minds of the more devout amongst them, What was to become of their religion ? There is

no record of what they did, nor indeed any probability
that as a community the captives either could or did
take any steps to answer the question forced upon them.
But it seems very natural to suppose that here and there
a few would meet together from time to time, neighbours
and friends who had known each other in the old homeland, and would encourage and comfort one another under
their present affliction. This is enough to account for
what may be called the germ of the Synagogue—the
occasional meeting of groups of people for religious purposes. Even this is pure conjecture, for there is no
contemporary record of any sort to show that such
meetings did in fact take place. But the conjecture has
at least this much in its favour, that the periodical meetings which developed into the Synagogue must have
begun some time, and the period of the Captivity provides a stronger determining cause than any other period,
because the people were then deprived of the Temple
and of any other provision for religion, if there were any
other, and were thrown entirely on their own resources,
and that, too, in a heathen land. It is obvious that some
means must have been devised by the exiles for the
maintenance of their religion, for otherwise there would
have been none left when the Captivity came to an end,
and the exiles would have gone the way of the Ten
Tribes. The same argument tends to show that the
origin of the germ of the Synagogue after the return
from Babylon is less probable, since the loss of the
Temple was in time made good by rebuilding it. Moreover, the type of meeting and form of worship of the
Synagogue, as it came to be known afterwards, point
to an origin independent of the Temple and conceived
on different lines. To attempt to imitate in Babylonia
the Temple in Jerusalem was unthinkable, and even to
symbolise its services by forms of prayer extremely
unlikely. If the circumstances in which the exiles found
themselves were at all like what I have suggested, then
prayer would find some means of utterance through the
mere need to pray ; speech on sacred themes and instruc-

tion in the way of righteousness would find their opportunity in any company meeting together. In such circumstances the usage of the Temple could give no guidance, and instead, the first beginning was made of a type of worship which outlasted the Temple and has come down to the present day, the type of congregational worship without priest or ritual, still maintained substantially in its ancient form in the modern Synagogue, and still to be traced in the forms of Christian worship, though overlaid and distorted by many non-Jewish elements. In all their long history, the Jewish people have done scarcely anything more wonderful than to create the Synagogue. No human institution has a longer continuous history, and none has done more for the uplifting of the race.

I place, then, in the period of the Captivity, the appearance of the germ of the Synagogue in simple meetings for worship and instruction. How these developed cannot be traced. But it is again reasonable to suppose that they gradually became regular by tending to association with the Sabbath, partly because that was the holy day from immemorial antiquity, and partly because it was the day of rest from ordinary work. If, as I have held to be probable, the original meetings began during the Captivity, the practice must have become so far established as to bear transplanting to Palestine after the return, for otherwise the process would have to have been started over again without its original determining cause. I am by no means suggesting that regular Synagogues were at once established by the returning exiles on their arrival, but only that the habit of meeting for worship and instruction, begun in Exile, was not wholly forgotten in the recovered homeland, and had sufficient vitality to take root and grow there. Such meetings do not necessarily imply a special building set apart for them such as became usual in later times. Synagogues as assemblies may have been far older than the House of Meeting, בית הכנסת, as it came to be called. There is no certain mention of these till long after the return from the Captivity; but when Ezra appointed the Torah to be read not only on the Sabbath but on the second and fifth day of the week (b. B.K. 82[ab]), it is hard not to suppose that he made use for this purpose of assemblies of a religious character already in existence, and already to some extent spread through the land.

It must be frankly admitted that the early stages of the development of the Synagogue are unknown, and that several questions of great interest must be left without answer in the absence of any evidence upon which an answer could be based. The Synagogue does not emerge into clear view until the time of the New Testament and Josephus; but how it came to be such as it there appears can no longer be determined. To attempt a conjectural history would be mere waste of time, for where nothing is known anything is possible. Yet from the study of the Synagogue, as it is first clearly seen at the beginning of the common era, something may be learned; not, indeed, of its history, but of its purpose and character. As regards its history, all that can be said is that at the time in question the Synagogue was already recognised as ancient. "For Moses from generations of old hath them in every city that preach him, being read in the Synagogues every Sabbath" (Acts xv. 21). As to its nature and purpose, it was a local assembly for the promotion of religion through the two main functions of worship and instruction. This twofold purpose has been characteristic of the Synagogue in all ages of its known history, and should never be lost sight of. It presents the earliest example on record of simple congregational worship, and in that capacity became the parent of the Christian Church. But it was also the place where the Torah was taught, and its lessons of religion and duty unfolded and applied for the benefit of the people. This function of teaching also was taken over by the Christian Church, but not to the same extent. No doubt the Church has always given instruction to its members; but the principal object of the Christian assembly in the sacred building has always been worship, whether praise, prayer or sacramental rite. The principal object of the Jewish assembly in the Synagogue has always been to realise in experience the blessing of which the divinely given Torah was the revelation and the instrument. Worship was one way by which that blessing was realised, for worship brought the worshipper into communion with God ; but meditation on the Torah was another way, and so was instruction, which brought forth and spread before the mind of the simple and unlearned the things which God had revealed in His Torah ; and amongst those things revealed were the lessons of plain duty, showing how the will of God was to be done in the acts of the every-day life. I have distinguished a twofold purpose in the Synagogue, for so it appears to the non-Jewish observer ; but I should imagine that to a Jew this double function would appear single, and that the Synagogue was, and is, the place where the divine revelation makes its strongest appeal to his higher nature ; an appeal, many-sided indeed, but yet coming to him from the one God through the one Torah. Whatever helped the Jew to feel that appeal and respond to it, had its rightful place in the Synagogue.

As the earlier history of the institution is unknown, it is impossible to say whether at any time a change from some earlier type took place in the fundamental purpose of the Synagogue as just described. That its true function came to be more clearly apprehended in course of time is only likely ; and with clearer apprehension would naturally come more adequate provision for the fulfilment of that function. But, assuming that Ezra did for the religion of Torah what has been shown in the preceding chapters, then the Synagogue, at whatever period it first became a defined institution, would naturally acquire some such character, and aim at discharging some such function as has been indicated above. Once it assumed that character it never afterwards lost it, and it keeps it still.

If such were essentially the character and purpose of the Synagogue, then it is clear that such an institution must have been entirely congenial to the Pharisees. Their one concern was the Torah and the religion founded on it—the exercise of that religion in worship, the practical application of it in the duties of life and the training of the heart and mind to be in accord with the will of God. If they had started *de novo* to create an institution to fulfil this purpose, they could not have improved on the Synagogue. If they found it in existence when they appeared they could only hail it with joy. Whether as a defined institution it was historically earlier or later than the appearance of the Pharisees under that name cannot be determined with any certainty. But it seems to me most probable that as the Pharisees inherited the spirit of Ezra and carried on the ideas concerning Torah which had come down through the Sopherim and the Ḥasidim, so those ideas found expression and application through such means as in course of time became defined in the institution of the Synagogue. The two went side by side, and each naturally influenced the other. There were those who were devoted to the religion of Torah from the days of Ezra onwards. They cherished and developed the Synagogue ; it helped and sustained them. That is the essential fact, and it is of but secondary importance to determine, if it were possible to do so, whether the Synagogue or the Pharisees first came by their definite and distinctive name.

Another question, of great importance, indeed, but to which no completely satisfactory answer can be given, is, What was the relation in practice between the Temple and the Synagogue ? The Temple was unique, the one central Sanctuary where the God of Israel could be worshipped with the due ceremony of sacrifice and ritual prescribed in the Torah. It was the visible symbol and outward expression of the religion of Israel for the whole nation. Round it gathered all the nobler emotions of the Jewish heart, from patriotic pride to the passionate devotion which finds utterance in so many of the Psalms. So long as the Temple stood, no other institution could rival its immense prestige. What place did the Synagogue hold beside that august shrine? That question gains additional point from the fact that there was a Synagogue in the Temple itself. This seems to me a significant and suggestive fact, and one which has received less attention than it deserves. The fact itself is vouched for by passages in the Mishnah (Joma vii. 1) and Tosephta (Succ. iv. 12), which refer to the "ruler of the Synagogue" (the ἀρχισυνάγωγος of the New Testament) and the "minister," ḥazzan (ὑπηρέτης). It was probably located in the Hall of Hewn Stones, Lishkath ha-gazith, where the Sanhedrin held its meetings.[1] In any case it met somewhere within the precincts of the Temple. Now it is generally admitted that the order of service in the Synagogue was made to correspond with that of the Temple, in so far that the prayers more or less represented the sacrifices. The comparison is made in the Talmud (b. Ber. 26[b]), and is not disputed. It is also generally accepted, on the evidence of Talmudic tradition, that the main elements of the liturgy, in their earliest form, were instituted by the men of the Great Synagogue, i.e. the Sopherim. Whether any of their work still exists in its original form is very unlikely, but it is quite in accord with what we know of the ideas of the Sopherim that they should have taken careful thought for these matters. It goes without saying that such directions as were given, such forms as were appointed for the conduct of public worship, were sent out from Jerusalem, presumably from the Sanhedrin, and if not from the Sanhedrin as a whole then from those who represented the strict adherents of the Torah. The Synagogue would not have possessed a uniform type of service unless its development had been guided by some central authority. So far all is clear. But it is also generally assumed that the prayers, Psalms, etc., which made up the Synagogue service, as it was known, e.g. in Talmudic times, were originally appointed for and formed parts of the Temple

[1] See Herzfeld, *Gesch. d. V. Israel*, i. 393, § 9. His location of the Synagogue in the Lishkath-ha-gazith is only conjectural, but his arguments seem to have much weight.

service, presumably interspersed with the various sacrifices and other ceremonies. That they were used in the Temple I am by no means prepared to deny; but it does not seem to me at all natural that they should have been combined with the ceremonial rites which formed the chief feature of the Temple service. If the prayers were to some extent modelled on the sacrifices, what need was there for both to be offered in the same service? That some of the Psalms were eminently fitted to be sung in a ceremonial service may be readily admitted; but it is no less obvious that many other Psalms were not. I suggest, therefore, that the institution of the prayers, etc., rightly ascribed to the Sopherim, was intended in the first instance for the Synagogue. The Temple already had its order of service in the ritual prescribed in the Torah. The Synagogue had not, and the Sopherim supplied its want by appointing an order, or at least the beginnings of an order. Whether the Synagogue in the precincts of the Temple already existed in the time of the Sopherim there is no evidence to show; but it must have made its appearance there at some point of time, and when it did it would bring with it such forms of prayer as were already customary in synagogues generally. From this time on it would be literally true to say that the prayers and Psalms, etc., were said or sung in the Temple, while yet their place would be in the service of the Temple Synagogue and not in the Temple service properly so called. Again I press the question, If these prayers, etc., were included in the regular Temple service along with the sacrifices, etc., why repeat them all (without the sacrifices) in the Synagogue a few yards away? I hold, therefore, that in all that is said in the Talmud and elsewhere about what was done in the Temple we may freely admit the fact of its all being done within the Temple precincts, but that we must distinguish between the ceremonial and the non-ceremonial elements, assigning the former to the proper ritual of the Temple and the latter, on the whole, to the service of the Synagogue which met within its walls.

As the Temple-Synagogue is known to the Mishnah, and no hint is given of its being recently established, it must have been already old at the beginning of the common era. Either it dates from the time (whenever that was) when first synagogues began to be organised, or else it was introduced into the Temple at some later time. Is it unreasonable to suggest that when the Pharisees enjoyed their golden age of power in the reign of queen Alexandra (see above Chapter II, pp. 47–8), and asserted that power in gaining control over the Temple services, they took the opportunity to plant a synagogue in the very Temple itself, so that their ideas of worship, of which the Synagogue was the embodiment, might be represented in the central Sanctuary? Some such intention seems to be suggested by the fact that there were very many [1] synagogues in Jerusalem itself; for, if there were so many, why add another one in the Temple which already had its organised worship, without the need of what the Synagogue provided? It is very different if the Synagogue were placed in the Temple to mark a certain new emphasis upon aspects of religion which the Temple was not historically fitted to represent. Further than this I do not venture to go, and must leave the suggestion for what it may be worth.

The Synagogue, however and whenever it actually assumed the form in which it is known at the beginning of our area, was a factor of the very greatest importance in the life of the Jewish people. There was a synagogue in every village, and probably many in each of the larger towns. It was the natural centre for the religion of the people living near it, not merely through the services on the Sabbath, but through its teaching and its charities. Its influence would be felt all through the week, and more or less by all the inhabitants of the place, even though not all were equally zealous or zealous at all for religion. The Pharisees were marked out by their

---

[1] The number 480, given in j. Meg. 73[d], cannot safely be relied on; but, unless the actual number had been considerable, the statement would have defeated its own purpose.

spiritual ancestry and their own principles as the natural leaders of the Synagogue. It gave them their opportunity of bringing religion home to the people in the form in which it was most dear to themselves. They were, indeed, apparently the only teachers who made this their object. There is no mention, so far as I know, of Sadducean synagogues. The Sadducees, as has been shown above (Chapter II, p. 43), were not at all keen on spreading the knowledge of Torah amongst the people. It was sufficient that the knowledge of it should be, as of old, reserved for the priests. The Pharisees were the only ones who brought the Torah to the people and helped them to realise the blessing of it. This is not to say that all the people became Pharisees, for we know from Josephus (Ant. xvii. 2, 4) that the Pharisees in his time numbered only some few thousands among the whole population. But it explains very well how it was that the great majority of the people sided with the Pharisees, followed their lead and held them in honour and reverence.

It should be remembered in this connection that the Pharisees represented the view that the Torah had been given to all Israel, and that the interpretation of it was not the exclusive privilege of the priests (see above, Chapter III, p. 62). This view influenced and even determined the character of the synagogue, for it was essentially an institution of laymen. Priests were not, of course, excluded, and no doubt many of the Pharisees were priests. But no priest as such had any controlling function in the management of the synagogue. The sole qualification there was piety, knowledge of Torah and ability to communicate that knowledge ; and that was not confined to any class of men, whether priests or not. There was no one who held the same position in regard to the synagogue which is held by the clergyman or minister of a Christian congregation in later times. A Rabbi, in the times when that title had become general, i.e. in the first century of the common era, was only a layman ; and such authority as he exercised rested on his own personal character and mental gifts, not upon any kind of ministerial office. A Rabbi was ordained to his office, it is true ; but that meant that he was recognised as competent to interpret and teach the Torah—it did not place him in a sacred caste apart from his fellowmen. The worship of the synagogue was regulated by the members themselves under the leadership of those who, by gifts and character, were best fitted to lead ; the prayers may have been usually recited by one person appointed for that duty, but members were called up to take part in the reading of the Torah and the portion from the Prophets. If a discourse was given after the prayers, it was given by someone in the opinion of the ruler of the synagogue best qualified to give it. There was no stated preacher. When Paul and his companions went to the synagogue in Antioch of Pisidia (Acts xiii. 15) they were given the opportunity of speaking to the congregation, being merely visitors, not regular members, much less its appointed officers. It was in some such way that Jesus had his opportunity of speaking in the synagogue at Nazareth (Luke iv. 16), though there, indeed, it is only said that " he stood up to read," presumably the ' haphtarah,' or portion from the Prophets.

This lay character of the organisation of the Synagogue was entirely in keeping with the principles of the Pharisees ; not from any hostility to priests as such, but as expressing the view that the function of the priests was restricted to the Temple, and consisted in the due performance of the ritual appointed for that place. A priest was held in honour for his sacred office ; but that did not suffice to qualify him for the widely different duties which had to be fulfilled in the Synagogue, and there was no reason why, merely *quâ* priest, he should expect, let alone claim, any position of privilege in regard to those duties. How far considerations of this kind were consciously present to the minds of those who developed the system of the Synagogue I do not know ; but this is clear, that it was the organisation of the Synagogue on non-priestly lines, as what would be

called now a laymen's church, which saved it from
destruction when the Temple fell. The altar and the
sacrifices could never be replaced unless or until the
Temple was rebuilt, and never anywhere out of Jerusalem ; but the synagogue could be planted anywhere
in the world where Jews were, and provide a local home
for the religion of Torah under every sky. Already,
when Jerusalem was captured, there were synagogues in
every land, probably in every considerable city, of the
then civilised world. And although from that day to
this Jews have continued to pray for the rebuilding of
Jerusalem and the restoration of the Temple, it is in the
synagogue that they have uttered their prayers ; and
if it had not been for the synagogues, the prayers would
have died into silence on the lips of a people dwindling
to extinction.

The Synagogue, as has been shown, was in full vigour
at the beginning of our era ; it was the only institution
which ministered to the religion of the people in their
daily and weekly life, and without making any extravagant claims on its behalf we may say with certainty
that it did fulfil its primary function with a considerable
measure of success. It is worth notice that Jesus, though
he said hard things about the Pharisees, never said anything against the synagogues ; and it is said of him that
it was his custom to go to the synagogue on the Sabbath
day (Luke iv. 16). Now, while it is quite true that we
do not know the exact date when the Synagogue first
appeared on the scene of Jewish history, nevertheless
its rise and development fall within the period covered by
the dominant influence of Torah established by Ezra
and the Sopherim. If that influence were of the kind
commonly supposed by Christians, and its effect had
been to sterilise the Jewish religion and turn its prophetic freedom into a legal bondage, then the Synagogue
would have felt the full force of that influence, and
would have been in no condition to keep alive the Jewish
religion, or serve as the natural model for the newly
formed Christian Church. It did both of these things, and

did them very thoroughly. If the influence of Ezra and the Sopherim, and the later Pharisees, were really a deadening influence, then the Synagogue must have grown up as a protest against that influence ; but there is not the slightest trace of any evidence to show that such protest was ever made, or the need of making it ever felt. The Synagogue is the organised embodiment of the religion of Torah or it is utterly meaningless. Whence the conclusion follows that the influence of Ezra and his later followers was not in the direction of reducing the Jewish religion to a barren legalism. The Synagogue was strong and flourishing at the beginning of our era. If it was then very ancient, dating back perhaps to the time of Ezra, then the supposed deadening power of the religion of Torah had not been able to stifle its vitality in all the centuries from his time to that of Jesus. And if the Synagogue were at this later date only of comparatively recent origin, then all the supposed deadening influence aforesaid was not strong enough to strangle at its birth an institution so full of spiritual vitality as it immediately proved itself to be. The sober truth of the matter is that the development of religion in terms of Torah was not the gradual petrifaction of the spiritual life that Christians have usually supposed it to be ; and the notion that it was should be put away as one of the errors which have too long passed for history.

If what has been said above is not sufficient, then this also is evidence bearing on the same point, that practically all of the Canonical Scriptures which are now known as the Old Testament were read and studied in the Synagogue. They were studied not merely, or rather not at all, for the sake of legal hair-splitting, but for the purpose of learning whatever they had to teach, whether for the practical conduct of life or for edification. It was the Sopherim who had most to do with the final collecting and arranging of those same Scriptures ; a thing they certainly would not have been careful to do if their own teaching stood condemned by the freer utterance of Isaiah and Amos. They believed themselves to be in

the direct line of succession to the Prophets (b. B. Bath. 12ᵃ
and Aboth i. 1) ; and if they did not speak in such
trumpet tones, at least they made their hearers attend
and take to heart what they said, to a degree which no
prophet had ever succeeded in doing. If the Prophets
could have done what Ezra did, there would have been
no need of the sharp lesson of the Exile.

The book of Psalms stands alone, not only in the Old
Testament, but in the literature of the world. The
collection of the various hymns in that book falls certainly
within the period of the rise of the Synagogue, whatever
may be the dates of the several pieces. Not only so,
but certainly some and probably many Psalms were
composed during that period. Psalm xix. and Psalm cxix.
have already been mentioned above as especially Pharisaic
in character. But all of them were part of the treasure
of the Synagogue, and many, perhaps most, found a
place in its services. They were not the hymns of poets
of another race and language translated and incorporated
into their service, like the Psalms as they appear in the
Roman Catholic and Anglican Prayer Books. They were
for Jews their own hymns in their own language ; and
though they have served to utter the devotion and
aspiration, the praise and penitence of millions who have
learned them through Christian use, they can say things
for the Jewish soul in its worship which are hidden from
the Christian, since no translation can exactly reproduce
the elusive turns of expression of the original.

I only refer to the Psalms here in order to use them
as additional evidence bearing on the character of the
Synagogue and of the worship offered there. If the
influence of Ezra and the Sopherim had tended towards
the petrifaction of religion, then it is strange that those
teachers who were most directly responsible for applying
the principles of Ezra should have taken the trouble to
collect the Psalms, if they did not write them, and should
have given them so prominent a place in the Synagogue
service. This they most certainly did, whatever they
may have done in regard to the Temple service. At the

time when the Synagogue was being brought into the form in which we know it first, the Psalms were fresh and new. They have never become stale from that day to this. And if they had been felt to be alien to the spirit of the Synagogue, out of keeping with its (supposed) barren legalism, then the Synagogue would have left the Psalms alone, as it afterwards left the Apocalyptic literature alone (see below, Chapter VII). Whatever may be the merits of that literature, its spirit was certainly alien to that of the Synagogue ; and though its influence can be traced in the Talmud and the Midrashim, it is, so far as I know, entirely absent from the liturgy. The Psalms were hymns of religion, felt to be fresh and living, and for that reason, and no other, the men who made the Synagogue and gave to its worship the means of utterance, turned to the Psalms to supply their need. The men who did this were those who followed the lead of Ezra ; and of the Synagogue as it was in the time of Jesus and the first Christians, the House of Meeting, the place of worship, the school where all the lessons of the Torah were taught, by men who believed in it to all who could be helped to share in its blessing, and learned by those who found that blessing—of the Synagogue thus living and ministering to the higher life of the Jewish people, the Pharisees were the devoted friends, and theirs the animating spirit.

CHAPTER V

THE TEACHING OF THE PHARISEES—I

In this and the following chapter I shall survey the religious and ethical teaching of the Pharisees; the answers which they gave to the various questions which present themselves to the thinkers and teachers of every religion, to all who ponder the problems of life on its higher side. That field of inquiry and study is open to all, and what it contains is fundamentally the same for all; but between the several bodies of thought produced by that study there is wide diversity, both in the form in which the fundamentals are apprehended and the terms in which the resulting answers are expressed. Comparison of one body of teaching with others is possible; but it is a mistake to try and force the concepts of one body of thought into the framework of another, and still more to condemn the mangled victim of such a process because it does not conform to a standard which it did not recognise and never attempted to reach. Pharisaic teaching deals with the same fundamental problems as those which form the subject of Christian teaching, but it approached them in a way and regarded them from a standpoint widely different from those of the Christian Church.[1] It will be my endeavour to set forth as clearly as I can, without partiality and without prejudice, the Pharisaic way and standpoint in regard to the treatment of theology and ethics, and to present the results at which they arrived.

[1] See an article by the present writer on "The Fundamentals of Religion as Interpreted by Christianity and Rabbinical Judaism," in the *Hibbert Journal* for January 1923.

An exposition of Pharisaic theology must necessarily proceed on lines very different from those which would be appropriate to Christian theology. The contents of both are indeed much more akin than is usually recognised, and fundamentally they are only attempts to apprehend and express the same spiritual realities ; but they differ in the terms which they use to describe those realities, in the conclusions which they drew from their premises, and in the emphasis which they laid upon the several factors involved. Pharisaic theology may be said to fall under the two heads of Halachah and Haggadah ; and if a division of Christian theology were made to correspond with the Pharisaic, it would have to be into moral theology and doctrinal theology. That would be, roughly speaking, correct as regards the subject matter ; but it would be entirely wrong as regards the emphasis laid on the respective members of the twofold theology. In the Pharisaic theology, as in the Christian, there is one department where agreement is required, where the results laid down by authority must be accepted and where individual liberty is strictly controlled ; and there is another department where, within wide limits, freedom is allowed, where acceptance of the declared teaching is not enforced, however much it may be desired, and where the individual has a considerable range of independence. But Pharisaic and Christian theology differ in this, that the one requires acceptance of what the other leaves free, and allows liberty where the other enforces obligation. The Halachah is indeed Law, though the Torah as a whole is not ; and the Haggadah is the free expression of the Pharisaic mind, its meditation upon spiritual things. The same restriction of individual liberty which was imposed by the Halachah is enforced in the case of the Christian creed and the dogmatic theology based upon it. And the same liberty, to the extent that implicit acceptance is not required, is found in regard to the Haggadah on the one side and moral theology on the other. Dogma is the Christian Halachah. And when, from the Christian side, the burden of the Law is con-

trasted with the freedom under the Gospel, it would be
well to bear in mind that the burden, if burden there
be, is only shifted, so to speak, from one shoulder to the
other. If to require acceptance and to enforce it by
strict discipline be good in the one case, it cannot be
justly condemned in the other; and if the Pharisee is
to be blamed for the Halachah, on what ground is the
Christian to be praised for the Creed? Each can say to
the other: " Physician, heal thyself ! " The two cases
are closely alike in substance though widely different in
form. For the Halachah served as the chief bond to
hold the Jewish community together, when every other
bond of national life was broken, and Jews were scattered wide over the face of the earth. And whether the
Christian Church, comprising men of many nationalities,
could have been held together without the Creeds, is a
question not to be hastily answered. The Church needed
a bond of union quite as much as the Jewish community
did. It could not, even if it had wished, have adopted
the Halachah for this purpose. Indeed, it very speedily
repudiated the Halachah, chiefly under the leadership of
Paul; and the early controversy with the Jewish Christians was the conflict of opinion between those who saw
and those who did not see that the Halachah was
impossible in a Church which was to consist almost wholly
of Gentiles.

But the Church, when it had shaken off the Halachah,
and said many hard things about it, very soon found
itself in just the same difficulty as that which the Halachah had been employed to meet. Some bond was
absolutely necessary to hold the Christian community
together, as the Church increased in numbers and in the
variety of its Gentile components. The result was the
Creed, and in time the whole body of dogmatic theology.
The Halachah was embodied in the Talmud, and was
the subject of Rabbinical casuistry more often condemned
than understood. The dogmatic theology of the Christian
Church has been worked out to a degree of minute
detail and subtle refinement fully equal, for good or

for evil, to anything which the Rabbinical literature
can show.

I leave the foregoing comparison without further elaboration and proceed to the more immediate subject of
this chapter—the study of the teaching of the Pharisees
so far as it found expression in the Halachah.

To survey the whole field of the Halachah is out of
the question, and would serve no useful purpose even if
it were possible. But certain questions arise in this
connection which ought to be answered if the student of
Pharisaism is to understand the true meaning of what he
studies. More especially if he is a Christian student,
not accustomed to the forms in which the Rabbis
expressed their ideas, and not without some preconceived
opinions about Pharisaism. Such questions are those of
the intention and effect of the Halachah as a moral discipline ; the function of conscience under the Halachah ;
the Pharisaic theory of merit and reward ; the relation
of Halachah to the teaching of the Prophets ; the relation of Torah to the Moral Law. It is upon these questions that criticism of the Pharisees is usually least
favourable and also least instructed. The reason being
that the Halachah is that factor in Pharisaism whose
results are most conspicuous to the outsider, and whose
inner meaning is usually hidden from him. I go on,
therefore, to the study of the questions enumerated
above.

(A) *The Halachah as a moral discipline.*[1]

Halachah has been defined above (Chapter III) as a
rule of right conduct, or collectively as a body of such
rules forming a coherent system. It was an opinion,
carefully thought out and deliberately pronounced, that
such-and-such was the right way of obeying the will of
God in a given set of circumstances. It was a direction
to the Jew showing him how the teaching of the Torah

[1] On the whole subject see an admirable essay by Lauterbach,
The Ethics of the Halakah, reprinted from the *Year Book of the
Central Conference of American Rabbis*, 1913.

was applicable to his particular case. Not that it was legislation merely *ad hoc*. It was a general rule laid down for the guidance of the whole community and of every member of it to whose case it might apply. And every member of the community was required to conform to it, or in the last resort he must cease to be recognised as a member of the community.[1]

To define Halachah was the task of the accredited teachers acting in consultation. No single teacher was competent to pronounce a binding decision by his own authority, however eminent he might be. It is true that a single teacher might declare that the halachah was so-and-so ; but that would be merely his own opinion until it was confirmed by a majority of his colleagues. They might accept it on the ground of his learning ; but unless it was accepted, it remained as his opinion, and had no binding force upon the community.

Halachah was not regarded as " judge-made law." It was assumed that upon every question which might come up for discussion there must be a halachah, a right way of acting in those circumstances. The task of the Rabbis was to find out what that right way was. It might be ready to hand in an existing tradition or custom, or it might be inferred from some text of Scripture, or it might be deduced from some other halachah ; but it was found, not invented, and it only became halachah, binding on the community, when it was accepted and ratified by the vote of a majority of the teachers present in the Assembly. This was called fixing the halachah. Thus it is said in a famous passage (b. Erub. 13[b]) that the School of Shammai wished to fix the halachah according to their view, while the School of Hillel wished to fix it according to their (different) view. The controversy, it is said, lasted for three years, and was only ended when a Bath Qol (heavenly voice)

---

[1] Excommunication, נדוי, was only applied in the case of teachers, at all events in Talmudic times. The two most famous cases were those of Akabjah b. Mahalalel, M. Edu. v. 6, 7, and R. Eliezer b. Horkenos, b. B. Metz. 59[b].

declared that each of the opposing parties had the words
of the living God, but that the halachah was according
to the School of Hillel. And, on the same page, it is said
that the two schools debated for two years over another
question, and they took a vote and decided so-and-so.

There is no reason to suppose that any other method
of fixing the halachah was ever employed at any period
in Pharisaic and Rabbinic history. The halachah which
was to bind the community was ascertained and declared
by the united voice of the teachers most eminent for
their wisdom and piety ; and its acceptance by the community was secured by their veneration of those teachers.
No teacher, however eminent, could impose his opinion
on the rest by sheer weight of authority. Even one so
great as R. Eliezer b. Horkenos had to fight for his
opinion by argument with his colleagues, and in the end
he was out-voted, and even excommunicated because he
would not conform (see the story in b. B. Metz. 59[b]).
And of R. Meir, somewhat later, it is declared (b. Erub. 13[b])
that, although there was no one like him in his generation,
yet the halachah was not fixed in accordance with his
opinion, so that no one should say that he had reached
the bottom of R. Meir's knowledge.[1]

The Halachah, or rather the whole *corpus* of halachoth,
formed the legislation for the community of those who
sought to live according to the Torah. It covered the
whole field of civil and criminal law, and also regulated
social and individual actions of private life in a great
variety of ways. It did not *include* morality and religion as separate departments, because it was all religious
and all moral. The fundamental idea of the Halachah is
that it teaches the right way of doing the will of God,
and that there is no department of life in which there is
not some opportunity, and therefore some obligation, of

---

[1] The meaning seems to be that R. Meir could give so many
reasons for and against any given opinion, that one could not be
certain what his own view really was. To declare the halachah
according to the supposed meaning of R. Meir might be to pronounce a wrong decision after all.

doing the will of God. This is the keynote of the whole Pharisaic conception of religion on its practical side, and between the Pharisees and the Talmudic Rabbis there is not the slightest difference of principle in this respect. By this fundamental principle Pharisaism stands or falls ; and it would need some courage, or some prejudice, to say that the principle was bad.

The Halachah was binding so long as it was not modified ; but it is important to know that it could be, and actually was, modified from time to time. It was never the cast-iron system which non-Jewish critics have usually supposed it to be, and so, misjudging it, have condemned it. The Halachah, fixed and declared by one Assembly, could be altered or repealed by another, if that other excelled the earlier one in numbers and wisdom. This is expressly declared in the Mishnah (Edu. i. 5), and there is no doubt that this maxim was sometimes acted on. The Halachah was never a rigid system, but always elastic, or, rather, plastic. It has been so from the days when Halachah was first formulated. As the Halachah in many instances modified and even annulled a Biblical precept in its literal sense, so the younger Halachah modified the older, in accordance with changes of opinion. And it was prevented from becoming a heavy burden by the wise provision that no Assembly might impose upon the community more than its members were able to bear (b. A. Zar. 36ᵃ). The reason of this was to safeguard the main object of the Halachah, viz. that the divine will should be done ; since that object would be defeated if the community could not perform the prescribed actions except at the cost of hardship or privation.[1] " Serve the Lord with gladness " has been the motto of those who framed and administered the Halachah, and no less of those who lived under it. No doubt there have been some who found it a burden and chafed under it or broke away from it ; but unless it had been substantially in accord

[1] For the general theory of the binding force of the halachah, see Maimonides, *Hilc. Mamrim*, chaps. i and ii.

with the real purpose and aspiration of the community, it could not have endured, still less could it have acted as the strong bond and protection of the community, as it has done for two thousand years. The joy in the divine commandments which rings in Psalm cxix, a purely Pharisaic psalm, as it were an Ode to the Halachah, has found an echo in Jewish hearts all down the centuries.

It was said above that the Halachah as a system was plastic and not rigid, and this is a fact of which non-Jewish critics are seldom aware. It is usually represented as a mass of fixed and unchangeable rules, under which there could be no liberty and no progress, and of which the only result must be the stagnation or petrifaction of the religious life. But in reality it was not so; that result did not follow, and least of all did it follow from anything that the Pharisees did in the century before the rise of Christianity. The Pharisees and the Rabbis were, before anything else, teachers; and what they set out to teach was practical religion, the doing of right actions for the service of God and man. They sought to strengthen the factors which make for unity and peace amongst men—the sense of justice, truth, purity, brotherly love, sympathy, mercy, forbearance, and the rest—in a word, to raise the moral standard amongst their people from age to age. They had this purpose mainly in view when they developed the Halachah and kept it from becoming a rigid system. They made it a means of ethical training by defining right conduct in terms of a progressive morality, a standard which was raised and not lowered in course of time. The ethics of the Halachah is not identical with the ethics of the Old Testament, and the change from one to the other was deliberately made, even to the extent sometimes of annulling some precept laid down in Scripture. Thus, to take a famous instance, the old law, " an eye for an eye and a tooth for a tooth," etc. (Exod. xxi. 24-5), was replaced by the enactment of a fine in money as the penalty for inflicting an injury (M.B. Kamma, viii. 1). The change, whenever it was made, is clear proof of the growth of a humaner feeling since the original law was framed, and the Halachah marks that progress. It is quite unjust to charge against the Pharisees, or the Rabbis or the modern Jews, that their religion still maintains the old *lex talionis*. That law has no more place in their religion than it has in Christianity, and it was discarded before ever Christianity appeared.[1]

If the Pharisaic teachers had not been so intent as they were upon raising the ethical standard and embodying their higher teaching in the Halachah, they would not have toiled so untiringly as they did at the work of interpretation of Torah, and ever fresh interpretation. Their aim was not in the least to set forth the meaning as understood by its first readers or hearers. What they sought to discover was its meaning for their own time and their own needs ; what it might have to teach which would help them and the community to serve God more fully and faithfully, with greater wisdom, more enlightened conscience, and more devoted will, in the circumstances of their own time. This could not be settled and written down once for all ; and only if it had been would that result have followed which is commonly charged as the main defect of Pharisaism, the reduction of religion and morality to a barren formalism. The Pharisees and the Rabbis were quite well aware of the danger, and they expressly guarded against it by refusing to make the Halachah a rigid system and by keeping it always open

---

[1] The words in Matthew v. 38 are : " Ye have heard that it was said," the reference being apparently to the text in Exodus, and not to anything being still taught. There is no evidence that the law " an eye for an eye," etc., was ever literally enforced. If it was, then that could only have been done by the Sadducees who adhered to the literal sense of the Torah and rejected the Pharisaic interpretation. If the Sadducees still enforced the *lex talionis* in its literal sense, the Pharisees certainly did not; and if even the Sadducees had abandoned the literal sense, the Pharisees would certainly not retain it. Now the Sadducean judicial code was abrogated in the reign of queen Alexandra (78–69 B.C.E.), and the event is noted in Meg. Taanith, 14 Tammuz. It is therefore clear that even if the *lex talionis* had been literally enforced up till that time it then ceased, thus fully a century before the time of Jesus. It may have ceased long before, and it may never have been operative at all.

to revision and amendment, always subject to fresh consideration.   That is why the whole of the Rabbinical literature included in the Talmud and the older Midrashim, especially of course the halachic Midrashim, is nothing but interpretation of Torah.   The Rabbis wrote no treatises of theology, philosophy or ethics till long after the Talmudic period.   And even when they did, the task of interpreting the Torah was not discarded.   Practically the whole of their literature in Talmudic times is one enormous answer to the question, How shall God be truly served in this present world ? the world being what it is, and man being what he is, and God being what *He* is.

The Halachah, then, was a system of law intended to direct and control action for a definite purpose.   At any given time it was binding upon all members of the community, the penalty for disobedience being public disapproval, or, in the last resort, excommunication.[1]   It was defined by the agreement of a majority of the accredited teachers in any given time and place, and it was accepted by the community on no other ground really than because the community trusted and revered its teachers.   It was always developed towards an ethical and not towards a ritual end, the object being not merely to prescribe certain acts to be done, but to teach men to serve God in doing those acts, and to foster the sense of human fellowship at the same time.   It did restrict liberty of action to a very considerable extent, and it did this deliberately.   By so doing, it served, and was intended to serve, as a means of holding the community together ; and further it provided actual practice in the doing of actions intended to be a service of God.   The theory was expressed in the words of an often-repeated maxim : " Let a man always employ himself with Torah and Mitzvoth, even though it be not for its own sake ; because while doing it not for its own sake, he will learn to do it for its own sake " (b. Pes. 50[b]).   It was a bold theory, and perhaps it did not always produce the intended result. But the Halachah as a system is justified by the experience

[1] But see above, p. 108.

of two thousand years, the experience of those who have lived under it.

What was the effect of the Halachah upon the moral character of the individual and the community who accepted it as binding ? [1] The answer from the non-Jewish side lies ready to hand, and has been given at any time since the New Testament was written. It is that the effect of the Halachah (here called the Law) was to impose a constraint upon individual action which on the one hand weakened the sense of responsibility in a man for what he did, by substituting an outward authority for the inward prompting of his conscience, and on the other hand, crushed him under an increasing burden of obligation from which he could find no release unless he came under the influence of the Gospel. Further, that the effect of performing so many prescribed acts necessarily tended to develop hypocrisy in those who performed them, hypocrisy being the pretence of piety without the reality, the form without the substance, typified by the whited sepulchre, which is outwardly fair and inwardly loathsome. The whole answer, for a good many people still, is summed up in the single phrase : " Scribes and Pharisees, hypocrites " ; and the question is dismissed as admitting of no other answer, considering who it was who uttered that deadly gibe. To those readers who may be more open-minded, I offer some considerations which may put the matter in a different light and a truer perspective.

First of all, it is to be observed that the Christian criticism of the Pharisees proceeds from men who were not Pharisees themselves, and, except at the beginning, were not Jews. Outside the New Testament it proceeds entirely from non-Jewish writers. Inside the New Testament, while Jesus and his immediate followers were

---

[1] See Montefiore's Hibbert Lectures, IX, pp. 464 *et seq.*, the most admirable and lucid treatment of the subject with which I am acquainted. It should be read again and again by those who want to know what the religion of the Pharisaic and Rabbinic Jews really meant to them.

certainly Jews, equally certainly they were not Pharisees.[1] Paul had been a Pharisee, but all his recorded utterances date from a time after he had broken with Pharisaism ; and it is common knowledge that a convert from one form of religious belief to another is not a reliable witness in regard to the system which he has left. The whole of the New Testament rests upon premisses, summed up in the supremacy of Christ, which render impossible an impartial conclusion from those premisses upon the merits or demerits of Pharisaism.

Moreover, whatever weight may be attached to the evidence of the New Testament, it is evidence collected from a period of time very short in comparison with the two thousand years during which Pharisaism, in its own name and under its later name of Rabbinism, has lasted. Most people think of the Pharisees, so far as they think of them at all, as the opponents of Jesus, in his ministry, and as authors of his death ; and they very naturally deem no condemnation too severe for the men who thwarted that ministry and helped to bring about that death. But, in the long history of Pharisaism, the public career and death of Jesus were hardly more than a passing incident, since the Pharisees naturally did not and could not estimate its importance from the Christian point of view. And as a matter of fact, the episode of Jesus and the rise of Christianity occupied but a very small place in the thought of the

[1] I cannot agree with the opinion of some Jewish scholars that Jesus was a Pharisee. It is perfectly true that much of his teaching is substantially what the Pharisees also taught. But Jesus did not teach from the basis of the Halachah, and by his declaration " But I say unto you " (Matt. v. 44) he virtually repudiated the principle of the Halachah. If he had been a Pharisee, why the sharp opposition between him and them ? I do not think that any of the categories of contemporary Judaism are applicable to him. He was *sui generis*. But, if he were to be placed in any one of those categories, I should be inclined to regard him as an Am-ha-aretz. Klausner, in his remarkable book, ישו הנוצרי, goes to to the extreme length in stressing the agreement between Jesus and the Pharisees (see p. 343, and especially pp. 396–401).

Pharisees, so far as their thought is expressed in their literature. To Christians this is no doubt surprising and deplorable. Yet how could it be otherwise, since the Pharisees were not Christians ?

Whatever, then, may ·be the truth in regard to the charge of hypocrisy, a question with which I shall deal immediately, the charge, so far as it rests on the New Testament, is brought by hostile witnesses, in this sense that they applied to Pharisaism a standard widely different from its own, and were seldom able, or apparently inclined, to make any effort really to understand it. The opposition was precisely in regard to the Halachah which the Pharisees maintained as the corner-stone, or rather the foundation walls and roof, of their system, and which the Christians definitely repudiated in favour of " the freedom with which Christ had made them free " (Gal. v. 1). There was sharp antagonism between the one side and the other ; and a calm, dispassionate and accurate judgment of the one by the other is as little to be expected and as seldom found as a calm, dispassionate and accurate judgment of the Roman Catholic Church by a Belfast Orangeman.

Much that is relevant to the charges brought against Pharisaism, and in particular against the Halachah, is contained in the preceding chapters ; for, if what has there been stated is true, Pharisaism cannot have been the barren formalism and organised hypocrisy which its critics allege that it was. Nevertheless, in the hope of getting to the real truth in this matter, I will deal with the charge expressly, and endeavour to show why it was made and why it was plausibly made, and yet not necessarily with justice.

First as to hypocrisy. The Halachah enjoined the performance of specified actions in a specified way. The intention was that men might thereby do the will of God exactly as He would have it done. For that result to be attained there must be along with the outward act the inward purpose. Without the inward purpose the outward act was worthless in a religious and moral sense.

The outward act alone was visible ; the inward purpose
was known only to God. It might, indeed, be discerned
by the sympathetic insight of a friend ; it could never
be perceived by an indifferent or hostile observer.

A system such as is here described is obviously one
peculiarly liable to abuse, in that it exposes its adherents
to the danger of formalism and hypocrisy to a much
greater degree than a system which has no Halachah.
The outward act can be performed, and all men see it ;
the inward intention may or may not be there, and even
when it is there none can see it in the same way in which
they see the outward act. There is, therefore, the constant danger that the outward act will be done without
the inward intention. Now the Pharisees and the Rabbis
were keenly alive to this danger, and perfectly aware that
it was real and not imaginary. They knew that it was
not always averted, that there were hypocrites in the
community who pretended to be pious,and they denounced
them with as much severity as can be found in the New
Testament, and with a much closer acquaintance with
the facts. The passage about the seven classes of false
Pharisees (b. Sot. 22[b]) has been quoted *ad nauseam*
and I will not repeat it. Less familiar is the passage, on
the same page, which gives the advice of King Jannai
(see above, Chapter II) to his wife when he was dying :
" Be not afraid of the Pharisees, nor of those who are
not Pharisees, but of them that are dyed to look like
Pharisees ; for their deeds are as the deed of Zimri, and
they seek the reward of Phineas." King Jannai was
a Sadducee, but at least he could distinguish a genuine
Pharisee from a false one. That his words were approved
by the Pharisees themselves is shown not merely by their
inclusion in the Talmud, but by the fact that they are
quoted in the immediate context of the seven classes of
false Pharisees, and the maxim about engaging in Torah
and Mitzvoth for its own sake. Thus explicitly did the
Pharisees recognise the danger to which the Halachah
exposed its adherents, and thus severely did they denounce
those who were false to their principles. Nevertheless,

they steadfastly maintained the Halachah, believing it to be indeed the right way of serving God, and not less right for being difficult and dangerous. But that on the whole the difficulty was faced and the danger sufficiently guarded against, is shown by the fact that the Jewish community has lived under the Halachah and by means of the Halachah for two thousand years. No community of hypocrites could do that.

The Halachah, then, involved the danger of hypocrisy, but it did not necessarily or in general produce hypocrites. Some there certainly were ; but in regard to others it must be remembered that the charge was brought on the ground of the performance of outward acts, of which the inward purpose and meaning was not and could not be seen by the onlooker. A Gentile, observing that a Jew did many things, in themselves apparently trivial, in a particular way and as a religious duty, would have no clue in his own religious experience to explain why the Jew did these things. He could not read the inner intention even when it was really there, and he had nothing to go upon except what he saw. It is obvious that he might easily put a quite wrong interpretation on what he saw, and declare that the Jew was a hypocrite when in reality he was perfectly genuine and sincere. And such outward observation alone is all that was possible to those who have maintained most persistently the charge of hypocrisy against the Pharisees.

Further, it is a matter of universal experience that in the case of every religion there are some who take it seriously and some who take it lightly, some who are conscious of its inner meaning and some who care only for the outward form. This is quite as true of Christianity as it is of Pharisaism. The results are different in appearance only because in Pharisaism definite action was required, which could be seen, while in Christianity definite belief was required which could not be seen. By the nature of the case no statistics are possible on which the question could be decided. In the absence of such means of proof, it seems to me reasonable to

hold that the proportion of hypocrites to sincere members
of the community was not greater amongst the Pharisees
than amongst Christians ; while the former were exposed
to the charge by the very form of their religious system
to a far greater extent than the adherents of any form
of Christianity.

Next, as to the alleged effect of the Halachah in weakening
the sense of moral responsibility in those who were bound
by it, the contrast being between the external authority
of the Halachah and the internal authority of the individual conscience. It is difficult for one who is not a Jew
and who has had no experience of life under the Halachah
to answer this question in such a manner as to carry conviction that his answer is right. I can only say how the
problem appears to me, and leave the reader to judge
whether the solution I offer is reasonable.

In the first place, a considerable effort of moral deter-
mination was needed if a man was to accept the system
of Halachah at all. The difference between an Am-ha-
aretz and a Pharisee (or one who followed the lead of the
Pharisees) was mainly this, that the former disregarded
the Halachah and the latter obeyed it. Such disregard
might amount to complete carelessness of any restraint
on the side of morality and religion, or it might be anything up to almost complete acceptance of the Pharisaic
position. There was nothing to compel anyone to accept
that position, and no one would accept it unless he took
his religion very seriously. If he did accept it, he did
so because he desired to serve God, and he believed that
the Halachah would help him to do this. That was
precisely what the Halachah was for. It was a moral
and religious discipline, and he voluntarily put himself
under that discipline, or remained in it having been
brought up under its influence. It is perfectly true that
the Halachah told him to do this and that and the other,
and in this sense an external command was laid upon
him ; whereas one who was not under the Halachah
would be guided by his own conscience whether he should
do that or something else or nothing at all. Yet the

obedience given to the Halachah was not a blind obedience, given merely to the letter of a law without regard to the intention with which it was fulfilled. The Halachah, *ex hypothesi*, was the defined will of God, and in obeying its precepts he had not truly served God unless he intended his act as a deed done for God. Merely to do the act without the intention of serving God in it was worthless, and even sinful. "Greater is the transgression (of a precept) with the intention of serving God than to fulfil one without that intention," was the bold declaration of a Rabbi (b. Nazir, 23[b]) ; and, whatever may be thought of the validity of that maxim, it does not leave much room for moral indifference.

In the case of a man not under the Halachah, but following the guidance of his own conscience, does he or does he not obey an external authority ? Apart from theories as to the function and meaning of conscience, the religious man believes that the authority which he owns in conscience is, in the last resort, the authority of God. It is certainly not his own. In obedience to his conscience he does various things which are difficult or dangerous, or in some way contrary to his inclination, and in doing them he yields to the authority of One higher than himself, whose right to command he owns. He recognises the intimations of that authority by the inward vision of his mind, known as conscience.

In the case of a man under the Halachah,[1] there is certainly an external authority, but here again it is the authority of God. It is not merely the authority of a book of rules or a code of laws enforced by social sanction, or a court of justice. It may be argued that the Halachah was, and could only be, an imperfect expression of the will of God. That is as it may be. But, given the

---

[1] The Halachah does not cover all the ethical teaching of the Pharisees. It is the development of the preceptive side of the Torah, but it does not include the moral and religious duties which were left undefined, "committed to the heart" (b. B. Metzia, 58[b]). These fall under the head of Haggadah. They will be dealt with in the next chapter.

fundamental conviction that the Halachah really was the defined will of God—and that conviction was of the very essence of Pharisaism—then the difference is but small between the one way of obeying the divine will and the other, and is a difference more of form than of substance. There is a difference in the way in which the inward energy of the soul is directed to right action, but there is no necessary difference in the amount of the energy so directed.   In other words, the individual responsibility of the Pharisee under the Halachah was not weakened, but it expressed itself in a different manner.

It must be further borne in mind that 'individual responsibility,' for the Pharisee, included his responsibility as a member of the community.   When he was faced with the question, What is my duty under these present circumstances ? he would feel that the answer depended not only on the fact that he was personally and directly accountable to God as an isolated human being in the presence of his Maker, but also on the fact that he was one of a community whose ideals of service he shared and whom he could either help or hinder in pursuing those ideals.   If there was present to his mind some indication of duty defined on behalf of the community by its accredited teachers, and accepted as being a true declaration of the will of God, then, being himself a member of the community, his sense of responsibility would incline him towards the particular action defined for the particular circumstances in which he found himself. And, unless for any reason his sense of communal fellowship were weakened, he would not naturally feel any opposition between the intimation of his own conscience and the injunction of the Halachah.   So far as I have observed, no case of such opposition is to be found in the Rabbinical literature, and I do not remember that the problem is ever discussed.   If I am reminded [1] of the

---

[1] This very point was raised against me by a Jew, one of my hearers when I lectured at The Hague on " The Pharisaic Point of View." I met it in the way set forth below, and another Jew, who took part in the discussion, agreed with me.

famous case of R. Jehoshua, b. Ḥananjah and R^n. Gamliel
(b. R. ha. Sh. 25^a), I claim that as a support of my contention ; because R. Jehoshua decided his course of action
precisely on the ground that he was a member of the
community, and not an isolated individual. Certainly,
he thought that R^n. Gamliel was mistaken in the view
which he expressed ; but if, in yielding against his own
judgment, he had also yielded against his own conscience,
he would have felt the pang of remorse as everyone does
who disobeys his conscience ; and there is no indication
that R. Jehoshua ever suffered remorse for what he had
done. In other words, the conflict of conscience with
Halachah did not arise in the case at all. Where alone
it would arise would be in the case of men whose allegiance to the system of Halachah was weakened or loosened,
as, for instance, by inclination towards the Christian
system, and who could no longer, with entire conviction,
regard the Halachah as the defined will of God. The
experience of Paul is a case in point.

I hold, therefore, that the effect of the Halachah was
not to weaken the sense of individual responsibility in
those who ordered their lives by its guidance, nor was it
to blunt their moral sensibility. The most that can
be truly said is that both individual responsibility and
moral sensibility showed themselves in ways different
from the ways which are to be expected under a non-
halachic system. I only add that the Halachah itself
was developed and elaborated as an ethical and not as a
ritual system. It was always the endeavour of those
who built it up to find an ethical meaning in the various
precepts and make even the most unpromising material
serve the purpose of a moral discipline.[1]

Finally, there is the fact that no branch of study has
been more zealously pursued by Jews in all ages than
ethics, as is shown by innumerable examples, from the

---

[1] The reader is referred again to Lauterbach's essay on *The
Ethics of the Halakah*, the very title of which is as suggestive
as the contents are illuminating. To illustrate the point fully
would be simply to quote the whole essay.

Pirkē Abōth at one end to the *Ethics of Judaism* by Lazarus at the other. Even Spinoza, though he went far from the traditional ways of thought of his people, bore witness to his ancestry by making ethics the subject of his greatest work. If the influence of the Halachah had been to weaken, let alone to paralyse, the moral sense of the Jew who lived under it, such age-long devotion to ethical study would be impossible, because self-contradictory. A comparison between Jew and Gentile, or Jew and Christian, in respect of morality would show that there was at least as much substantial virtue on the Jewish side as on the other. If this was due to the Halachah, then its influence as a moral discipline was beneficial. And if it was not due to the Halachah, then the influence of that system was not injurious to morality. Whatever the Gentile may think, the Pharisees and the Rabbis knew what they were about when they elaborated the Halachah, and made it the chief means for the moral training of their people. Two thousand years of experience may provide the answer to the question whether their labour was in vain.

(B) *Merit and Reward.*[1]

It is beyond question that a great deal of the ethical teaching of the Pharisees turns upon the ideas of ' merit '

[1] The reader should consult the essay of Marmorstein on *The Doctrine of Merits in the Old Rabbinical Literature*, which forms No. 7 of the Jews' College publications. Dr. Marmorstein has ransacked the Haggadic literature and given an immense collection of illustrative passages. I am not convinced that the theory which he maintains, of distinct views held by separate schools amongst the Rabbis, is well founded ; but this does not detract from the value of the work as a thesaurus of information. A non-Jewish reader would perhaps feel, as I have felt, the want of a fuller discussion of first principles. For want of such guidance, I have had to do the best I could to get to the root of the matter, and to find an explanation of what seems to me to be the real difficulty. To a Jew I should imagine that the difficulty does not exist, because the doctrine of merit and reward is the natural outcome of the theory of Halachah. It has taken me long to understand what, after all, is very simple. That is, if I have understood it.

and ' reward,' and thus provides the basis for the charge of self-righteousness so often brought against them. And while it is perfectly true that most of the relevant passages which may be quoted are the utterance of individual teachers, expressing only their own opinion, yet they are in harmony with the general Pharisaic view, otherwise they would not be included in the Talmud and the Midrashim. It is not the fact that every Pharisee believed, still less that he was required to believe, that God kept a ledger account of merits and sins for every individual Jew, and apportioned reward or punishment accordingly. R. Akiba made use of a very similar figure of speech on one occasion, and it was included as a striking utterance in the ethical anthology known as Pirke Aboth (iii. 16). The figure of speech was his own ; the meaning of it, for which a better figure might have been chosen, was what every Pharisee would endorse. All the utterances of individual teachers about merit and reward are the varied expression of a few ground principles, fundamental conceptions, inherent in Pharisaism itself. I shall try to show what those fundamental conceptions were, and how the Pharisaic system, more particularly the Halachah, necessarily produced a theory of merit and reward. Of course these words have a disagreeable sound when used in connection with acts done in the service of God. " Doth Job serve God for nought ? " was the question of the Satan in the poem. And it might well be that the same question should be asked concerning the Pharisees, who certainly did believe that a man could acquire merit by serving God, and certainly did hope for a reward as the result of so doing. But, however it may have been with Job, the case of the Pharisees is not disposed of until it is seen why they came to use these words in connection with the service of God, and what they meant by them.

The Pharisaic doctrine [1] of merit and reward is, like

---

[1] I use the word " doctrine " for convenience, to denote the general way of regarding the subject. There was never any clearly defined statement of that general way, which could be regarded as the authorised and accepted Pharisaic teaching. See above, Chapter III, on Haggadah.

nearly everything else in their system, a development of what is found in the Old Testament. The idea of reward appears in the Decalogue, attached to the Fourth Commandment. Deuteronomy is full of it, expressed in the oft-repeated phrases : " That it may be well with thee," " That thou mayest prolong thy days," etc. The intention obviously was to induce observance of what was commanded by the promise of substantial benefit ; in short ' reward ' in the plain meaning of the term. Moreover, in the Old Testament there was no hesitation in describing the reward in terms of material welfare, nor in associating prosperity with virtue, and misfortune with sin. The chief moral problem which finds a place in the Old Testament is that presented by the occasional failure of this theory, as in the ease of Job, and the Servant of the Lord (Isa. liii).

The idea of ' merit ' is far less prominent in the Old Testament than that of ' reward,' if indeed it can be found there at all. The word ' zāchūth,' זכות, which is constantly used in the Rabbinical literature, does not occur in the Old Testament ; and the verb from which it is derived, though it is found in the Old Testament. has not there its later Pharisaic meaning. It may be said, therefore, I believe with substantial truth, that the doctrine of ' merit ' is mainly due to the Pharisees, and that while they inherited the idea of ' reward,' they developed it along lines of their own towards a conclusion very different from that reached in the Old Testament. Whatever they meant by ' reward,' a question which will be considered presently, they did not identify it with merely material prosperity.

The Pharisaic doctrine of reward and merit is a conclusion drawn from three fundamental convictions, axioms of their religious belief : first, that God is just ; second, that there is an intrinsic difference between doing right and doing wrong ; third, that the whole duty of man is to do the will of God. These are axioms of Judaism in general, and not peculiar to the Pharisees. What is distinctive of them is that they developed those axioms, especially the last one, in terms of Torah. Upon the first two little needs to be said. That God is just, perfectly righteous, is the final word of Judaism in regard to human apprehension of the divine nature. Jews believe strongly in the love of God, and have much to say about it ; but they do not regard love as being the highest attribute of God discernible by man. After all, perhaps the difference is only in the form of expression, and the divine righteousness and the divine love may be in reality one and not two. No less fundamental in Judaism, of whatever type, is the distinction between right and wrong, as a moral and not merely a prudential or utilitarian distinction. It was the perception of this moral distinction as an integral element of belief in God which marked the divergence of the old Hebrew religion from that of " the peoples round about " ; and mainly by insisting on the close connection between religion and morality did Judaism rise to the great height which it attained. This was the constant theme of the Prophets, and the no less constant theme of the Pharisees and the Rabbis. Moreover, the distinction between right and wrong was no mere theoretical opinion, but the basis of a practical demand. It was to be acknowledged in act, by the doing of right and the refraining from wrong. Not otherwise could God be owned as God, let alone served. " Ye shall be holy, for I am holy " (Lev. xix. 2) has been in all ages since its utterance one of the watchwords of Judaism. This is really the third axiom mentioned above—that the highest duty of man is to do the will of God.

These three axioms express the essence of Judaism, as a religion which places before everything else the *doing* of the will of God because He wills the right and abhors the wrong, being in Himself perfectly righteous, just, holy and good. There is much else in Judaism besides what is here indicated, but there is nothing more fundamental. Christianity, no doubt, has always believed in a righteous and holy God, has always insisted on the distinction between right and wrong and has always taught the duty of doing His will; but Christianity, as expressed in the teaching of the Church, has not put these *before everything else*. The first place has always been given to right *belief*.[1] If the Church had dealt with sinners as she dealt with heretics, her history would have been very different from what it has been.

Upon these three axioms the whole structure of Judaism rests; and one part of that structure is the doctrine or theory or general conception of merit and reward, which must now be more closely examined. If God is righteous, then He cannot be indifferent to the distinction between right and wrong. That is no arbitrary human distinction, but one inherent in the ultimate reality, in the very nature of God. Not that there is evil in God, but that the Good is what He is and evil is the contradiction of it. The distinction between them is contained in the idea of God, as the presence of both to the apprehension of man is within the scope of his creative action. " I make peace *and create evil*. I am the Lord which doeth all these things " (Isa. xlv. 7).

When this distinction is expressed in conduct, there arises the distinction between the righteous and the sinner. And the conclusion follows that because God is just He will not treat the righteous and the sinner in the same way. There must be some difference between the condition of the man who does right and that of the man who does wrong. In some way it is better with the former than with the latter; and not only *is* better, but *must be* better, through the justice of God. In what way it is better is another question, variously answered; but of the fact of a divinely appointed difference between the condition of the righteous and the condition of the sinner there has never been any doubt in Judaism. It is, indeed, confirmed by general human experience, wherever that experience includes the recognition of the conceptions, goodness and sin.

Now this fact of a divinely appointed difference between

[1] See below, Chapter IX, p. 231.

the condition of the righteous and that of the sinner, is what the doctrine of 'reward' in any of its forms sought to express. The reward was ultimately that better condition, whatever it might be ; and the worse condition was the negative of the reward—the punishment or retribution—or in whatever way it might be conceived.

It is only natural that this 'better condition' should be described in various ways, ranging from the grossest material prosperity to the purest spiritual bliss. That was but the result of the slow process of moral development in the Jewish people. The most obvious method is to connect the difference between the 'better' and the 'worse' condition with the difference between prosperity and adversity. So it is found in numberless passages of the Old Testament ; and it may be called a first rough approximation to a true explanation of the meaning and nature of the 'better condition.' Even in the Old Testament this explanation was challenged, as in the Book of Job ; but the fact remained for which the explanation was sought.

The development of Pharisaic and Rabbinical thought was towards a higher and more spiritual conception of the 'better condition.' The old idea of material prosperity was never indeed abandoned, but other conceptions were brought in beside it, with no attempt at consistency, but just as each individual teacher thought that he could best represent it. And perhaps the highest point was reached by Rab, in his great saying that in the world to come " there is neither eating nor drinking, but the righteous . . . enjoy the radiance of the Shechinah " (b. Ber. 17ᵃ; and cf. Matt. xxii. 30, for a very similar utterance of Jesus). That the Rabbis could rise high above the old materialist conception is shown by the great saying of Ben Azai (Aboth iv. 2): " The reward of a mitzvah is a mitzvah ; and the reward of a sin is a sin " ; a 'mitzvah' being an opportunity of serving God by fulfilling a precept. In these and many other sayings which might be quoted, the Rabbis used the term 'reward' without hesitation, and they used it always [1] to denote the ' better condition,' which was, through the justice of God, the certain accompaniment or result or consequence of doing right. That was the meaning of ' reward ' in the thought of the Rabbis. They did not teach that a man could, still less that he should, make a bargain with God and stipulate that for such-and-such a service he should be paid so much. Possibly some teacher amongst the many hundreds whose words are recorded in the Rabbinical literature may have used such language ; but it certainly was not habitual. It is emphatically contradicted by the famous saying of Antigonos of Socho, an early Pharisaic teacher, quoted in Aboth i. 3 : " Be not like servants who serve their master on condition of receiving a present " ; where the word for ' present ' is different from the usual word for ' reward.'

Such being the real meaning of ' reward ' as understood by the Pharisees and the Rabbis, it is evident that those who based their actions on such a conception cannot fairly be condemned as mere traffickers, serving God for what they could gain by doing so. If there is a ' better condition,' divine blessing in some form, for those who serve God the best they know, then on what ground is it to be thought wrong if a man hopes to please God by what he does, if he hopes that he may in some way be made aware of the approval of God ? Is it wrong to hope for the blessing of God ? When it was said in the parable (Matt. xxv. 21) : " Well done, good and faithful servant . . . enter thou into the joy of thy Lord," will any Christian say that it is wrong to hope that such a greeting might be given to him ? Yet a Pharisee would

---

[1] The ' reward ' of a sin, in Ben Azai's saying, is indeed not a ' better condition ' ; but, alike in regard to precept and sin, it is the justice and even the goodness of God which determines the subsequent condition of the man who does the one or the other. And if it is the justice of God which appoints for a sinner such weakened will that he more easily sins, still it is ' better ' for the sinner to be so dealt with than if his sin were passed over. It is the *mercy* of God which " renders to every man according to his deeds " (Ps. lxii. 11).

have said, "that is exactly what I mean by 'reward.'"
And it was not a Pharisee who used the words. Moreover,
Jesus in several of his sayings used the word 'reward'
apparently with as little hesitation as the Pharisees
did ; and Christian readers have often felt uneasy when
they have read " Thy Heavenly Father shall *recompense*
thee " (Matt. vi. 4), " Great is your *reward* in heaven "
(*ibid.* v. 12), " He shall in no wise lose his *reward* " (*ibid.*
x. 42). Is such teaching on a low moral plane ? If it
is not, then that is because Jesus and the Pharisees meant
precisely the same thing when they used the term 'reward.'
He and they made it the essential of their respective
teaching to do the will of God, whatever be the difference
between their respective conceptions of the will of God.
And he, no less than they, recognised that there was a
'better condition' for the man who did the will of God
than for the man who did not do it.

Before leaving the subject of 'reward,' it should be
noted that the tendency of Rabbinical teaching was to
defer the actual reward, whatever it might be, to the
future life. No one knows what form the reward will
take, if it have any form at all beyond the inward peace
of the divine approval. And R. Eliezer the Great warned
against serving God for the sake of what could be gained
by doing so, when he explained the text (Ps. cxii. 1) :
" Blessed is the man who delighteth greatly in his commandments " to mean " delighteth in his commandments,
but not in the reward attached to them " (b. A. Zar. 19ᵃ).
The Pharisees were quite aware of the abuse to which
their theory of 'reward' was liable, and they sought to
guard against that abuse ; but they held to their fundamental conception of the 'better condition' through
the justice of God, because they were convinced of its
truth. And true it surely is, though it be hard to find
the exactly fitting words in which to set forth the truth.

So much for 'reward'; now for 'merit.' This is,
as shown above, a conception more distinctive of Pharisaism than that of 'reward.' To understand what the
Pharisees meant by 'merit,' we must go back to the three

fundamental axioms explained above. If a man, in any given set of circumstances, does the will of God, he is obviously more pleasing to God that if he disobeyed or did nothing. This must be so if God be just, and if He desires that His will may be done. When, therefore, an opportunity comes to a man of doing the divine will, there an opportunity is given of serving God, of becoming more pleasing in His sight. By performing the act in question he has done something for God ; and while what he has done may make no difference to God, who does not need what man does for Him, it makes this difference to the man, that he has in that instance definitely exerted his will, acted out of himself, on the side of God. If that opportunity of service had not presented itself, he would have been by so much the less effective in his service of God than he became by doing the duty. Now God has made known what is His will, in such-and-such circumstances. On Pharisaic lines the Halachah is the defined statement of the divine will. It gives directions how the several ' mitzvoth,' precepts, are to be performed. When an occasion arises in which a ' mitzvah ' can be performed, three courses are open to a man : either he can obey it, or he can remain neutral doing nothing, or he can disobey it. If the neutrality line be taken as the basis of the argument, then the man who obeys the divine will by performing the mitzvah, rises above that line, while the man who disobeys sinks below it. The position of the man who rises above the neutrality line is what is meant by ' merit ' in the Pharisaic theory.

What is here described under the figure of a change of position does correspond to something real. The doing of an act of service to God does make a difference to the character of the man who has done it—adds something to his character which was not there before. That ' something added ' is the ' merit ' acquired by doing the act. Of the fact, in any given case, that the act was done, there could be no question, it spoke for itself. The Pharisees accordingly accepted the ' something added ' as a psychological fact, and made full use of it.

Whether the word 'merit' is the best rendering of 'zachuth' is perhaps open to question, though I am not able to suggest a better. But the word 'merit' tends to obscure a fine distinction which the Pharisees drew, and which relieves their theory of merit from what has been felt to be objectionable in it.

Suppose a man does some act of service to God, performs a 'mitzvah,' or does a work of charity or the like. It may have cost him some effort of self-sacrifice, or even suffering or hardship. He did it by the help of God in whom he trusted and to whom he prayed. In the act so done there are two factors, the will of the man expressing itself in the act, and the help of God which enabled the act to be done. Now zachuth, 'merit,' applies to the first factor and not to be second. The Pharisee would put the case to himself thus : "I have done this act, and thereby I stand higher than I did before ; but it was God who made me able to do it, and I do not claim for myself what is His alone." The Pharisee did not say: "See how good I am"; he did not mean that at all when he believed that he had acquired merit. He meant that a change had been effected in his position as a moral being ; that was an objective fact of which he could be aware as he could of any other fact. But he knew quite well that it was the help of God which had made his act possible. The use of the word 'merit' to include both these factors, turns what is entirely harmless into what is morally objectionable.

This subtle distinction, though it is nowhere, so far as I know, expressly drawn, was evidently recognised because it explains how it was that a Pharisee, or a Rabbi, could be quite aware that he had done such-and-such acts of service to God and yet could be humble in mind. There is hardly any virtue upon which more stress is laid in the Rabbinical ethics than humility ; and what is more, their literature, a most honest disclosure of the Pharisaic mind, does not indicate that self-righteousness was their special fault. Of course, the theory of 'merit' exposed the Pharisee to the danger of self-righteousness, just as the theory of the Halachah exposed him to the danger of hypocrisy; and I am not going to say that the danger was always avoided. But in the one case as in the other, the theory was perfectly clear and sound, and the practical working of it did not, on the whole, lead to the deplorable results which non-Jewish critics have usually ascribed to it. After all, the Pharisee knew what he was about much better than his non-Jewish critics have usually known.

Both 'merit' and 'reward' were consequent upon the doing of an act of service to God, 'merit' being the 'something added' and 'reward' the 'better condition.' And both conceptions were the inevitable products of a system which placed actual *doing* of the will of God before everything else. The Pharisee stated his theory of 'merit' and 'reward' in terms of Torah, by teaching that a man could acquire 'merit' by performing the 'mitzvōth' and might justly hope for a 'reward' for doing so. The whole intention of the theory was summed up in a famous saying:[1] "The Holy One, blessed be He, was pleased to make Israel able to acquire merit; wherefore He gave them much Torah and many mitzvōth." Those who are in the habit of talking about the burden of the Law and of imagining the Jews as helpless captives in its iron fetters, would do well to study the meaning of this saying, for it expresses truly, as the other never did, the way in which the Pharisee looked upon Torah and mitzvōth, and thanked God for both.

After what has been said in explanation of the term 'merit' as understood by the Pharisees, it will be easy to understand their further development of the idea in the conception of vicarious merit, and especially the merit of the Fathers. Merit being taken to be a psychological fact, and not a boastful assertion of personal excellence, it was held that the merit of one who had much

[1] The saying is found in M. Macc. iii. 16, and its author was R. Ḥananjah b. Akashia, of whom nothing is known. The saying is usually printed in the editions of *Pirke Aboth* at the end of each chapter.

could be available for those who had little or none. There were two reasons which led to this further development, both arising out of the fact that Israel was a community whose members had a certain responsibility for each other. One reason was that one member who had much merit could by imparting it help his brethren who had less. And the other was the consideration that since the community had often, in spite of its sins and failures, been delivered from danger, and in various ways received the blessing of God, this must have been due to the merit of the holiest and best among them. The merit was there, and it was there not to be wasted but to effect some good under the providence of God. Rabbinical speculation spent much time in dwelling on the connection between the merit of the faithful and the blessings which had been received.[1] The connection traced is often fantastic, as no doubt the teacher was quite well aware ; but what he taught was the solidarity of Israel, the truth that " no man liveth to himself alone," and that Jews are members one of another. He taught that everyone, by his own faithful service of God, could thereby also serve his fellow-man ; and that one who had little or no merit of his own could think gratefully of those who had, by faithful lives, done much for him. That was the real outcome of the doctrine of imputed merit, a lesson of mutual service and brotherly love, and not at all a mere calculation of self-righteousness. He who pleads his own merits before God is answered for the merits of others ; and he who pleads the merits of others is answered for his own (see b. Ber. 10[b], and Marmorstein, pp. 17–18). In this saying, and many others, the necessary warning was given against the danger of relying on the merits of others as an excuse for one's own slackness. Here, as elsewhere, the Pharisaic theory is exposed to moral dangers, and made severe demands upon the men who lived under that system. But the dangers were pointed out and carefully guarded against ; and, whatever might have been expected from an *a priori* view of the theory, in

[1] For details see Marmorstein's essay, *passim*.

practice it met the needs of men who took both their religion and their morality in deadly earnest, and were not afraid to serve God in the perilous way which they believed He had shown to them.

(C) *The Relation of Pharisaism to the Teaching of the Prophets.*

The contrast between the Prophets and the Pharisees in their manner of teaching has often been pointed out. It is indeed obvious, even to the most casual reader. The Prophet delivered his message freely, and owned no authority other than that of God, whose word he proclaimed : " Thus saith the Lord." The Pharisee, and after him the Rabbi, went no further than : " Thus it is written," or " Thus the Wise have taught." The contrast is fully admitted, for what it may be worth ; but it is worth little or nothing, if it be intended as an answer to the question, What was the relation of Pharisaism to the prophetic teaching ? There was a close relation, as will be shown, and the contrast referred to has a certain bearing upon that relation ; but it is hardly more than a superficial detail.

The Prophets, whatever else they did, were preachers of righteousness, messengers of God declaring His nature and calling His people to turn from their sins and serve Him. They spoke as their inward vision of the divine compelled them to speak, regardless of all human opposition or restraint. They gave such lofty and magnificent teaching that their words have been carefully recorded as Holy Scripture, and " have gone out through all the earth " wherever the Bible is read. Their power is still felt, and what they have left is part of the imperishable treasure of the human race.

But what of the people to whom they delivered their message and cast forth their winged words ? The evidence is chiefly negative ; for there is nothing to show that the people took seriously to heart the rebukes and warnings and pleadings of the Prophets, and there is nothing to show that the people, or any of them, used the " great freedom of speech " of the Prophets. This second point would not be of any importance except for the fact that the contrast referred to above is usually taken to mean that the prophetic freedom is preferable to the Pharisaic constraint, and that an ordinary member of the community stood higher, morally, under the former than under the latter. If " all the Lord's people were prophets," as Moses vainly wished they might be, there would be something to be said for this comparison. But they were not, either by divine calling or by their own character. The prophetic heroes shine out against the background of a people not worthy of them, having many vices and by no means willing to serve the Lord according to the rigorous standard of the Prophets. Whatever the moral position of the people was, before the Exile, whether they exercised a prophetic freedom themselves, or went to the priest for instruction, or listened to the Prophets and then went their way and " burned incense to the Queen of Heaven," matters nothing. Such as they were, the Exile was their fate : and they had no power, as their later descendants had " to withstand in the evil day." The teaching of the Prophets, so far as the mass of the people of the time was concerned, had utterly failed.

The sharp lesson of the Exile was not lost upon the men who, after the return, became the leaders and teachers of the newly established community in Jerusalem. It became clear to them that if Israel were ever to be made into a holy people, serving God fully and faithfully, some other method than that of the Prophets must be applied. Their teaching had been the highest and best that was possible, and just for that reason there was no further need of any more Prophets. What was urgently needed was some way of training the people to obey that teaching. What was the good of hearing lofty declamations about God, His righteousness, His sovereign power and wisdom, if there were no real attempt to bring the life and character of the worshipper into harmony with that teaching ?

This was what Ezra saw, and it strikes the keynote of Pharisaism. The one thing needful, in his view, was to put the teaching into practice, to lay the whole stress upon *doing* the divine will, to make the Torah, which contained the essence of revelation, the one supreme concern for the Jewish community, and for every single member of it. The Torah, in the written text of the Pentateuch, contained a great number of commands, express declarations of the divine will. Before everything else these things must be done, the will of God must be obeyed, the teaching must be applied. There was no contradiction between the Torah and the prophetic teaching ; both alike came ultimately from God. But the definite precepts of the Torah provided a more effective means of discipline than the rapt utterances of the Prophets, while at the same time, the moral energy, developed under the influence of the Prophets, was not lost but directed to its proper object.

Between the Prophets and the Pharisees there was no breach whatever. There was a change of method, but not of principle. The Pharisees and the Rabbis took note of the fact that the line of the Prophets had come to an end, and that they had been followed by the Wise, and they claimed that they were not merely *de facto* but *de jure* the successors and heirs of the Prophets. " Prophecy was taken from the Prophets and given to the Wise ; and it has not been taken from these " (b. B. Bath. 12ᵃ). The Pharisees never dreamed of repudiating the prophetic teaching. On the contrary, they desired to make it effective, to bring out, in the lives of those whom they could influence, the fruits of " godly, righteous and sober life " which the Prophets would have brought out if they could. Pharisaism is applied prophecy ; and to treat it as the negation or repudiation of the work of the Prophets is to make the largest error of which the case seems to admit. The Pharisees, in relation to the Prophets, " came not to destroy but to fulfil " ; not to depart from a high ideal in order to set up a lower one, but to make a more effective approach to the higher one ; not to hide it from the gaze of those who once had seen it, but to make it seen by those who had never beheld it, felt and obeyed by those who had disregarded it, to enforce its authority and control upon those who (or whose fathers) had been content merely to listen to the Prophets and go their own way.   Unless it be contended that the practical application of the prophetic teaching to life was a matter of slight importance, it must be allowed that Pharisaism was the direct sequel and necessary completion of the work of the Prophets. The Pharisees were precisely those who saved the work of the Prophets from being wasted, by infusing the spirit of their teaching into the moral and religious character of the people.

That the Halachah was developed on ethical, not on ceremonial lines, was due to the lead of the Prophets, which the Pharisees followed as a matter of course.   If they had not done so, if according to the usual view they had repudiated the prophetic teaching or even merely ignored it, then the Prophets would have laboured in vain, and presumably would never have been heard of. For it was the Pharisees, more particularly the Scribes, to whom alone is due the preservation of the writings, prophetic and other, which form the Old Testament. If there had been no Prophets there would have been no Pharisees.   If there had been no Pharisees, the Prophets would have " perished as though they had never been."

(D) *The Torah and the Moral Law.*

Part of what might properly be included under this head has already been dealt with when considering the relation of the Halachah to the moral responsibility of the man who lived under it (see above, in this chapter, section A).   But a fuller treatment is necessary of the question, What is the relation of the Torah as a whole to that moral responsibility ?   This question includes several subordinate inquiries, such as, What is the function of conscience in a system of morals expressed in terms of

Torah ? What is the nature of the authority which is obeyed in the doing of right actions ? How is this authority recognised ?

Whatever innovations the Pharisees may have made, they certainly did not introduce a new morality. To understand the position of the Pharisees and those who received their teaching in regard to the fundamentals of morality, we must look to the Prophets and the Pentateuch. The Prophets (including, of course, Moses) gave the moral lead which made the religion of Israel a new thing, and not a mere development of Canaanite nature-worship. The Pentateuch contains various more or less definite expressions of the moral teaching of the Prophets, in the form of divine commands. For my present purpose it does not matter whether the Pentateuch be ascribed to Moses or be regarded, on the lines of the modern theory, as a combination of several documents of different dates. The point is that both the prophetic writings and the Pentateuch contain moral teaching, of the most direct and emphatic kind, the only difference being in the manner of its presentation. The Prophets gave it as the word of the Lord, that which God had bidden them to say, and which as His chosen messengers they forthwith said. The Pentateuch gave it as commands from God to Israel, communicated to them through Moses : " Speak unto the children of Israel and say unto them, Ye shall " do this and that. Alike, therefore, in the Prophets and the Pentateuch the source of knowledge in regard to right and wrong was God Himself, directly or indirectly communicating to Israel what it concerned them to know ; that is, what was essential to their true service of Him. The Teaching, *par excellence*, was that contained in the Pentateuch, which was on that account called the Torah. To call it the ' Law ' is to lay the emphasis on the wrong point, besides being in every respect incorrect. Neither the ancient Israelite, nor the Pharisee, nor the Talmudic Rabbi, nor the mediæval nor the modern Jew has regarded the Pentateuch as a code of laws, comparable with the Institutes of Justinian or the Statutes at large, or even with the Shulhan Aruch. Doubtless it might in some respects serve the purpose of a code of laws, but it was in itself something other and higher. It answered, for Israel, the question, What has God taught us ? What does He bid us do ? And whatever Israelite or Jew might do by way of carrying out that teaching, he did as an act of service to God, not as the result of looking up a statute-book and following its directions.

On the lines of Judaism in all ages, morality and religion are inseparable ; there could not be a morality apart from religion, or a religion without morality. Historically, of course, there was often a wide interval between them, both religion and morality being variously corrupt. Of this the prophetic writings give abundant evidence. But in theory, religion and morality were inseparable ; and it is precisely this truth which gave to the Prophets the ground of their vehement denunciation of the sins of the people.

The essence of the teaching, alike in the Pentateuch and the Prophets, was an appeal, or demand, or challenge, to the moral nature in man on the ground of a similar moral nature in God. " Ye shall be holy, for I am holy " (Lev. xix. 2) is the key to it all. " He hath showed thee, O man, what is good " (Mic. vi. 8). And that was shown to man, not as something new and strange, but as something which he could own and recognise as being in accordance with his own nature, the object of his aspirations, the ideal towards which he was inwardly drawn. And the effect of the teaching, alike of the Pentateuch and the Prophets, was gradually to develop the religious and moral nature of those who received it, and to train them in the right way of living as the people of God. That the effect, in this respect, of such teaching was great and lasting, is not disputed, nor open to dispute, whatever may be thought of the influence of the Pharisees as responsible for some supposed unfortunate modification. Both the Pentateuch and the prophetic writings (to say nothing of the other Scriptures of the Old Testament) were regarded as the chief guarantee of the truth of the religion and morality combined in Judaism. They were the written record of that truth, the source from which it might be drawn without limit. But always as a revelation from God, and never as a mere impersonal code of law, or an abstract system of morality. For this reason the usual terms found in treatises on Ethics do not occur in the Old Testament. The Moral Law is nowhere referred to under that name, and there is no word for conscience. There is no attempt to define the *Summum Bonum*, nor to explain the sense of moral obligation. No need was felt for these theoretical terms, or the explanation of them, simply because the facts denoted by them were all present and were all included in the revelation which God had given, and in the awakened human consciousness which received and responded to that revelation. When a prophet said " Cease to do evil, learn to do well " (Isa. i. 16), he implied the Moral Law, but he did not name it ; he took for granted that those whom he addressed knew the difference between good and evil, though he did not refer to conscience ; he assumed that they owned the obligation of duty, or the constraint of the moral ideal, though he did not use those terms. All these lay outside the consciousness alike of his hearers and himself. What was present to the minds of both was the thought of God as revealing to them His nature and His will concerning them. The authority which lay behind the command was His authority, and the command itself was received not as the arbitrary order of an irresponsible power which might conceivably be unmoral, but as the expression alike of the divine will and the divine nature. The good was not good because God commanded it, but He commanded it because He was good. He made known, to that extent at all events, what He is, in order that those to whom He made it known should themselves be (to that extent) like Him, in discerning, choosing and doing the good.

Such a revelation, with its challenge and demand for fulfilment, could only be addressed to moral agents who were free to choose whether or not they would comply with the demand. The freedom of the will is one of the pillars of Judaism, though the term is not found in the Old Testament or the Talmudic literature. Obedience was given not on compulsion but on persuasion ; and though at the lower stages of moral development it was reinforced by the promise of reward or the threat of punishment, at the higher stages the promises and threats were discarded, and the ideal held up of obedience through love, the children on earth doing the will of their Father in heaven.

Under the influence of the Pentateuch and the Prophets, the development of the moral sense of Israel was carried on for centuries ; and while it is true, as has been shown above, that the actual results in life and conduct left much to be desired in the period before the Exile, that was not because the teaching given was unintelligible, but because the demand it made was felt to be too severe. The temptation to make terms with the religion and morality of the neighbouring people was too strong. Yet if there had not been some real moral progress, some lasting result of that discipline, there would have been nothing to serve as a basis for a new beginning after the return from the Exile. That there was such a moral basis is due in part to the work of Ezekiel and other teachers in Babylonia whose names are unrecorded. But even they would have had nothing on which to work unless the discipline of the Prophets and the Pentateuch (so far as it was in existence) had produced some lasting effect.

At the period, therefore, of the return from the Exile, we may assume that the moral consciousness of at least the more highly developed members of the community included a clear perception of right as distinguished from wrong, of the obligation to do the right and refrain from the wrong, of the freedom to choose between them, of the authority of God as the source of the obligation to obey, not by arbitrary enactment but by revelation of His own nature and His will.

In a word, there were present all the essentials of a

strongly moral religion, or of a religious morality ; in Judaism the terms are identical. And the truth of this statement is not affected by the fact that the revelation on which it all depended was recorded in written words The words alone could not have conveyed any revelation, unless there had been the awakened mind, the enlightened conscience, to apprehend what was revealed, that which formed the meaning and contents of the written words. There was, at least in the loftier minds, a real perception of God through the inward vision of the soul, and not merely a blind subjection to the letter of a command. And it is to be noted that the general moral consciousness as above described showed itself in ways for which there was no specific commandment, or only the most general. Such virtues as kindness, sympathy, pity, brotherly love, were the natural products of a moral consciousness so developed ; and although there might be specific precepts to practise them in this or that way, in such-and-such circumstances, yet the virtue did not wait on the precept ; it was the spontaneous motive of the heart and found its opportunities for itself. The precepts merely pointed out some ways in which the virtue might be shown. The source of the virtue was the mind itself enlightened by the divine teaching and warmed by the divine love.

Now the question arises, What was the influence of Pharisaism on all this ? Did it modify the moral position as described above, and if so, in what way ? Did it reduce the moral freedom hitherto enjoyed to a legal compulsion, substituting for the light of conscience the letter of the law ?

It will not now be difficult to answer these questions. The one definite innovation which the Pharisees made was to lay the strongest possible emphasis on the *doing* of the will of God.   That before everything else.[1]   But,

---

[1] The Rabbis emphasised the fact that when the Torah was proclaimed at Sinai (Exod. xix.) the people answered (v. 8) : " All that the Lord hath spoken we will do," even before they had heard what it was.   The Haggadah picturesquely embroiders this passage. —b. Shabb. 88ª.

no less for the Pharisees than for the Prophets, the moral
fundamentals as described above remained unaltered.
They assumed that same foundation, the recognition of
the difference between right and wrong, the obligation
of duty, the inward vision of conscience, the authority
of God, the revelation of His nature and His will. Not
a single one of these fundamentals did they deny or dream
of denying ; as indeed these have been owned and maintained in Judaism down to the present day. The Pharisees
would have said, if the question had been put to them :
" This is all true ; but what is needful is that these things
shall be made more effective in life and conduct than
they have been so far. God's will must be done by a
whole people who really mean it, and who will put the
doing of it before everything else : God has made known
His will ; it is for His people to do it exactly as He would
have it done. If the right way is known, then the only
thing left is to do it. If the right way is not known,
then it must be sought till it is found." That, I believe,
truly describes the way in which the Pharisees regarded
the moral-religious problem of their time. They brought
to the solution of it their conception of the Torah, written
and unwritten, as the full and inexhaustible revelation of
God, and the system of the Halachah. The effect of them
was this : the Torah was made to include not merely a
static but a progressive divine revelation, as more and
more of its meaning was discerned and interpreted from
age to age. And the Halachah was the definition of the
will of God, for the purpose of carrying it out in action,
not by way of substituting a mechanical constraint for
an inward obligation. All that there had been before of
the fundamentals of morality remained under the Halachah
in unimpaired clearness and strength, nay, even with
growing clearness and strength, as it was the aim of the
Pharisaic teaching to develop the Halachah in the ethical
rather than the ritual and ceremonial direction. And it
is to be noted that the Halachah did not touch, or if it
merely mentioned it did not modify, the general virtues
such as those named above, kindness, sympathy, brotherly

love, etc.[1] These were precepts certainly ; it was the
will of God that men should be kind and merciful and the
like, because He was so Himself. But they needed no
explanation, nor any reinforcement beyond the heart's
own instinct—its natural response to the love of God
which it felt and owned. The Jew, under the Pharisaic
discipline, remained as much a free moral agent as he had
been before. What he had, in addition, was a more
detailed instruction of how the divine will was to be done
in regard to precepts which were not clear, or in circumstances which were not usual. As regards any individual
Jew, much of the Halachah never touched him at all ;
but he was not on that account bereft of morality. He
was a free moral agent, serving God according to his
conscience and the dictates of his heart. If the circumstances arose in which the Halachah did prescribe his
action, he still remained a free moral agent serving God
according to his conscience. And that being his intention,
he would not feel the Halachah as a burden, but he would
thank God for those who had taught him, out of their
wisdom, exactly how, in his present circumstances, the
divine will was to be done. Something will be said in
the next chapter about the specific ethical teaching of the
Pharisees and the Rabbis upon the main elements of right
living. They gave that teaching chiefly in the form of
Haggadah, as will be there explained. But the foundation
on which they based it all was the moral nature of those
whom they taught. If those who are not Jews find it
difficult (as the present writer for a long time found it
very difficult) to understand how the Moral Law was
related to the Torah, and how the freedom of the conscience could keep its place under the constraint of the
Halachah, I believe that the difficulty arises from the
fact that in Judaism religion and morality are not two,
but one and the same. It may be philosophically more
correct to distinguish between religion and morality, and
of course the regions of thought denoted by the two terms
are usually separated for the purpose of study. But no

[1] These are the " duties committed to the heart."—b. B. Metz. 58ʰ.

CHAPTER VI

THE TEACHING OF THE PHARISEES—II

IT is the purpose of this chapter to give some indication of the Pharisaic teaching upon those topics of religion and morality which did not form the subject of Halachah, the results obtained by interpretation of Torah on its non-preceptive side.

The Halachah was the defined will of God, intended as a means of training those who lived under it in the way of rightly serving Him. Here are implied the existence of God and of man, and the fact of some relation between them. The Halachah threw no light on that relation ; it assumed the duty of obedience on the part of man towards God, and unfolded the implications of the duty so assumed. It said nothing about the nature and attributes of God, nor of the nature and characteristics of man. And, as the Torah was, *ex hypothesi*, the teaching which God Himself had given, the contents of that teaching upon these other subjects must obviously be learned by those who had received the revelation. The Pharisees and the Rabbis were not idle in that study, being, as they were, religious men intent both to learn and to teach. The Rabbinical literature contains an enormous quantity of their recorded teaching, so that the material is not lacking for a just appreciation of it, if only the reader knows how to use it in the right way. For it must never be forgotten that there was no requirement of doctrinal uniformity ; the Haggadah was not imposed on the community as the Halachah was (see above, p. 105). There was never any idea of working out a consistent system

of theological doctrine, and the attempt to construct
one, as Weber did in his *System der alt synagogalen Palestinischen Theologie*, is intrinsically futile and historically false.
That one haggadic utterance contradicted another did
not distress the Rabbis or those who learned from them.
If both came out of the Torah, then that only showed
how much the Torah contained. God could say many
things at once.[1]

At the same time it is possible to trace broad lines of
general agreement, so that the religion of the Pharisees
can be distinguished, e.g. from that of the Greeks or
Romans ; or, again, from that of the Christian Church
which had its origin in Judaism. It is possible to observe
that in Pharisaism certain beliefs were almost universally
held ; and thus it is possible to arrive at a presentation
of Pharisaic theology which should rest on a *de facto* agreement, but always with the reservation that there was
never any official definition of a doctrine, to be accepted
on pain of excommunication if it were rejected. The
nearest approach to such an official definition, dogma in
the true sense of the word (to be clearly distinguished
from doctrine), is the declaration in the Mishnah (Sanh.
x. 1) : " And these are they who have no portion in the
world to come : He who says that the resurrection of the
dead is not [taught] in the Torah, and that the Torah
is not from heaven ; and the Apikūrōs." It is worthy
of note that nothing is said here of those who denied the
existence or the unity of God. The conclusion would
seem to follow that this statement of the Mishnah was
intended not as a definition of the outer boundary of
Pharisaic Judaism, because it is manifestly incomplete,
but merely as a declaration that the boundary passed
through the points there specified, wherever else it might
be drawn. Probably the statement in the Mishnah was
an official pronouncement upon some controversy of the
time, deemed to be of special importance. If anyone
denied the existence of God, he could not possibly be a

[1] This is shown by an ingenious haggadic combination of
Jer. xxiii. 29 and Ps. lxii. 11.—b. Sanh. 34[a].

Jew, let alone a Pharisee ; if he denied the authority of the Torah, as the supreme revelation of God, he could not be a member of a community whose religion was inseparable from that belief. The same exclusion would follow if he denied that there was a life hereafter—the world to come. But within those wide limits there was no obligation in regard to belief, while yet, as above remarked, there was a general agreement upon some main heads of doctrine. Such agreement is not after all wonderful, though it may seem so to those who are accustomed to the requirement of doctrinal uniformity as expressed in the acceptance of a creed. For the Pharisees started from the same premisses and applied to them the same principles, so that it need cause no surprise if they arrived at the same or similar main conclusions. Others, in later times and in quite a different region of the field of religion, have done much the same and have arrived at substantial agreement in their conclusions, while under no obligation to do so.

The fact that Pharisaic and Rabbinic theology is quite unsystematic is mainly due to the circumstances under which their teaching was given. It has been shown above (Chapter IV) that the Pharisees were beyond everything else the religious teachers of the people, especially in the Synagogue and the School. The Rabbis worked on the same lines. They taught, therefore, in forms suited to the capacity of their hearers, by parable and exhortation, appeals to the heart and the imagination as well as to the reason ; in short, as preachers, not as theologians. Most of the Haggadah contained in the chief Midrashim consists of what was presumably spoken to a congregation or to a band of disciples. A theological treatise, as every preacher knows, or ought to know, would have been entirely useless for such work. And if it be said that the teacher ought to have a systematic compendium of the subject-matter of his teaching, the answer would be that for the Scribe and the Rabbi the Torah itself was the treatise or compendium, and no other was needed. But whatever the reason may be, it was not till long after the Talmudic period that theological or ethical treatises began to be written. Of any such in Pharisaic times there is not a trace. Those who taught the people in the synagogues unfolded to them some portion of the Torah, now this passage, now that ; and pointed their lessons of religion and morality by such illustrations and appeals as their own spiritual experience and knowledge of human nature suggested. It was all very simple and direct, and it certainly produced very substantial results in the training of Jewish character in the ways of piety and right living. It has often been remarked that there is something childlike in the ideas and utterances of the Talmudic Rabbis as expressed in their Haggadah. The remark is certainly true, but that does not justify the rather contemptuous intention with which it is sometimes made. After all, these ancient religious teachers were men precisely like those whom they taught, men who for the most part had to work for their living, and who had no higher position or advantage over their flock than that which their own self-denying toil of thought and study afforded them. They were lay-preachers, and they devoted themselves to that difficult service of God and their fellow-men for no other reason than the desire to bring some of their brethren in Israel to a fuller knowledge of the truth and a deeper trust in God.

It will now be possible to survey the field of Pharisaic and Rabbinic theology in its main aspect, and to bring out into special clearness such features as were most characteristic. For it needs hardly be said that the Pharisees made no new beginning in theology ; they were the heirs of the Prophets, and the whole of the Old Testament Scriptures were their inheritance. The main religious and moral teaching of the past was handed on to them, and they brought to the learning of it a devotion and untiring zeal which were all their own. In some respects they modified the older teaching, laying greater stress on some features and less on others, and introducing yet others which in the older teaching were hardly if at all known.

Substantially, the Pharisaic belief in God [1] was that found in the Old Testament. Of course it is true that in the older Scriptures there are widely different conceptions of God, ranging from the hardly more than local deity of the earliest legends to the High and Lofty One of Isaiah and the great Prophets, the Creator of all things, the Sovereign Lord. And, equally, of course, the Rabbinical teachers did not reject anything about God which the Scriptures contained. But they laid the weight of emphasis upon the higher and more spiritual conception, as the Prophets had done ; and with it they combined an insistence upon the nearness of God, His close personal relation with human beings, as of father and children, which was less prominent in the Prophets though by no means absent. Of God as the Creator and Lord of all, the Prophets had left them little more or higher to say. For the Rabbis, God was the One and undivided Supreme Being, without qualification or reserve. Such, in Jewish belief, He has always continued to be, no matter what evidence might be alleged to the contrary from apparent personification of divine attributes, speculations about angels, etc., of which more will be said presently. On the other hand, the Rabbis insisted no less emphatically upon the nearness of God ; and it is well to remember that the term " Our Father who art in heaven " was first used in Pharisaic circles. No doubt the Old Testament prepared the way for it, but it does not occur there in so many words. It was certainly not new either in the time or on the lips of Jesus. If it had been, it would have been at once challenged as a daring innovation. When it was first used there is no evidence to show ; but the reason why it came into use was surely that it served to express the personal relation of God to man more truly than any other term. Those who first used it did so presumably because their own religious experience made them feel the need of some term that would do this ; and so well

[1] On the whole subject of the Rabbinic conception of God the reader should study Abelson's masterly book on *The Immanence of God in Rabbinical Literature* (Macmillan, 1912).

did it serve its purpose that Jesus, when he came, made no change and suggested no improvement. His religion was by no means identical with that of the Pharisees ; but the points of difference did not touch the belief in God as the Father in Heaven.

God was thus, in the belief of the Pharisees, both transcendent and immanent, though they never used any such philosophical terms in which to express their thought. Neither did they attempt to solve the problem of reconciling these two opposite conceptions. Both were necessary to their thought, the former to their intellect, the latter to their inner experience of immediate communion with God. Both, therefore, were held together as of equal truth ; and how they were to be reconciled was doubtless God's own secret. But of the two, the Rabbis dwelt, I think, more often and with more delight upon the nearness of God than upon His sole sovereignty. And it is a decided error to say that the tendency since the time of the Prophets was to set God more and more at a distance, separated from the world and humanity by a widening gulf which needed the ministrations of angels and semi-divine beings to maintain intercourse between the Creator and His creation. Whatever Philo or the Gnostics may have believed and speculated on this theme, the Pharisees and the Rabbis did not follow that line ; and the proof of it is their insistence on the nearness of God. A Father, though He be in heaven, does not need angels by whom to communicate with His children. " From earth to heaven," said a Rabbi, " is a five hundred years' journey ; yet when a man whispers or even meditates a prayer, God is at hand to hear it " (Debar. R. ii. 10.)

It is of course true that in the Rabbinical literature there are several terms used in reference to God, as modes of addressing Him or speaking of Him, which have been thought to lend some support to the view that the God of Pharisaic belief was a remote and unapproachable being. The ancient personal name of four letters was of course avoided, but even the usual word for God, ' El ' or ' Elohim,' is less frequent than such terms as " The

Holy One, blessed be He," " Lord of the worlds " (mostly in direct address), "ha-Makōm," "The King of the kings of the kings," and again the somewhat different terms, Shechinah and Mēmra. It is these last two which have most often been appealed to in support of the theory of subordinate divine beings, emanations of the Supreme God, the implication being that the Shechinah was in a sense God and yet other than God. If the Pharisees and the Rabbis had been theologians, or exponents of a philosophical theory, there would be more force in the argument. But it is surely not needful to seek for any more profound reason than the natural hesitation and unwillingness of God-fearing men to bring in the divine name unveiled, so to speak, into their ordinary discourse. The Rabbi spoke of the Shechinah when he meant the near presence of God. The phrase might and did lend itself to imaginative representation, especially in the vivid oriental mind. But what lay behind it was the thought of God, making His presence known and felt. That was the truth to which Jewish belief has always clung in its heart, whatever some may have said in picturesque utterance.

Somewhat the same may be said of the belief in angels, as divine messengers and intermediaries. Doubtless a good deal is said about angels in the Rabbinical literature ; and one does not need the assurance of Josephus that the Pharisees believed in them, as they believed in hosts of good and evil spirits. But the place of the angels is in the imaginative, not in the essential region of religion. They served to give form and picturesque expression to the thought of God as the King of kings ; they were the ministering attendants of His court, the messengers to do His bidding. And the good and evil spirits were creations of folk-lore and popular fantasy. Neither the one nor the other class of beings held a place in the real fundamental belief of the Pharisee or the Rabbi in the nearness and personal influence of God Himself. " If trouble comes on a man " (God is represented as saying) " let him pray, not to Michael, and not to Gabriel, but to Me, and I will deliver him " (j. Ber. 13ᵃ.) The

Pharisees and the Rabbis, being simple teachers of simple folk, may very probably have believed in angels and spirits and the like ; but, after all, their main concern was to teach a plain, direct and sincere religion, of which the strength and inspiration were the undivided sovereignty of God, and His Fatherhood, His righteous will and His pitying love. Abelson, in his book above referred to, on the Immanence of God, has given an exhaustive classification of all the variants in the use of the terms Shechinah and Holy Spirit, and the contents of a volume cannot be condensed into a paragraph. But all that is there set forth in minute detail goes to show how central, in Rabbinical belief, was the thought of the nearness of God. In this respect, Rabbinical Judaism had nothing to learn from Christianity, while it avoided, to its own very great advantage, the peculiar and bewildering doctrinal form in which, for most Christians, the nearness of God is expressed.

The fundamental attributes of God in Pharisaic belief were the same as those indicated in the Old Testament, foremost among them being His justice and His love. It would be possible to imagine a Judaism which left out the love of God (though in fact it never did) ; but a Judaism without a deep and even passionate conviction of the justice of God is inconceivable. If any knowledge of God at all was vouchsafed to the intuition of Prophet, Pharisee or Rabbi, it was the knowledge of Him as just and righteous ; and, in this direction, Judaism has said the last word that so far ever has been said.

The omniscience and omnipresence of God were divine attributes never questioned in the Pharisaic theology. So also His omnipotence. And there was never any idea of distinguishing between His attributes and Himself, although the Haggadah sometimes allowed itself to represent the attributes in more or less personal form. Whatever His attributes, it was always God who possessed them, and the distinction of attributes was never allowed to suggest a distinction of persons (in any sense) in the Godhead. Whatever to the Jewish mind was divine was to be ascribed to the one sole supreme undivided God.

Next, of the nature and characteristics of man in Pharisaic thought. Here, again, most if not all of the main lines were the continuation of the teaching of the Old Testament. Man was a created being, differing from other creatures in that he was made in the image and likeness of God. He was a conscious moral agent, able to look up to his Maker, to own the authority of his Lord, and to love Him whom he learned at last to call his Father. He had freedom to choose between good and evil, righteousness and sin, service and disobedience. He was thought of as a soul dwelling in a body ; but both soul and body were from God, and if the soul were that which bore the divine image and likeness, the body was to be treated with care and reverence as its earthly dwelling-place. The asceticism which made a practice, for spiritual ends, of defying, chastising and tormenting the body, never found a place in Judaism, not even amongst the older Ḥasidim.[1] There was, in some Pharisaic circles, an austerity of living which bore a close outward resemblance to asceticism, but it was the expression of a quite different principle. The Hasid never forgot that " the earth is the Lord's, and the fulness thereof " (Ps. xxiv. 1) ; and the real ascetic never remembered it.

Perhaps the most characteristic development which the Pharisees made of the teaching of the Old Testament as to the nature of man, was in the doctrine of the two Yētzērs—impulses, inclinations, tendencies—the Yetzer ha-tōb, the good inclination, and the Yetzer ha-rā, the evil inclination. The sources of this conception are found in the Old Testament, but it was elaborated by the Rabbis with a wealth of illustration and a keenness of psychological discernment which were all their own. Every human being was thought to be under the influence of these two inclinations, though not the helpless slave of

---

[1] See the admirable monograph of Büchler, *Some Types of Ancient Jewish Piety*, Jews' College Publications, No. 8, 1922, the most exhaustive treatise I know upon this subject. It is not too much to say that Büchler understands the character of the Ḥasid in every detail.

either of them. Man's will was free to choose which of the two leadings he would follow, and moral victory consisted in overcoming the evil inclination ; indeed, the ideal of the perfect life, morally, was the final and complete subjugation of the Yetzer ha-ra. In the Rabbinical theology the whole of the moral life of man is described in terms of the two Yetzers, and it is to be observed that both are regarded as having been implanted in man by the Creator Himself. There was never any question of a dualism, even in the creation of a world which includes evil or of a human nature which makes room for sin. The Rabbis were painfully aware of the moral corruption of human nature, which they accounted for by the presence in every man of the Yetzer ha-ra ; but they were not to be shaken out of their confident belief in the fundamental righteousness of the Creator, and they taught that even the Yetzer ha-ra had, so to speak, its divine side.[1] God planted it in human nature not that man should yield to it—He never willed that anyone should sin—but that man should have the frequent opportunity of exercising his will on the side of good and against evil, and thereby realise more and more that likeness to God in which he was made.

The doctrine of the two Yetzers, though it be cast in a form unfamiliar to modern thought, was no childish conception. It served as the vehicle of the teaching of men who were severe moralists and intent on the service of God, and whose main purpose as teachers was to help those they taught to live " a godly, righteous and sober life to the glory of His holy Name." For the philosophy of the problem they cared little, if indeed they knew anything about it ; but no one who has any knowledge of their teaching will deny that they did understand its practical realities.

[1] This is one of a series of sayings, paradoxical in form but only for the purpose of emphasising their truth, recorded in Ber. R. ix. The particular reference to the Yetzer ha-ra is given *ibid.* ix. 7, where the Yetzer ha-ra is included amongst the things which God had made, " and behold they were very good."

Apart from these two inclinations, the other characteristics of man present little that is distinctive of Rabbinical thought.   The capacity for knowledge, the power
of reason and reflection, the various affections, belonged
to his nature as a spiritual being ; and his bodily powers
were those of a creature whom God had endowed with
life.   All were from God, and all were to be used as being
His gift, for ends not contrary to His will.   Yet the
powers of mind, soul, spirit, were recognised as higher
than those of the body ; and though the body might in
various ways be made to serve the divine will, as in the
doing of right acts, yet the real service of God was rendered
by the will, thought, affection, conscience, the devotion
of the spiritual nature of man to God, known, adored,
reverenced and loved.   This is the keynote of Baḥya's
wonderful book on The Duties of the Heart ; and anyone
who has been accustomed to think of Rabbinical Judaism
as arid and unspiritual, should read that book, and
especially the last chapter, on the love of God.

Such, in outline, were the conceptions in the mind of
the Rabbis concerning God and man.   We have now to
consider their beliefs concerning the relation between
them.   The general character of that relation is indicated
in the terms already indicated as applied to God—Maker,
Lord, Father.   The first and second are found in the
Old Testament, and the third is clearly foreshadowed
there.   But it is to be noted that, whatever may have
been the usage in earlier times, the Rabbis applied these
terms to the relation between God and men in general,
all men and not Israel alone.   This indeed is obvious
in regard to the first ; the human race is the handiwork
of God and of none other.   So, too, all men are morally
accountable to Him, under His sovereign authority,
whether they owned Him or not.   But it is not so obvious
that God was regarded as the Father of all men ; and it
has usually been claimed that Christianity first taught
the extension of the range of the Fatherhood of God
from Israel to mankind in general.   It would not be
true to say that the Rabbis thought of God without

qualification as the Father of all men ; neither would it be true to say the same of Christian teaching. In each case there is a limitation, to be pointed out presently. But, in the main aspects of providence, loving-kindness, pity, the Fatherhood of God extended to all mankind, and was not reserved for Israel alone. " His tender mercies are over all his works," said the Psalmist (Ps. cxlv. 9), and the thought was not only accepted but dwelt on in the Rabbinical literature.[1] It was recognised and taught that not only all Israel but the good amongst the Gentiles have a share in the world to come (T. Sanh. xiii. 2). And this great utterance of R. Jehoshua b. Hananjah, delivered in answer to the narrower declaration of R. Eliezer, was never repudiated. It may be freely admitted that this more general conception does not find frequent expression in the Rabbinical literature. And here comes in the limitation referred to above ; and the clue to it is given by a saying of R. Akiba (Aboth iii. 18) : " Happy are Israel in that they are called children of the All-Present ; but it was by a special love to them that it was made known to them that they were called children of the All-Present." That is to say, the relation of children to Father was only effectively realised by those who belonged to the community of Israel. All others were indeed potentially His children, but could have no knowledge of their true relation to him except through the revelation made to Israel. That revelation had been offered to all the nations, but only Israel had accepted it (Mechilta, 62[a]). Those outside the community of Israel, the Gentiles of every race, could only become effectively children of God by joining the community, or at least by sharing in the revelation made to Israel. And it was the mission of the " chosen people," that for which alone they were chosen, to bring such knowledge to the Gentile world. That there was a good deal of quiet missionary work done by Jews in the last century before the common era is evident from the fact that Christianity spread rapidly, and always began from some Jewish centre, or

[1] See Abelson, *Immanence of God*, pp. 300 ff.

at all events in places where the ground had been prepared by Jewish influence. The great disasters which befell the Jews by the capture of Jerusalem in 70 C.E., and the final overthrow of the Jewish national existence in the War of Bar Cocheba, 135 C.E., put an end to all missionary work on the Jewish side. The sorely stricken community had all it could do to maintain its own existence. But, so long as missionary effort was still possible, it was the aim of the Jewish teachers to spread the knowledge of the God who had revealed His will in the Torah, and to bring as many as could be persuaded to come "under the wings of the Shechinah."

Thus, the conception of the Fatherhood of God was only realised consciously within the community of Israel, and to the Gentile mind it was not present; while yet, in the intention of God and in His general providence, it was universally true. This is certainly a limited conception of the relation of man to God. But it is to be observed that Christianity only replaced one limitation by another. For Christians were taught that they became effectively children of God only through faith in Christ. Doubtless, *in Christ* "there is neither Greek nor Jew, circumcision nor uncircumcision, barbarian, Scythian, bondman, freeman" (Col. iii. 11). But what of those who were not "in Christ"—the great mass of mankind who never heard of him? Were they, or were they not, children of God while still in their ignorance and blindness? The teaching of the Church was that men became sons of God by adoption (Rom. viii. 15), and were not so already by birth. And whether or not that has been the consistent teaching of the Church, it has certainly guided her practice. Neither Judaism nor Christianity has ever, unless in recent times, taken up the position that all human beings are God's children, Torah or no Torah, Christ or no Christ. In the early centuries of the common era, such an unqualified universalism was perhaps hardly conceivable, certainly it was not often or clearly expressed But it is not for Christianity to reproach Judaism with the absence of it.

To come back to the fact of the relation between man and God, as represented in Rabbinical teaching. It was a necessary element in that relation that there should be intercourse between them, communication of some kind from God to man and from man to God. These are represented by revelation and prayer. For the Pharisees and the Rabbis, revelation was summed up in Torah. Not that they denied for a moment that revelation had been made to the Prophets, but that they held that all which had been revealed to the Prophets was contained in the Torah. As, of course, it was ; meaning by the Torah all that the Pharisees meant by it. Revelation, in the last resort, was a purely spiritual process, communication from the divine mind to the human mind ; and what was communicated was knowledge, both of the nature of God and of His will. It has been shown in the chapter on Torah and Tradition how the original meaning of Torah was enlarged by the Pharisees, and it will be sufficient here to lay stress on the fact that the real Torah was that which was apprehended in the minds of those to whom the revelation had been given. The written word was the record of it, a priceless record but not to be so read that its literal meaning exhausted all that there was in the Torah. And whatever may be thought of the validity of the Pharisaic theory of Tradition, as a theory, in practice it made all the difference between a living religion and a dead one. A fact of which the Pharisees were very well aware. The Torah, to the Pharisees, was the full revelation which God had made, for ever inexhaustible, because the mind which received that teaching, studied it, meditated on it, prayed over it, was looking at "things unseen and eternal" and beholding them by the light of God. The revelation had been given to Moses, and in a lesser degree to the Prophets ; but to study Torah was, in a manner of speaking, to follow in the train of Moses and the Prophets, and by their help to see something of what had been shown to them. When it is taught, in countless passages in the Talmud and Midrash, that a man should ever be diligent in studying

Torah, what was intended was not the mere turning the pages of a book, or repeating words learned by rote ; that was only the lower end, and perhaps some never got beyond that lower end ; but the upper end and the higher meaning were reached in some such contemplation of heavenly truth as I have faintly indicated.

If revelation was confined to a few chosen to receive it, prayer was for all ; and prayer was the intercourse of spirit between God and man. On the human side it was aspiration, petition, entreaty, praise, thanksgiving ; on the divine side it was blessing, help given, mercy bestowed, forgiveness granted. It is needless to enumerate the main elements of prayer, because they are the same fundamentally in all religions which can be called spiritual. With other religions we have here no concern. The essentials of prayer were known in the experience of Pharisees and Rabbis no less than in that of Christians ; and if that statement be challenged, then two great witnesses can be called in support of it, the Book of Psalms and the Jewish Liturgy. The former was arranged and in part composed by Pharisees, and the latter is the creation of the Rabbis ; both, therefore, the devotional expression of the Pharisaic mind. No one will dispute the supremacy of the Psalms, as the utterance of the devout aspirations of the soul ; wherever they are known, the words of the Psalmists have become the sacred and loved words of worship. The Jewish liturgy is but little known outside the community of Israel. If it were, there would be less said about the mechanical formalism of Jewish prayers. Of course, any fixed form of prayer can become a mere form, and the recital of it a soulless repetition. No doubt it has been so in Jewish worship. No doubt it has been so in Christian worship. But neither on the one side nor on the other does this alter the fact that the thoughts, feelings and aspirations which found expression alike in the Jewish and the Christian liturgies, were deep and sincere. As in the case of the Halachah, so in the case of prayer, the Rabbis were keenly alive to the danger of formalism, and were careful to guard against it. As they taught that the mitzvoth were only rightly performed if done with the conscious purpose of serving God thereby, so they taught that prayer without devout intention, kavvānāh, was no prayer and was spiritually worthless (cp. M. R. ha. Sh. iii. 7).[1] A liturgy, by the necessity of the case, is intended to utter the prayers of a community, not those of an individual as such. The Jewish liturgy, though not uniform for the entire multitude of Jews in all lands, is uniform for large groups of them, some following the Ashkenazi Order, some the Sephardi, and so on. And there is a good deal, both in the material and the arrangement, which is common to all the various types. To name only one point, the recital of the Shema is an element in every Jewish liturgy. But it has not been, so far as I know, the custom amongst Jews, unless in recent times, for a synagogue or a local group of synagogues to have a private liturgy, compiled and arranged to suit its own taste. Throughout the greater part of the history of the Synagogue, the theory of the liturgy has been, if I understand it aright, that it should utter the prayers of the whole community of Israel, the one people adoring the one God, and should not merely voice the worship of this or that particular group of Jews. The function of the Halachah in serving to hold the community together was shared by the liturgy. And that was no doubt the reason why the Rabbis who framed it were so minutely careful in deciding what should be included in it, what should be said, and when, and where, and by whom. The Halachah has been deemed a rigid yoke of bondage which crushed out the life of religion in the Jewish soul, and the Jewish ordering of public prayer has been condemned as the reduction of devotion to a deadly formalism ; but those who comprehend the inner meaning of the Halachah and can discern the radiance that shines from within the liturgy,

---

[1] On kavvanah, see the essay by H. G. Enelow in the *Kohler Festschrift*, pp. 83 ff. And on the general Jewish conception of prayer, the article " Das Gebet in Judentum," by Felix Perles, in his *Jüdische Skizzen*, pp. 129 ff.

will own that the Pharisees and the Rabbis knew well
what they were about, and in Halachah and liturgy
built no unworthy temple for the service and worship
of God.

We have so far, in our study of the relation between
God and man as presented in Pharisaic and Rabbinical
theology, regarded that relation as unbroken, the relation
between Creator and creature, Lord and servant, Father
and child, united by love and obedience, blessing and
trust. Man is made in the image and likeness of God ;
the perfect life of man would be the *Imitatio Dei*. The
actual facts of experience show a very different state of
things. The harmony that should exist between God
and man is broken by sin, evil in the individual and in
mankind at large. We have now, therefore, to inquire
how the Rabbis dealt with the problem of evil, or rather
not with the problem of evil as a philosophical theory,
but with the actual facts of human nature discerned in
the lives of their fellow-men and read in their own experience.

The need of the soul was for harmony with God, perfect
accord between the human will and the divine. To attain
to that harmony was the constant aspiration of the soul ;
and the ideal was a harmony perfect and unbroken.
Whether that ideal had ever been reached in known
human experience, is a question which no religious teacher,
Jewish or other, would be hasty to answer. But the
Pharisees and the Rabbis held that it was not intrinsically
impossible, and that harmony, interrupted indeed but
nevertheless restored, could be attained by the faithful
doing of God's will. That which broke the harmony was
sin, and the means of restoring the broken harmony was
repentance answered by forgiveness. Sin and repentance
occupy a very large place in Pharisaic theology ; and the
reason is that Pharisaism as a religion turns wholly on
the doing of God's will. Sin was the disobeying of the
divine will, the defiance or disregard or neglect of what
God had commanded. Moreover, just as the mitzvah
was not truly performed unless there was the conscious

intention of serving God thereby, so a sin was gravest when it was intentional, though it did not cease to be a sin if it was done in ignorance or by oversight or carelessness. If an act had been done which was forbidden, or left undone which was commanded, then there was a failure, from whatever cause, to carry out the divine will in that particular instance, and that was sin. But further, just as there was goodness not defined by the prescriptions of the Halachah, the natural virtues of the good heart, so there was sin in the failure of those virtues, or the exercise of the corresponding vices. Hatred, jealousy, cruelty, and the like, all that implied the refusal of sympathy and love towards one's fellow-men, the active exercise of ill-will, all came under the head of sin, and, where they were present, broke the harmony between the soul and God.

Before going on to speak of repentance and forgiveness, it may be well to make two remarks which will serve to throw light on the Pharisaic conception of sin.

It has often been said in disparagement of Pharisaism that its idea of goodness is fear of sin, a negative and not a positive idea. Like many criticisms of Pharisaic teaching, this is true in form but not in substance. It is true that the Pharisees did, to a large extent, identify goodness with ' fear of sin ' ; but it is not true that they meant by ' fear of sin ' a merely negative attitude of mind which could be attained by inaction. It has been well shown by Büchler in his recent monograph on *Types of Ancient Palestinian Jewish Piety* (see especially p. 30), that ' fear of sin ' is " the religious readiness of the mind to realise the law " ; in other words, the effective desire to fulfil the will of God under all circumstances. To fear sin is not merely to refrain from wrong acts, or words or thoughts, it is to guard against the failure to do at any moment what at that moment would be the truest service of God. The form of the expression is negative ; the meaning is intensely positive. And that this is so is shown, or confirmed, by the saying of R. Joḥanan b. Zaccai (Aboth ii. 13), in which he commended his disciple, Eleazar

b. Arak, for declaring that the secret of the " good way " in which a man should walk was that he should have a good heart. There is a positive source for goodness, approved by a great Pharisee, who evidently found no contradiction between such a conception of goodness and that implied in ' fear of sin.'

The other remark which needs to be made is that Pharisaism never drew such conclusions as to the irreparable effects of sin as were drawn by Paul in the Epistle to the Romans. It was never for the Pharisee true that once a sinner always a sinner, in the sense that a man who broke even one mitzvah was thenceforth under a burden of sin from which there was no release ; since the Torah could not release him, and there was, on Paul's lines, none that could, except Christ. Doubtless, an act once committed could not be undone ; and if it was a wrong act it remained so. And if the Pharisees had been philosophers they might have speculated on the problem of the irrevocable past. But their concern was with the living present, and more particularly with the living soul. They taught that repentance and forgiveness opened the way of escape from the grip of the past, and prevented it from becoming the mere futile encumbrance which it would be if the Pauline theory were true. Moreover, the Pharisees were not in the least distressed by the fact (if they knew of it) that the Torah could not bring them release. To do that was not what the Torah was for. It did not itself give them release, but it told them that God could and would. And they needed no other help than His, as indeed why should they ? All that Paul said about the burden of the Law, and of man being sold into bondage under sin, was presumably true of himself ; but it did not correspond to anything in the experience of the Pharisees. They knew as much of the psychology of sin as he did, while they had a quite different theological conception of it. Paul is the very last person who ought to be relied on as a witness to the nature of Pharisaism.

Individual sin, by which the harmony between God and man was broken or prevented, had its remedy in repentance and forgiveness. Repentance is the act of the soul seeking to return to God after having, through sin, turned away from Him. That essential meaning of repentance is better expressed by the Hebrew word ' teshubah,' (תשובה), one of the great words of the Pharisaic theology. It was both natural and inevitable that, in a religion which required the doing of the will of God before everything else, the doctrine of repentance should become of immense importance. If, under any circumstances, repentance were impossible, the result would be spiritual disaster. In other words, if the harmony between God and man, sought in the doing of His will and broken through sin, could not be restored, there would be the end of all religious and moral life. Repentance, accordingly, was presented in the Pharisaic theology as always possible, no matter how great the sin or how vile the sinner. But, at the same time, repentance must be a real turning of the soul to God, not a mere verbal or formal profession ; and, where possible, it must be accompanied by acts of reparation and amends.[1] So much the sinner could do ; more he could not do, to restore the broken harmony. What remained was the act of God in freely forgiving the penitent. As repentance was always possible, so, in the Pharisaic teaching, God always forgave the sinner who truly repented. There has never been in Judaism, Pharisaic or any other, an unpardonable sin ; and such a doctrine would never have got into

---

[1] As long as the Temple stood, the sacrifices for sin were still offered ; but the sacrifices did not cover the whole field of possible sins, and even where they were applicable it was held that they were insufficient without repentance. They were offered because it was the direction of the Torah that they should be offered. But the deeper insight, of which the enlarged conception of the Torah is the witness, was already in times while the Temple was still in existence, recognising the spiritual value of repentance and attaching less importance to the ancient sacrificial system. When the Temple fell, the sacrifices had only a historical importance. If they were minutely discussed in the Mishnah, that was because they were part of what was ordained in the Torah, not because they were still of primary importance.

Christianity if those who based it on the words of Jesus (in Matt. xii. 32 and parallels) had known more than they did about the language which Jesus spoke and the common phrases which he used. That ignorance has produced a theological monstrosity in the doctrine of the Unpardonable Sin for which Jesus ought not to be held responsible, and of which the Pharisees and the Rabbis never had the remotest notion. They always taught that God forgave one who truly repented ; and they did not complicate this simple conception by introducing the mediation of any third person. For the essence of repentance and forgiveness was not the cancelling of a debt, but the renewing of personal relations between the soul and God, the restoring of the harmony which sin had broken. A mediator might plead that a debt might be forgiven, might offer to pay it himself, and the like ; and no doubt illustrations of that kind may be found in the abundant material of the Midrash. But no mediator could come into the direct personal relation of the soul to God, which was that of child to father. The Pharisaic doctrine of repentance and forgiveness assumes that relation as its basis. If it was true (so far as human word and thought can express divine reality), then the forgiveness of God meeting the repentance of man was the natural way in which love went out to meet love, and there is no more to be said.

But individual sin was not the only factor in the disordered moral condition of man. The sight of the Gentile world as it presented itself to Pharisees and Rabbis, to say nothing of the Jewish people of whose moral defects they were well aware, showed a state of moral corruption which could not be accounted for merely by individual sin. There were ignorance and blindness as well, superstition and degradation, cruelty, lust, selfishness, and all human vices. There was, in short, a human race which showed but faint traces of the divine image and likeness in which it was made, so that the idea of a harmony between God and man seemed reduced to a futile mockery. Christian theology has extended the word sin so as to include all this mass of evil in human nature and life ; and has dealt with it on the lines of the doctrine of the atonement.[1] Pharisaic theology took a quite different line. It did not apply the word sin to the general evil in the human race, but accounted for that condition by pointing to the presence and active influence in every human being of the Yetzer ha-ra, the evil inclination described above. The Yetzer ha-ra was not itself sin, but it was the occasion of sin, providing both the temptation and the opportunity, or rather providing the temptation when the opportunity was offered. If the Yetzer ha-ra was present in every human being, and if there were not also present the means of controlling it, viz. the knowledge of God and the desire to do His will, and the divine help sought and given, then the result on the great scale of the human race would be such an appalling moral confusion as in fact was there.

Such in its essence was the Rabbinical conception of human evil in general, a simple, clear and profound reading of the facts of the case. There is nothing strained or artificial about it ; and while it has none of the dramatic force of the corresponding Christian doctrine of the Fall and the Redemption, it escapes the pitfalls and perplexities of that doctrine. It is a sane and sober treatment of a grave problem by men who were accustomed to think deeply on the perplexities of life, and who took religion and morality in deadly earnest. So, of course, did Christian teachers, from Paul downwards ; but, if the Christian teachers were obliged to bring in Christ as the governing factor in their solution of the problem, that is not to say that the Jewish solution, from which that factor was necessarily absent, was any the less valid for want of it.

The Jewish solution assumed no sudden entrance of evil into the world, nor any sudden defeat of its power ;

[1] On this point, and on much of the contents of this chapter, see an article by the present writer, " The Fundamentals of Religion as Interpreted by Christianity and Rabbinical Judaism," in the *Hibbert Journal*, January 1923.

no total depravity through the sin of Adam, no deliverance through a special agent conceived as both divine and human. It assumed the influence of God slowly working in all human lives, to bring about in the course of ages the harmony which ought to be, between the Creator and His creatures, the Father and His children. There was no other way, if the fundamental facts were as Pharisees and Rabbis believed them to be. But it was the duty of every true servant of God to work with Him towards that great end, by spreading the knowledge of God, and winning men to His service. The end of that gradual process of salvation was far off, how far was known only to God ; but its attainment was as certain as that the power and the love of God were sufficient. It did not depend on some sudden exercise of divine power, in a form and through an agent hitherto unknown. The factors remained the same throughout—God and man ; and the immeasurable length of the process was due to the infinite complexity of the human lives involved, age after age. The note of hope has, therefore, always sounded in Rabbinical Judaism, in regard to the future of mankind, an unconquerable optimism based on unshakable trust in the goodness and righteousness of God.

Hope, in the Pharisaic theology, did not confine itself to an expectation so vague and general as that just indicated. It gradually defined its object in a twofold form, the life hereafter and the reign of the Messiah. To the consideration of this twofold expectation the remainder of this chapter will be devoted.

This expectation for the first time became definite in the teaching of the Pharisees ; but, like most of what they taught, it had its roots in the Old Testament, particularly in the writings of the Prophets. The references indeed to a future life, other than that of the shadowy existence of departed spirits in Sheōl, are in the Old Testament but few and doubtful. Certainly they cannot be taken to indicate a general belief common to all Israel. And when that general belief did emerge into the Jewish consciousness, it did not do so in the form of a belief in immortality. It took the form of a belief in the resurrection of the dead, the recalling to life at some future time of those who had died previously, and who, until that future time, were as much dead as if there were no resurrection. Immortality means, of course, that the soul does not die with the death of the body, but lives, whether there be a resurrection or not. The belief in immortality, so defined, is indicated, though only faintly, in the Rabbinical literature ; but it is beyond question that the prevailing expectation was that of resurrection, of the body with the soul, the two being united again as they had been in the former life on earth.

The belief in the resurrection of the dead had already become general at a time so early as to be definitely expressed in the second benediction of the Shemoneh Esreh, i.e. probably in the Maccabean Age ; and there must have been a long period during which it was assuming definite form. It is generally held to have been largely due to Persian influence, and if this means only that the form or forms which came to be used in defining the belief were to a considerable extent borrowed from Persia, the statement is no doubt true. But if it means that the belief itself, or more particularly the spiritual longing which found expression in the belief, was borrowed from Persia, then I hold that the statement is not true. Partly because it is intrinsically improbable that a wholly new religious conception should be adopted from a foreign source by a people who up till then knew nothing about it, and partly because there is enough in the Old Testament to explain the appearance of such a belief sooner or later, and enough in the teaching of the Pharisees to explain why they should be the ones to develop this particular belief. This is an aspect of the question to which less attention has been given by writers on the subject than the details of strange and fantastic imagery in which the belief was clothed. The Haggadists gave free rein to their imagination in describing the things that should happen in the end of the days ; and still more the Apocalyptic writers made this, as was natural, one of their main themes. But all these lie on the surface, so to speak ; and whatever worth they have (it is not much) is gained from their association with deep-seated hopes and convictions in the Jewish mind. It is these last that alone are of real importance, as is shown by the fact that it is these which find utterance in the Jewish liturgy, from which the Apocalyptic imagery is almost if not entirely absent.

If the Old Testament contains enough to prepare the way for the belief in the resurrection, and if the principles of Pharisaism are sufficient to explain its actual appearance, there is no need to discuss the question where this or any other religious belief was ever taken over by one nation from another. I shall confine myself accordingly to the first and second points, though in the reverse order. That is, I shall try to show why the Pharisees, and they alone, developed the belief in the resurrection, and how in doing so they were building on the foundation of the Old Testament. That they held the belief in the resurrection is attested by Josephus (Ant. xviii. 1, 3), who, in the next section, says that the Sadducees did not share the belief. The reason for this difference was surely not a mere petulant opposition of the one party towards the other, but is to be found in the fundamental principle of Pharisaism which the Sadducees did not accept. The gradual result of the Pharisaic teaching was not at all the sterilising of religion, as usually supposed, but, so to speak, the intensive culture of it. Religion, as the conscious service of, and devotion to the holy, righteous and loving God whose will was to be done, was made the supreme concern of those who followed the Pharisees. Both as an individual and as a member of the community, the Pharisaic Jew felt that religion came much more closely home to him than ever it had done in earlier ages. Which is one reason, though not the only one, why many of the Psalms show such depth and power of religious feeling. They may not have been written by Pharisees, though some of them were ; but they were written in a time when religion, personal and communal, was strongly felt and vividly expressed, when it was the subject of devout meditation, and when religious experience was becoming more intimate and profound. Whatever influences there may have been in the national life to bring about such a condition of the Jewish mind, Pharisaism was certainly one of them, also the strongest and most definite. The Sadducees had nothing to contribute in the least likely to produce such a result.

Such being the position arrived at under the influence of Pharisaic teaching, it would be only natural to expect that new ideas, or new forms of old ideas, of religion should be developed. Now the Prophets had said much about a future time when the power of God should establish a reign of peace and righteousness on the earth, had spoken of a great day of the Lord when judgment would be passed upon good and bad, and had declared (in the earlier prophetic writings) that a man chosen by God, and anointed (Mashiaḥ—Messiah) for his great task, should appear in the last days and bring in the Golden Age. These prophetic utterances had remained from the time of the Prophets, as it would seem, merely as lofty eloquence and the expression of an only general hope. To the Pharisees they were, though not included in the written Torah, yet part of what God had revealed to His special messengers, and therefore to be studied and laid to heart. That these declarations were and must be true followed from the fact that God had sent the Prophets to make them. But there was more than that. God was just and righteous, and His promise could never be broken. His will was holy and good ; and it was, as the Pharisees taught, the supreme duty of man to do His will. There was ' reward '[1] to be enjoyed and ' merit ' to be acquired through the doing of His will. There was retribution to be expected for sin ; in short, there was the certain conviction that the disorder and moral confusion of the world, as seen in actual fact, must give way in the end and be replaced by the order and beauty of a

[1] For the meaning of merit and reward, see above, Chapter V, pp. 128 ff.

world where God is the only ruler, and where all who dwell in it join in serving and adoring Him.

But when the end of the days shall at length have come, and the Messiah shall have established the kingdom of peace and righteousness, if then only those who shall be living at that time shall enjoy the blessing, what of those who died long ago and who yet in their day served God as faithfully as any of their posterity ? Especially, what of the martyrs who had laid down their lives, as in the Maccabean time, rather than be unfaithful to the God whom they served ? According to the ancestral belief, their departed spirits were in Sheōl, to remain there without hope of any change in their condition. What became of the justice of God in their case ? Why should the mere accident of living in one age rather than another make so tremendous a difference between them in regard to their ultimate condition ? Such questions could not but arise in minds which, under Pharisaic influence, were acquiring a deeper insight into the problems of religion and life. And gradually the answer began to take shape that when the new order was established God would call back to life, from Sheol, the righteous of former times, in order that they also might share in the blessing of the reign of peace and righteousness. And this is the resurrection, in its simplest meaning, apart from all the imagery with which it was set forth by Haggadists and Apocalyptists. By some such line of thought as that just indicated, the belief in the resurrection came into the Jewish, and more particularly the Pharisaic mind. It is impossible to say precisely when or by whom it was first conceived or first put into words. But we shall not be far wrong in supposing that the few passages in the Old Testament which seem to refer to a future life were, so to speak, momentary glimpses of the great idea which was coming into view. I say the great idea, although the resurrection as first conceived was limited in its scope, and clothed in imagery usually of a grossly material character. Nevertheless, it is from such a beginning that there has grown up all that is loftiest and purest

in the belief in the future life, for Christians as well as
for Jews. That height was not reached, unless by a
very few saintly souls, in Talmudic times ; but the important fact is the emergence into consciousness of the
belief in a future life at all. That marked a change from
a vague hope to a definite expectation, a sudden ray of
heavenly light into the dim region of Sheol, the assurance
that the departure thither at death was not the final end.
It is not wonderful that, once the idea had been suggested,
it was rapidly developed into a firm belief, for it satisfied
a spiritual want which had only come to be keenly felt
under the influence of the Pharisaic teaching, and its
insistence upon the supreme importance of religion.

Henceforth, in Pharisaism and Rabbinical Judaism the
twofold belief in the resurrection of the dead and the
coming of the Messiah held its place and holds it still,
although the contents of that belief have been conceived
in different ways at different times and by different
teachers. The belief has been set forth with an extravagant
abundance of detail, drawn from various sources, Persian
and other, or simply from the imagination of the writer.
Even when all these are laboriously arranged and classified
and compared by scholars, as is done in most books which
deal with the subject, little or nothing is gained for the
better understanding of the real significance of the under-
lying belief. Doubtless such things served to impress
the hearers, and give to the imagination what the reason
was not trained to receive in abstract terms. There was
endless room for inventive fancy, in picturing the incidents
of the coming of the Messiah, his overthrow of the world
powers of evil, the length of his reign, the bliss of the
righteous and the punishment of the wicked, and the
other topics which are included in eschatology. Doubtless,
also, these things were eagerly listened to and immensely
popular ; but, for all that, the real significance of the
belief was that it gave a new meaning to the fundamental
belief in the eternal God, Holy and Just and True, a new
meaning to Israel's passionate devotion to Him and entire
consecration to His service ; a new meaning to the hope

which dwells in the inmost heart of Judaism. In the course of ages, the outward trappings of the belief have been cast aside ; but the hope has remained, and the belief founded on it has taken on diviner forms and a loftier meaning. The ancient prophet had declared, in the name of God, the great word, "All souls are mine" (Ezek. xviii. 4). The Pharisees took up the word, and taught something of what it meant ; and they opened the way along which, to the human race and not to Jews only, has come the vision of life hereafter of immortal souls in the nearer presence of God.

With this I conclude the survey of Pharisaic theology comprised in this and the preceding chapter. I have intentionally refrained from going into details, because it seemed of greater importance to set forth the main lines along which the Pharisees and the Rabbis laid out their conceptions of divine things. The details are innumerable, and there was never any requirement that they should be mutually consistent. What the Rabbis said upon the chief subjects of belief was what they had the wisdom or the imagination or the insight to say, each as he best could. Where they were all at one was in their belief in the One God, the sole supreme Lord, who had called them to His service and given them in the Torah the revelation of His nature and His will. Halachah and Haggadah together are their reading of the meaning of Torah. And the whole of Jewish life, on the lines first traced by the Pharisees, is the answer, wrought into actual deed into the very fabric of life, to the challenge of the Torah, the call of God to Israel to be His witness to the world. Wherefore, the greatest of all the watchwords of Judaism is : "Hear, O Israel, the Lord our God, the Lord is one ; and thou shalt love the Lord thy God with all thy heart, and with all thy soul and with all thy might."

CHAPTER VII

PHARISAISM AND THE APOCRYPHAL
LITERATURE

No account of Pharisaism would be complete which
omitted to deal with the question of the relation between
that body of teaching and the Apocryphal, more particularly the Apocalyptic literature. The profound study of
this literature, which has been made by eminent scholars
in recent years, renders it unnecessary to survey it in
detail ; but the conclusions drawn by some of those
scholars, after minute examination of the Apocryphal
literature, would be of more value if they were based
upon a corresponding knowledge of the Rabbinical literature. For the exposition, indeed, of the positive contents
of the Apocryphal books, their religious and ethical
conceptions, to say nothing of questions as to their date
and authorship, such self-contained study is sufficient,
and has produced results of great value. But more is
needed if the Apocryphal literature is to be shown in its
true relation to the other elements in contemporary
Judaism, in particular to Pharisaism. The Apocryphal
literature is readily accessible and easily read by every
Greek scholar, and for practical purposes by those who
know no Greek but have access to the great Oxford edition.
The Rabbinical literature is not easily accessible, still less
easily read, still less easily understood when it is read.
But read and understood it has got to be if the Judaism
of the early centuries before and after the common era is
to be truly portrayed.

It may have occurred to the reader of the foregoing pages to ask why the Apocryphal literature has not been there referred to and used as evidence for the illustration and explanation of Pharisaism ? It was a contemporary literature, for there were Pharisees (in fact if not yet in name) when the Book of Jubilees was written, and there were Pharisees after IV Ezra was written. Moreover, the contents of the Apocryphal books have a greater resemblance to some elements at least in Pharisaism than to any Sadducean ideas or even to those of the Essenes, for which a better case might be made out. We need not consider a Sadducean or Essene affinity for the Apocryphal literature. That was not Sadducean, and probably not Essene. It has, indeed, been generally assumed that it was Pharisaic. Why then not use it ?

It is a fact, known to every Rabbinical scholar that, whatever the reason, the Apocalyptic type of writing is only very scantily represented in the Rabbinical literature.[1] There was plenty of occasion for such topics and such treatment of them, if there had been the desire to introduce them. What there is of such material in the Talmud and the Midrashim (at all events the earlier ones) is but small in amount, and not for a moment to be compared with the elaborate works like the chief Apocryphal books. There must have been some reason for this, though for the moment I do not offer any suggestion as to what the reason might be. And the reason must have been strong enough to warrant the leaders of Pharisaism in leaving those books out of the Canon of Holy Scripture, a point on which more will be said presently. Since, therefore, it is obviously the duty of the scholar who studies

---

[1] The two passages richest in Apocalyptic material to be found in the Talmud are b. Ḥagg. ii and Sanh. x (xi). To which may be added M. Sotah ix. There are some few other passages quite short, as b. Ber. 7ᵃ (according to Zunz, *Gott. Vortr.* 164, later than the Gemara), b. Joma 10ᵃ, b. Shebu. 6ᵇ. These certainly include the most important Apocalyptic passages in the Talmud, and they are only trifling in amount compared with the whole mass of the Talmud. The disproportion is very striking and significant.

Pharisaism to go in the first instance to the literature which embodies their own teaching of their own principles, and since that literature discloses ideas with which the Apocryphal literature, for whatever reason, was not wholly congenial, it would not be justifiable to use the latter as evidence for the character of Pharisaism. To say that the Apocryphal, and still more the Apocalyptic, writings were the work of Pharisees is a pure assumption, only to be explained by the idea that every writer who displays a profound veneration for Torah was necessarily a Pharisee. I shall hope to show that that assumption is mistaken, chiefly on the ground that Pharisaism had main principles which could not find natural expression in such literary forms.

I have, therefore, in the preceding chapters, tried to describe Pharisaism as the Pharisees intended it, and expressed its meaning in their own literature. If I have failed, there is nothing more to be said, and the work must be done again by some more competent hand. But if I have not failed, then the Pharisaism so portrayed is the standard by which to judge of approximations to it such as are found in the Apocryphal literature, and still more such unfavourable representations of it as are contained in the New Testament. These latter I shall consider in the next chapter. My task in the present is to consider the relation between the Pharisaism already ascertained, as I believe with substantial truth, and the body of religious ideas and conceptions set forth in the Apocryphal literature.

One point may be dismissed in very few words. I have heard the opinion expressed that the Pharisees did not know the Apocryphal and Apocalyptic writings at all. I cannot share that opinion. For it is beyond question that those writings were widely read and extremely popular. If they had been only obscure productions, meeting no real or even imaginary want, they would not have been translated into other languages as they were. All, or nearly all, were translated into Greek, and Greek could be read by someone in all parts of the then known world. Moreover some, and perhaps most, were originally written in Hebrew; and it is not probable that the Pharisaic teachers would or could be ignorant of books written for a religious purpose in the sacred language. In the case of Ben Sira it is beyond a doubt that they knew the book well, as there are several quotations from it in the Talmud. They may, and probably did, disapprove of the others; but they could not disapprove without knowing something of what they disapproved. And why should Ben Sira be the only book known to them out of the many which in fact shared its fate ? The Mishnah (Sanh. x. 1) says that R. Akiba included amongst those who had no part in the world to come " him who reads in the external books." It is not, indeed, stated what those ' external books ' were, and it only amounts to a declaration that there were external books, and that the reading of them was disapproved. R. Akiba, who made that declaration, knew very well what Apocalyptic was ; and if he made his famous entry into Paradise (b. Hagg. 14[b]) whatever that may really mean, he did not do it for nothing. He was the only Rabbi of importance who took a leading part in the War of Bar Cocheba, which was entirely a Messianic effort, inspired by Apocalyptic ideas of which Akiba himself was the most distinguished preacher. If such a man denounced the reading of ' external books,' he could hardly have been ignorant of writings with whose teaching he was, from some points of view, in such close agreement. If, on the other hand, it be still maintained that he knew nothing about them, then how strange is that ignorance in a man who had travelled even as far as Ginzak in Media, who had visited Africa and been in Rome.

I put aside, therefore, as wholly improbable, the view that the Apocryphal literature was unknown to the Pharisaic leaders, and proceed to the examination of the question, now become actual, What was their relation to it ?

The known writings of this class were produced in a period extending from the Maccabean Revolt, when the Book of Daniel was written, to some time after the capture of Jerusalem, 70 C.E., an event which is implied in IV Ezra. The lower limit may be extended without affecting the argument. For the Book of Jubilees, the Book of Enoch, the Testaments of the Twelve Patriarchs, the Psalms of Solomon and IV Ezra fall within the period specified, and they will supply sufficient material for a conclusion.

It may be freely admitted that the Apocalyptic literature is founded on the prophetic writings, " the true child of prophecy," in Charles's picturesque phrase (Pref. to his edition of *Enoch*, 1912). Whether the only child is another matter. The prophetic writings, e.g. Joel, Deutero-Isaiah, Haggai, Malachi contain enough to show clearly where the Apocalyptic writers got their ideas from, and whom they took as their models. What prompted them to write in this manner can only be guessed ; but it seems reasonable to suppose that the later writers wished to do for their own age what the Prophets had done in the older time. No doubt they did their best, with a high purpose and a genuine desire to help their readers. But a prophet cannot be made to order, and no amount of study and imitation of prophetic models will bring the divine afflatus. The Apocalyptic writings make but a poor show beside the words of the great Prophets. It is held by Charles (*loc. cit.*) that the " absolute autocracy of the Law . . . made the utterance of God-sent prophetic men impossible, except through the medium of pseudepigraphs, some of which, like Daniel, gained an entrance, despite the Law, into the Old Testament Canon." It is no doubt true that the ' Law ' did acquire a supreme place in the Judaism of the centuries since Ezra. But, if there had been, during those centuries, any real prophets who felt that they had a word of the Lord to declare, they would have declared it. Who would have prevented them ? Certainly not the ' Law,' nor those who expounded it. Rather, who *could* have prevented them ? Amos said what he had to say in spite of the priest and the king ; and, if there had been an Amos in the centuries now in question, he would have spoken his word regardless of Pharisee or

Scribe, in the very unlikely case of their wishing to prevent him. Also, if there had been a second-century Amos, there would have been some trace of him. But there is no trace. The Pharisees recognised the fact that prophecy had come to an end, and drew their own conclusion from that fact. And the Apocalyptic writings are a witness, not to " the tyranny of the Law," but to the feebleness of those who aspired to wear the mantle of Elijah. If their writings had appeared under their own names, it is quite conceivable that no attention would have been paid to them ; their device of introducing their works under the shelter of great names—Enoch, Moses, Solomon, Ezra— was one which men of original genius would not have needed nor condescended to use. Did John the Baptist fear " the tyranny of the Law," or let it prevent him from delivering his message ? Yet he spoke without concealment of his own identity, and there was never any doubt about his gaining a hearing. The Apocryphal writers included neither an Amos nor a John the Baptist, else they would not have written anonymously. Their works bear out this opinion, for their want of original power is conspicuous. They are obviously based on the prophetic writings ; and, what is more, the peculiar type of Apocalyptic writing is repeated in its main features over and over again. It is true that they contain some ideas which were not directly due to the Prophets, e.g., the belief in immortality ; and they worked out the details of their eschatology far beyond the range of the prophetic vision. Also, as in the Testaments on the Twelve Patriarchs, the ethical standard is very high ; and if the ethical teaching be not purer it is certainly more fully developed than that of the Prophets. I am by no means contending that the Apocryphal, and more particularly the non-Apocalyptic, writings are devoid of religious and moral value. I am contending that the want of original power in their writers gives a sufficient explanation of the manner of their appearance and the nature of their contents.

These writings, with the one exception of the Book of Daniel, were not included in the Canon of Holy Scripture.

It is affirmed that this exclusion was due to " the tyranny of the Law," and that only the Book of Daniel managed to gain a place in the Canon, in spite of that tyranny. (Charles, *loc. cit.*) That, with the one exception mentioned, they were excluded from the Canon is true, and that the supreme influence of the Torah had a good deal to do with their exclusion is also true, though I hold that the phrase " the tyranny of the Law " is an incorrect description of that influence. Yet, accepting it for the moment, I would ask, Is it not strange that a book which contains so much Torah as Jubilees, should be rejected through the tyranny of the Torah itself ? The whole book is in form a Midrash on Genesis, and the writer is so loyal in his devotion to Torah that he is usually supposed to have been a Pharisee. Why should the Scribes reject a Pharisee ? The same may be said of the other Apocryphal books ; there is enough of devotion to Torah expressed or implied in them to suggest some other explanation of their exclusion from the Canon than " the tyranny of the Law," and some other account of their authorship than that they were the work of Pharisees. I go on, therefore, to investigate these further questions.

Apart from the Apocalyptic passages in the Prophets, the Book of Daniel is the first known example of this special type of writing. It appeared in close connection with the Maccabean Revolt. What its actual effect was can only be guessed, but it is reasonable to suppose that such a book appearing at such a time would produce a great impression and do much to encourage and inspire the nation in its resistance to Hellenism. Now the Book of Daniel was a new thing, a type of writing which till then was unknown. To that extent, its author was a man of original power ; he saw and supplied what was wanted in the circumstances of his time, and presumably found an eager hearing for his message. His book was allowed a place in the Canon of Holy Scripture, though not among the Prophets. The reason may have been, as usually said, that the Canon of the Prophets was already closed. Yet that is not a wholly conclusive reason ; for

those who, in the first century C.E., debated whether
Ezekiel should be reckoned as in the Canon or not
(b. Shabb. 13[b]) could no doubt have included Daniel among
the Prophets if they had seen reason to do so. In the
Greek Canon, indeed, Daniel was included among the
Prophets, as he still is in the Christian Bible ; but that
is not to say that he held that place in the Pharisaic
Canon. If at the first he did, then all the more remarkable
is his subsequent relegation to a place only amongst the
Hagiographa. However this may be, the Book of Daniel
did get into the Canon ; and if it be said that this was
because the author wrote under an assumed name, on
what ground were the other pseudepigraphs excluded,
whose authors wrote under names which carried greater
weight than that of the apparently hardly known Daniel ?
The reason why it was included may be only that it was a
book which had a profound effect at a critical time, and
could not well be excluded. Moreover, since it was the
the first of its kind, any grounds of objection felt later
towards imitations of its peculiar form and manner would
not at once have become definite. One might say that
Daniel took his position by storm, and that later attempts
to repeat his exploit failed.

Why did they fail ? That question goes to the heart of
the matter. To find the answer, or such answer as is
possible, we must recall from Chapter II the history of
the time beginning with the Maccabean Revolt. That
event was an uprising of the adherents of Torah against
the Hellenists. The victory meant the triumph of the
Torah, and the conquerors were, to a man, fervent in their
allegiance to it. But not all in the nation were of the
type to which afterwards the name Pharisee was applied.
When that name came into use, it was borne only by a
small fraction of the nation, some six thousand in all,
according to Josephus, writing of his own time. Which
means that there could be, and was, enthusiasm for Torah
on other lines besides those of the Pharisees. Now anyone who wrote a book, at all events a religious book, in
such a time must of necessity have written from the

standpoint of devotion to Torah. If we knew more of
the details of this period, we should probably find a considerable variety of types amongst those writers who
represented the Judaism of their time. We do not know
all the details, but when we find books like Enoch
and Jubilees, written wholly or partly in the period
under discussion, we are not on that account entitled to
call them Pharisaic, but ought to regard them as representing one amongst various types of religious thought
then present in Judaism, and by no means necessarily
to be identified with Pharisaism. Of course there was a
good deal of common ground, since all united on Torah ;
but there were differences nevertheless quite sufficient
to mark a distinction. I am not saying that when
Enoch, or Jubilees, appeared it was received with disfavour by the Pharisees, for I do not know. It is likely
enough that when those books appeared they would be
read with eagerness by all who could read, and that
objections on the part of the Pharisees would only gradually
become definite. The books were certainly of a kind to
be popular ; they were easy to read, they were full of
Torah, they stimulated curiosity, they had a flavour of
mystery in them, they professed to disclose secrets, both
of earth and heaven, and they pleased the sense of national
pride in being the chosen people, whose God would triumph
over their enemies and his. Such a literature, whether
represented by Enoch and Jubilees or by later works,
could not fail to make a strong appeal to its public ;
as indeed is shown in the fact that so many Apocalyptic
writings appeared in which the main ideas and forms of
description recur with so little variety. Even IV Ezra,
with its mournful and despairing tones, yet keeps to the
conventional lines of Apocalyptic description. It would
seem that the popular taste was never satiated with
this kind of religious nourishment, notwithstanding its
abundance and its want of variety.

But in spite of their popularity, very natural under the
circumstances, these books did not find a place in the
Canon of Holy Scripture as that was arranged under

Pharisaic guidance. If they did at first, and there is no evidence so far as I know to show that they ever did, they lost that place when the Canon was finally closed. Now it is perfectly true that the Pharisaic opinion about these books is nowhere expressly defined. So far as I am aware they are nowhere mentioned in the Talmud or the Midrashim. We can only judge from the known principles of the Pharisees what that opinion was likely to be. That it was unfavourable goes without saying ; so much follows from the mere fact of final exclusion of these books from the Canon. But it will be remembered that the Pharisees placed before everything else the doing of the divine will ; their aim was to apply a moral and religious discipline in order to train the people to live as the people of God ought to live. They taught and elaborated the Halachah for this main purpose. The Halachah was intended to be the means towards the consecration of life, the discipline of the will, the guidance of action. And though the Haggadah was its indispensable accompaniment, yet it was the Halachah which, so to speak, gave the word of command. Now the Apocryphal, and especially the Apocalyptic, books were by no means on the lines of Halachah, and seemed to have a different end in view. They were not unlike Haggadah, and yet not quite the same. Even if they had been, no Pharisee would admit for a moment that Haggadah was sufficient without Halachah. It was the peculiar genius of Pharisaism that developed them both, and that put Halachah first. If the Pharisees had admitted the Apocryphal books to Canonical authority, they would have undermined their whole position, and taken the driving force out of their own teaching. They may have been right or they may have been wrong, though for my part I believe they were entirely right ; but, from their own point of view and on their own principles, they could not do other than they did, in looking with disfavour upon these books. That the books could have been written by Pharisees is a contradiction in terms.

The explanation here offered, of the exclusion of the

books in question, has this also in its favour that it applies to all the Apocryphal books and not alone to those which are specifically Apocalyptic. For there is not one of them in which the Halachah is mentioned, still less its fundamental authority recognised. The comparisons between the older and the later Halachah, suggested by Charles in his edition to Jubilees are in the notes, not in the text; the author of Jubilees said nothing about Halachah, and, if he had intended to do so, he would have expressed himself very differently. If the Apocryphal literature alone had been preserved and the Rabbinical literature perished, little or nothing would have been known of Halachah or of the Pharisees who created it. The former would have remained to represent some prominent types of contemporary Judaism, and no one would have had any reason to identify them with the vanished and unknown Pharisees. But, as the Rabbinical literature exists in enormous amount, the conclusion to be drawn is not that its authors are to be identified with those of the Apocryphal literature, but that they represent another of the prominent types of contemporary Judaism. All had common ground in the Torah, and in a varying degree in their ethical conceptions; but the Pharisees stood apart from the others in their definite affirmation of the Halachah, and the religious and moral conceptions which they intended it to express.

This I hold to be the fundamental and irreconcilable difference which marks off the Pharisaic from the Apocryphal literature, But it is not the only one, and I go on to show what further reason there was why the Pharisees should look with disapproval upon that literature. If I am right, the explanation will throw some light on the real character of the Apocalyptic writings, though not necessarily of the others.

It has been shown in Chapter II that the Pharisees were in the main a non-political party, whose chief aim was to ensure the peaceful exercise of religion. From the time when the Maccabean princes began to develop the political side of their victory, down to the final overthrow of the Jewish State in the War of Bar Cocheba, the Pharisees had stood aloof from politics so far as they could, and in all the troubles which threatened or resulted in war, they had been consistently on the side of peace. We have seen, also, that gradually, under the pressure of adversity and especially the cruelties of Herod, a protest was made against the passivism of the Pharisees by the party to whom the name of Zealots was given. The main division of the nation in regard to Torah, at the beginning of the last century B.C.E., was that between Pharisees and Sadducees ; but looked at more closely this appears as a division between the Sadducees on the one side and a composite group on the other, of whom the Pharisees were the most conspicuous member, though not the most numerous. All in this composite group, comprising the majority of the nation, were united by devotion to Torah, and to that extent were in close agreement with the Pharisees. But other tendencies and types of thought were also represented, and gradually found expression. There were those who disagreed with the peace policy of the Pharisees and finally broke away from it, becoming the party of the Zealots. They were as zealous for the Torah as any Pharisees, but they could no longer be content to defend it by peaceful submission. They were ready to fight for it, against its enemies and those of God— the heathen oppressors whose yoke lay heavy on the neck of Israel. They longed for the day when the Gentile, Roman or any other, should be overthrown and when God should establish His kingdom on earth. Now it was persecution, no doubt, and oppression which gave the occasion for such ideas to become articulate and pass from word to deed. But it is clear that the material for them lay ready to hand in the pseudo-prophetic, Apocalyptic writings. These had much to say about the final overthrow of the Gentile world, the deliverance and victory of the Saints, effected by the intervention of God himself through the Messiah. They showed the future bliss of the righteous and the torments of the wicked, and drew both pictures in bold lines and glaring colours.

They were full of religious zeal, but it was the religion of
fanatics, in which sincere piety was allied to hatred, and
the sacred consciousness of being the chosen people of
God became a bitter national pride—blind, fierce and
cruel. The Apocalyptic writings are full of such ideas ;
and the fervent devotion of the writers to their religion,
the lofty aspirations which they utter, the zeal for holiness
which they display, cannot disguise the baser elements
which are mingled in their thought and feeling, the spirit
of hate and vengeance which darkens the whole. In a
word, the Apocalyptic literature is Zealot literature. It
shows the inspiration, the ideas and religious and ethical
conceptions of the Zealot Movement, alike on its good
side, for it had a good side, and on its bad side, its very
bad side. The Apocalyptic literature and the Zealot
Movement went hand in hand, the one providing the
dangerous food and the other feasting on it and calling
for more. Of course there was excuse, if not justification,
for the Zealot Movement in the suffering of an oppressed
people, driven to fury by a Herod or a Gessius Florus.
In a sense it was only natural that such treatment should
have such results. But that is not a reason for saying
that the literature which embodies the ideas of the Zealot
Movement was noble or beautiful or sublime. If it echoes
some, but not all, of the tones of the ancient Prophets, it
breathes a very different spirit ; and if Apocalyptic were
indeed " the true child of prophecy," it is permissible to
doubt whether the parent would recognise the child, or
care to acknowledge the paternity.

Now the Zealots were an offshoot from the Pharisees, or,
more correctly, a branch of the original Torah stock which
had grown on other than the Pharisaic lines. The
Pharisees never coalesced with the Zealots, and only under
stress of circumstances shared in the war against Vespasian.
Even then they were the peace party, and would have
avoided war if they could. This is evident from the
example of R. Simeon b. Gamliel during the siege of
Jerusalem, and R. Joḥanan b. Zaccai and his colleagues
after it. In the last great war, the Pharisaic leaders, with

only a few exceptions, stood aloof. R. Akiba, certainly the greatest of all the leaders, was almost the only one to greet and support the Messianic king, Simeon Bar Cocheba. The whole Zealot Movement was contrary to the ground principles of Pharisaism. The Pharisees, for all the respect they enjoyed as the religious leaders of the people, could not stem the furious rage of the Zealots. Is it then in the least degree probable that they should have approved the writings which inspired and fostered the Zealot Movement, or should have recognised as Holy Scripture books which taught, along with devotion to Torah, a religion and an ethic widely different from their own, a religion which adored a God of vengeance and an ethic which turned the hand of the Jew against his fellow-man if the fellow-man was a Gentile? The Pharisees had their faults, doubtless; but they stood for nobler ideals than these. Truly, their fate has been a hard one, at the hands of the world. Not alone have they been branded for nineteen centuries as hypocrites, but they have been made to bear the blame of all that is repulsive in the Apocalyptic writings, whose whole spirit was repugnant to them.[1]

In expressing the opinion here offered of the Pharisaic disapproval of the Apocalyptic, i.e. Zealot literature, I do not forget that some of its elements are to be found in Pharisaism also; for instance, the belief in the resurrection and in the coming of the Messiah, beliefs which are

[1] The latest instance of this is to be seen in *The Lord of Thought*, by McDougall and Emmet. It is there taken for granted, owing to an entire ignorance of the Rabbinical literature, that the Apocalyptic writings represent the ideas of the Pharisees; whereas the Pharisees would have agreed with all, or nearly all, that is said there by way of condemnation of Apocalyptic, both on its religious and its moral side. There was in the synagogues and the schools a far higher and nobler teaching, though no doubt the Apocalyptic style made a more telling appeal than the austere simplicity and the severe moral challenge of Pharisaism. Jesus himself must have been perfectly well aware of this; and he showed it in his own teaching. That had much in common with the Pharisaic teaching, though it was based on a different principle. But that he should have stooped to the low level of Apocalyptic, as seems to be thought by many scholars, is to me inconceivable.

very prominent in the Apocalyptic literature. In the presentation of those beliefs, the Pharisees, for anything I know to the contrary, would not be averse from using such figures and illustrations as those which abound in the Apocalyptic books. Examples can be found in the Talmud and the Midrashim. And if the Apocalyptic books had contained nothing more, the Pharisees would have had no reason, on this ground, to object to them. So, too, the Pharisees believed in the coming of the Messiah, to set up the kingdom of God upon earth. But they differed from the Zealots in holding that belief as a pious hope, not as a call to action. The Messiah would come, when it pleased God to send him ; it was not for man to try and force the hand of God, or even to inquire curiously when the great day should be.[1] The action of the Zealots was an attempt so to force the hand of God, and the Apocalyptic literature inflamed them with the desire to make the attempt. There would have been no particular harm in the Apocalyptic books if they could have been kept free from the spirit of national pride and vindictive hatred which finds expression in them along with their nobler aspirations. The Pharisees condemned alike the literature which fostered such a spirit and the men who acted in accordance with it. They could not stop the men from dragging the nation to its ruin ; but they could and did refuse a place to that pernicious literature in the Canon of Holy Scripture.

It is, of course, true that the Apocalyptic literature has maintained its popularity, not only in Christian, but also in Jewish circles till far down in the Middle Ages, and has served to keep hope alive in dark times of suffering. I say " of course " because I am not prepared to deny the

[1] See b. Sanh. 97ᵇ, where there is a good deal about calculating the time when the Son of David, i.e. the Messiah, should come. Several examples are given, based upon Habb. ii. 3. Then is given the dictum of R. Jonathan, reported by R. Samuel b. Nahmani, " may they perish who calculate ends ; for they said, As soon as the end is reached and He has not come, He will not come any more." R. Jonathan (b. Eleazar) was a Palestinian living about the end of the third century c.e.

assertion. Yet, allowing that hope has been kept alive
or revived by such means, how often has the flame died
down and the hope been disappointed ! Apocalyptic is
full of promises, but it has never kept one of them. Its
immediate effect may have been exhilaration, but it has
left despair behind it. And if Judaism had not held in
its heart a nobler faith and a stronger trust, a deep passion
of devotion to the will of God, not all the Apocalyptic
that ever was written would have sufficed to keep it alive.
Apocalyptic uses the words of hope but its message is
despair, despair of all human means for establishing the
kingdom of God on earth, the anxious longing for God to
intervene and the distrust of the slow waiting for His
purpose to be fulfilled, the hasty casting of the responsibility for the future of the world upon God and the disowning of His command to serve Him in the passing time.
All these find voice in Apocalyptic, as it was only natural
they should ; but that does not alter the character of the
literature which expresses them. The Pharisees and the
Rabbis set their faces against all that, being well able to
see the effects of it in their own time. They saw the two
great wars against Rome, both probably and certainly
the last inspired by Apocalyptic ideas. And if they had
wanted an example to give point to their disapproval
they had one ready to their hand in IV Ezra, written
soon after the fall of Jerusalem in the first war. To read
that book is to understand the close connection between
Apocalyptic and despair. It is indeed a mournful book,
and the writer plainly indicates his perplexity that devotion to Torah should have ended in such colossal disaster.
But to say that IV Ezra represents the answer of Pharisaism
to the problem presented by that disaster is to go about
as far from the truth as is possible. The answer of
Pharisaism is precisely what IV Ezra does not give. The
answer of defeated and disheartened Zealots, yes ; but
the answer of Pharisees, never. The Pharisees had not
shared in those wild hopes ; and, though they grieved for
Jerusalem, as every Jew must do, they did not feel the
same crushing weight of despair. Their answer, in effect

if not in words, was to take up again their old task of building up the religious life of the people, a task which the war had made for the time impossible, to keep Israel together as the holy nation set to do the will of God, now that the political dream of triumphant nationality had been shattered. The Zealots had twice broken loose, and twice their effort had ended in utter failure. The Pharisees had done what they could to cherish a nobler hope, and a truer faith in God than that which found utterance in Apocalyptic, and made mad fanatics of the Zealots. They could only wait till the storm had spent itself, and then bind up the wounds and share the sufferings of their people. They preached again, and practised, the serving of God in the daily doing of His will ; and it is highly significant that the two centuries which saw the final discomfiture of the Zealots saw, at their close, the completion of the Mishnah, the official declaration of the Halachah. That book, for those who can understand, is the real answer of Pharisaism to the problem of Israel's twofold overthrow. The Mishnah, the embodiment of Pharisaic devotion to the will of God, conceived in their own characteristic manner, built up on the foundation of a living faith and an unconquerable trust, the Mishnah, and not IV Ezra or any of its kind, represents the life and soul of Judaism, its answer to the counsels of despair and the futile wailing of disheartened visionaries. This is obvious to those who know the inner spirit of the Rabbinical literature in general, and of the Mishnah in particular. And it is just because they did know it that Jewish scholars have usually placed the Rabbinical far above the Apocalyptic literature as representing the real and essential Judaism of the time. Of course Apocalyptic represented one type of Jewish thought and belief prevalent in that age, and for that reason deserves to be studied, just as the Sadducee, the Essene and the Am-ha-aretz deserve to be studied, if only the necessary material existed for such study. But when it is a question of relative worth and importance, then it is only those who know but little of the Rabbinical literature and who have not read its deeper meaning, who will give any high place or worth to the Apocalyptic literature in comparison with that of the Pharisees. Child of prophecy in some sense it doubtless was, as there are children and children ; but the true child was that Halachah in which the Pharisees sought to apply in the act of the conscious will the faith and devotion of the Prophets.

I have tried to show that in regard to the Apocalyptic literature there was a fundamental difference of principle which made it impossible that the Pharisees should regard it with approval. But in regard to others of the Apocryphal books there was no such fundamental ground of objection. The Psalms of Solomon and the Testaments of the Twelve Patriarchs (omitting the Christian additions) may very well have been the work of Pharisees. Why they were excluded from the Canon of Scripture I do not know, nor do I know if there was ever any suggestion that they should be included. After all, perhaps no other reason need be sought than the one usually given, that they appeared too late in time to be added to a Canon which was regarded as virtually, if not finally, closed.

As to the Testaments of the Twelve Patriarchs, I gladly accept the judgment of Charles (Oxford Apocrypha II, p. 293) that the book " shows that pre-Christian Judaism possessed a noble system of ethics on the subject of forgiveness. By the early school of the Ḥasidim, or the pious ones of the Psalms, the best elements of the Old Testament had been taken up, studied and developed, and the highly ethical code of conduct deduced therefrom had been carried out in actual life by these ancient Quietists." That is admirably put, though it should be remembered that if these Ḥasidim be identical with the " pious ones " of the Psalms, they, too, could " indulge in resentful feelings or even in personal vengeance " (loc. cit.).

But Charles follows up the statement just quoted with another, which in my judgment presents an entirely wrong view of the nature and the development of Pharisaism. He says : " But when Pharisaism, breaking with the ancient ideals of its party, committed itself to political

interests and movements, and concurrently therewith
surrendered itself more and more wholly to the study of
the letter of the Law, it soon ceased to offer scope for such
a lofty system of ethics as the Testaments attest, and so
the true successors of the Ḥasids and their teaching
quitted Judaism and found their natural home in the
bosom of primitive Christianity." Pharisaism did not
break with the ancient ideals of its party, though it may
have adopted other ways of realising those ideals. Neither
did Pharisaism at any time " commit itself to political
interests and movements." Of course, as the Pharisees
were not recluses, they could not help being involved
in the political turmoil in whose midst they lived ; but
that was wholly against their will, and that exactly marks
their difference with the Zealots, who showed what
Pharisaism would have been turned into if ever it had
become political. Neither is it true that Pharisaism
" devoted itself more and more wholly to the study of
the letter of the Law." What the Pharisees did do in
that respect, and how strenuously they sought the spirit
behind the letter, and therefore prized the letter as indicating the spirit, has been shown in Chapter III ; and if the
assertion at present under discussion be true, then that
chapter, and indeed this whole book, have been written
in vain. What is true is that the Pharisees devised
and developed the Halachah as a religious and moral
discipline. They did not use the method of written
treatises, they chose the method of practical action under
guidance and instruction. And they got very substantial
results from their methods, by way of moral and religious
development of the character of the people, at least of
those who followed and obeyed their teaching. The written
treatise, in this case the Testaments, certainly does contain
a noble ethic, but not nobler than that which the Pharisaic
literature also contains. Which, indeed, is not wonderful
if a Pharisee wrote the Testaments. Certainly, the book
passed over into Christian use, and found a welcome there.
Whether it remained as a subject of Jewish study I do not
know ; but, whatever became of the book, the ethical

teaching it contained did not quit Judaism. The Pharisees had their own way of arriving at the same results, and found all they needed in the Torah, interpreted as they interpreted it. When the Christian Church arose, it repudiated the method of the Halachah, which indeed was not capable of being applied to Gentiles. But the need for ethical teaching had to be supplied ; and it is only natural that the Apocryphal books of an ethical character should meet that need and be adapted to that use by teachers who had broken with the Pharisaic way. How much real effect they had in the practical discipline of character when applied to Christians is another matter altogether. It is easy to read a book and say how beautiful it is, how pure and lofty its teaching. The Pharisees would not be content with anything less than the doing of right acts and the refraining from wrong ones ; and they did not get this out of books, however excellent.

It may be that this really is what underlies the Pharisaic attitude towards the Apocryphal books in general, apart from the Apocalyptic writings in particular, towards which there were special grounds of objection. But in regard to the others, while the fact remains that the Pharisees did not allow them a place in the Canon, and apparently took no particular notice of them, the reason may be found, not in any special objection to their teach ing, but in the unsuitability of written books as such to the Pharisaic method. They had, in the older Scriptures, and above all in the written Torah, all the books they needed ; their sole concern was to draw forth what they believed to be the real contents of those books. They were not out to construct a system of ethics or theology or anything else, but to study and apply the teaching contained in the Scripture—especially to apply it. How they did this has already been shown. For their purpose the books outside the Canon were of no use, though their teaching might be in itself admirable. With the practical result that they left those books alone. Pharisaism elected to stand or fall with the Halachah ; that was its own creation, the fruit of its own peculiar genius. They developed the conception of Halachah to the furthest possible limits, and made it the central feature of their whole body of religious and ethical thought. The end and purpose of it all was action, the consecration of will and deed to the service of God ; it placed this before everything else, knowing well the difficulty and danger of its task, yet deliberately choosing it, and with unwearied patience and strenuous toil fulfilling that task through the centuries. The choice was one which no other body of religious teachers has ever made, unless the teachers of Islam have learned from them ; but the choice the Pharisees made places them outside the comparison with other religious bodies who have followed other methods. These others have had natural recourse to books setting forth religious truths or ethical principles, and have formulated their beliefs in doctrinal treatises. Pharisaism did not express itself in that way, nor feel the need to do so. Not till after the creative age of Pharisaism (under its later name of Rabbinism) had come to an end with the closing of the Talmud, did any treatises appear dealing with the chief concepts of Judaism.

Saadiah wrote to defend Judaism against attack from without, not to supersede the Halachah from within ; and the same is true of the great writers who followed him in later ages. The Halachah, even when incorporated in the Mishnah and elucidated in the Gemara, is not a treatise, and is therefore not to be judged along with works that are specifically treatises on religion and ethics. In the Mishnah and the Gemara the religion and ethics are present in abundance, but so to speak in solution, not distilled out or rather precipitated into definite propositions and formal doctrines. It is the failure to comprehend this radical difference between the Halachah and other methods of religious and ethical teaching which makes so much of the current criticism of Pharisaism not merely unjust but irrelevant. When that difference is understood, then it is also seen why the Apocryphal literature, though interesting and important as an element in the history of the times to which it belongs, is of little or no value for the knowledge of the real essential Judaism which alone survived. The Pharisees alone had got the secret of vitality ; they developed it in the centuries after Ezra, and gradually succeeded in making it supreme in Judaism. The Apocryphal literature represents elements which for one reason or another did not assimilate with Pharisaism, and therefore sooner or later passed into other regions of the religious world. If Christianity has benefited by taking them over, and has found spiritual nutriment in old Jewish Apocalypse, so much the better. It was not these which any Pharisee would have grudged to the Christian Church. It is enough that Christians should set great store by these ancient writings, if they really seem so admirable, without going out of the way to disparage the Pharisaism which did not share that admiration, and whose ways and thoughts and inner meaning no amount of study of the Apocryphal literature will ever disclose.

Prophecy had two children and not one only. Like Jacob and Esau they parted and went their several ways. And as between Pharisaism and that type of thought represented in the Apocryphal and especially the Apocalyptic literature, so to speak Jacob and Esau, the inheritance remained with Jacob, not with Esau—Jacob who was called Israel, and Esau who in the Midrash typifies Rome and the Gentile world.

CHAPTER VIII

PHARISAISM IN THE NEW TESTAMENT[1]

IF there was reason for dealing with the relation of the Apocryphal and Apocalyptic writings to Pharisaism only when the main lines of Pharisaism had been drawn on the witness of its own literature, there is even more reason for placing last of all the discussion of the questions raised by the presentation of Pharisaism in the New Testament. The Apocryphal literature expressed ideas wholly within the circle of Judaism, though not wholly within the circle of Pharisaism. But the New Testament expressed ideas the most important of which were entirely outside the circle of Judaism. The outlook of its writers, and those whose words they record, was from a standpoint wholly different from that of Judaism, and most of all different from that of Pharisaism. It is true that Jesus and his earlier disciples were Jews, and it is true that in his teaching he had a good deal in common with the Pharisees. If he had not had this common ground to begin with, he would never have been in a position where a breach would have been possible. But neither he nor any of his immediate disciples were Pharisees; and Paul, who had been brought up a Pharisee, left Pharisaism behind him when he turned to follow Christ. The New Testament as a whole is the product of a religious move-

---

[1] The reader should study in connection with this chapter the ישׁוּ הנוצרי of J. Klausner, Jerusalem, 1922, and not be deterred by the fact that it is written in Hebrew. The book is highly interesting as coming from a Jew with no leaning towards Christianity, though he assigns a high place to Jesus, well read in all the latest literature of his subject and scrupulously fair in his treatment of it.

ment which, *ex hypothesi*, was not Jewish, and its general attitude towards Judaism, apart from individual Jews, is nowhere friendly, and often hostile. The Christian Movement which produced the New Testament, and the Church which adopted it, stood in a relation to the Judaism from which it had come forth, which was that of opposition towards a rival, a discredited rival who could be a dangerous enemy. There was certainly never any question of mutual friendship between Christianity and Judaism in or since the century which saw the rise of the former. Therefore the evidence of the New Testament upon the subject of Pharisaism is at best only the evidence of outsiders who could see its effects but had not the means of knowing from within what produced those effects ; and who, for want of that knowledge, were not in a position to judge rightly what they did see. It is, moreover, the evidence of partisan witnesses, honestly partisan no doubt, intensely convinced that they were in the right, but none the less partisan, even when not definitely hostile. This is not to say that they were on that account false witnesses ; it is to say that their evidence is only of secondary value for deciding the question of the real meaning of Pharisaism, and cannot be admitted till that of the Pharisees themselves has been heard.

Moreover, Pharisaism was already some centuries old, in principle if not in name, when Christianity appeared ; and it has continued, in principle if not in name, down to the present day. The evidence of the New Testament is drawn from a period of perhaps a century and a half ; and the particular evidence presented in the Gospels relates to a period of not much more than a year, or three years if the Gospel of John be admitted. What the Pharisees may have said and done during the time of the public career of Jesus, affords but a slender base for a judgment upon their real nature and character, their conceptions of religion and morality and the results which they worked out from those conceptions. In any other connection this would be readily admitted. So far as evidence goes, the case is rather the other way, namely, that only when the ground principles and main conceptions of the Pharisees are understood on their own showing can the meaning of the New Testament evidence be justly appreciated. To begin the study of Pharisaism with the New Testament, to help it out with Josephus and Apocalyptic, and only at last, if at all, to make some little use of the Talmud and Midrash, is indeed the easiest way and therefore the one most commonly followed.[1] But it does not lead to a real knowledge of Pharisaism. If that be indeed the object sought, and not rather the defence of the New Testament view of Pharisaism, then the only way is to begin with the Pharisaic literature, and learn there Pharisaism from the inside, with its ideals and its convictions, also its limitations and defects, its own conception of its task, and the difficulties and dangers, spiritual if not material, which confronted it in the fulfilment of that task. Those difficulties and dangers were well known to its exponents, and not always successfully overcome or averted. As how should they be, since the Pharisees were only human and liable to fail ? But when, by this way, Pharisaism has been learned from the inside, it is only then possible rightly to understand how it could appear in such an unfavourable light as it does in the New Testament.

For what is presented there is not fundamentally a conflict of mere jealousy and ill-will, " envy, hatred and malice and all uncharitableness," though all these are present, and not on one side only. They are there simply because human nature was there, and was influenced by

---

[1] This is the line followed in the small book of A. T. Robertson, *The Pharisees and Jesus* (Duckworth Studies in Theology Series). A considerable display is made in this book of acquaintance with Rabbinical literature ; but the list of passages cited is sufficient to show how slight and superficial that acquaintance is. Anyone who has looked up the references there given will know that many of them are incorrect and some impossible, and will have some idea where they came from. Of any comprehension of the real meaning of Pharisaism there is not the slightest trace.

a disturbing cause immensely powerful and by no means understood. Whatever it was, its influence was felt very deeply, and affected the most vital issues of religion and morality. Where religion is thought to be in danger, fear and anger are awakened, and in their train the baser passions of human nature readily follow to make the mischief worse. So it was when Christianity appeared, and so it has been many a time since. But only the partisan (of either party) will maintain that all the right was on one side and all the wrong on the other. The student who wishes to be fair to both will seek rather to understand what each side stood for, what it considered to be at stake, and will neither excuse nor justify the deplorable elements in its defence. Pharisaism and Christianity faced each other in an opposition which was fundamentally irreconcilable, and the disturbing cause which created the opposition was Jesus.

Pharisaism, after already a considerable length of existence and development, suddenly found itself confronted by Jesus. I say " suddenly " because there had been nothing in the past history of Judaism to prepare men for the appearance of one such as he. It is true that John the Baptist had come and gone, and Jesus at the outset took up his message (Mark i. 14). But Jesus was far other than a second John ; and it may be truly said that he took the Pharisees entirely by surprise, when they began to be aware of his presence in their midst. And not the Pharisees alone. Until Jesus actually appeared, the like of him had never been known. Prophecy might be thought to point to him ; but prophecy drew no picture beforehand by which Jesus was actually recognised when he did come. When the first attempts were made to write down the earliest recollections of what he had said and done, the ancient prophecies were quoted in order to show that this and that was fulfilled in Jesus. So especially in Matthew. But the prophecies had been read for centuries ; and, in spite of them, no one was prepared for Jesus.

The effect of his coming into the world has been greater

than that made by anyone else in history ; and since it was the effect produced by one who, at the outset, was entirely unknown and unexpected, it can only be understood as due to the impression made by a personality of tremendous force and intensity. If there be in every human soul a divine element, if there be a point of contact (so to speak) where the soul is in touch with God, then I would say that in Jesus this became no longer a mere contact but a deep and overwhelming consciousness of God. Whatever of spiritual force is inherent in the human soul as such, in virtue of its origin from God, was in Jesus raised to an intensity unknown in any other person. So much may be said without bringing in theological distinctions and definitions, which I wish to avoid as unnecessary to the present argument. Less than this cannot be said, if any *vera causa* is to be found for the results which actually followed from the presence of Jesus in the world. To assume in him a personality marked by spiritual force and intensity to a degree unknown before or since is, I believe, the one and only clue to the right understanding of the significance of Jesus. If this be so, then it is vain to estimate the significance of Jesus by ranging him under the categories of Teacher or Messiah or Prophet, let alone such purely theological conceptions as Saviour, Redeemer and God-man. All these are attempts to bring the central fact of the intense spiritual energy of Jesus into relation with more or less familiar concepts. That central fact is what alone matters ; with it, the attempts at definition are needless, without it they are useless and misleading. That Jesus was a teacher is certainly true ; that he taught many things which the Pharisees taught is also true ; but the vast difference in the effect produced in each case must have been due to a difference in the personality of those who gave the teaching. The teaching itself was, by comparison, of hardly any importance. And the same is true, more or less, of any other function, real or supposed, which has been assigned to Jesus.

In every other respect than that of his intense spiritual

force, he was a man of his time and country, sharing in the common ideas of his fellows, not exempt from their limitations. So much one of themselves that his neighbours asked : Is not this Joseph's son ? (Luke iv. 22), and yet with something about him which made them ask the question. He shared many of the usual religious beliefs ; he was never challenged for saying that God was the Father in heaven, or for assuming the approach of the end of the world, or for believing in evil spirits and the reality of the power to cast them out. I know of nothing in the Gospel records to show that his mental outlook extended beyond his country and, in the beginning at all events, beyond his own nation. One who is reported to have said (Matt. xv. 24), to a woman of a neighbouring people, " I was not sent but to the lost sheep of the house of Israel," would surely have expressed himself differently if he had had any clear conception of mankind as a whole, let alone of himself as having any function in relation thereto. That he had any far-reaching views upon any subject of thought whatever, a comprehensive theology, a profound philosophy or an elaborate theory on social questions, does not, so far as I can see, any-where appear ; though of course philosophies and theories in abundance have been constructed upon the foundation of his words. He moved amongst the ordinary persons, and met the ordinary experiences of his time, as belonging to them ; but his words and his actions were what they were by reason of the intense spiritual energy within him. Those who saw and heard him appear to have instinctively felt that there was some dominating power in him (see Luke iv. 30, and indeed the Gospels *passim* ; for it is the prevailing feature of all that is told about him).

To say, *a priori*, what is and what is not implied in such a personality as that indicated above would be a rash undertaking ; but it will probably be admitted that one in whom there was so vivid a consciousness of God would neither seek nor recognise any human authority for what he said or thought or believed in regard to

religion. The ultimate authority is, of course, in every
case, that of God himself, however it may be apprehended.
It was so for the Pharisees no less than for Jesus ; but,
while for them it was apprehended through the Torah,
and its injunctions, defined by intellectual process and
moral discernment, derived their binding force in fact
from human enactment, by him the authority of God
was owned and felt in immediate experience. This is, if
I understand it aright, what is meant when it is said
(Mark i. 22), that " he taught as one having authority
and not as the Scribes." And if so, this is the point of
collision between him and Pharisaism, the irreconcilable
difference which admitted of no compromise. Once Jesus
had appeared, being such as I have tried to indicate,
then, unless he had lived in seclusion and kept silence,
a collision sooner or later was certain to come.

It would seem that neither the Pharisees nor Jesus
sought a collision, or perhaps even expected it. Naturally
the Pharisees did not, because they knew nothing about
him until his fame began to spread, so that they then
for the first time heard of the new teacher and took
notice of him. But it is noteworthy that Jesus himself
did not at the outset challenge the Pharisees, or apparently
have them specially in his mind. It is said (Matt. ix. 36)
that " When he saw the multitudes he had compassion
on them, because they were distressed and scattered as
sheep not having a shepherd." And he said of himself
(Matt. xv. 24) : " I was not sent but to the lost sheep of
the house of Israel." This would seem to show that he
found his first call to service in the needs of the uncared-for
masses, and not in the shortcomings of those who had
not cared for them, who at all events had not prevented
them from getting into that lost condition. They were
outside the Pharisaic circle, and so also was he. He
gave them " out of the abundance of his heart " such
" good treaure " as is contained in the Sermon on the
Mount and the Parables, and it is not wonderful that
they " heard him gladly " (Mark xii. 37), and that " the
people all hung upon him, listening " (Luke xix. 48).

We may safely suppose that people were more impressed and overawed by him than by any definite message which he proclaimed, as that the kingdom of God was at hand. However this may be, he did not, as it would seem, at the outset throw down any challenge to Pharisaism. His concern was to speak out of himself what he had it in him to say, and not to ask what others might think of it. The challenge came from the Pharisees, when they heard of his preaching to the multitudes, and themselves heard him in the synagogues. They heard him say many things which were in accordance with their own religious teaching, but he said them as from himself with no appeal to traditional authority. They saw him do things which were not in accordance with the Halachah, simply on his own authority, because he thought fit to do them. In the incident of the paralytic who was healed in Capernaum (Mark ii. 12), it is told how " certain of the Scribes were sitting there, and reasoning in their hearts, Why does this man thus speak ? He blasphemeth : Who can forgive sins but one, even God ? " Whether this was actually the first awakening of suspicion and alarm in the minds of the Pharisees, I do not know ; but it shows clearly how that awakening must have come about. The challenge was definitely made when (as recorded in Mark vii. 5) the Pharisees asked him : " Why walk not thy disciples according to the tradition of the elders ? " The challenge was met by a repudiation of the tradition of the elders, pointed by a quotation from Isaiah and addressed to " you hypocrites." He accused them of rejecting the commandment of God that they might keep their tradition, and he gave as an example the practice of evading the commandment " Honour thy father and mother " by the plea of " Corban." This incident, if indeed it be correctly reported in the Gospel, is very instructive in regard to the attitude of Jesus towards the Pharisees. In the first place it is the attitude of an opponent. He flashed out a sharp retort to a quite natural question, and thereby showed himself wholly aloof from the Pharisaic position. He made no attempt to reason with them and show them where, as he thought, they were in error. He denounced them straightway as hypocrites, " making void the command of God by their tradition." If he really gave the practice of Corban as an example, and if this be not due to later manipulation of the Gospel material, then the inference is legitimate that Jesus had no close acquaintance with the tradition which he denounced. The tradition of the elders is of course the Halachah. The alleged practice of evading the fifth commandment is nowhere known in the recorded Halachah (see especially M. Nedar, ix. 1, and the commentaries on the passage), and is, besides, entirely at variance with the Pharisaic practice of laying the greatest stress upon honour to parents. If Jesus had had any inside knowledge of Pharisaism on its Halachic side he would never have given an example so entirely beside the mark. But it is quite in accordance with what we know of the circumstances of his life that he should have had no inside knowledge of Pharisaism in general or of Halachah in particular. His sympathies, and his affinities, were with the multitude who were outside the Pharisaic circle, the Am-ha-aretz class if that term may be taken in a very wide sense. And, so far as he was outside the Pharisaic circle, he himself was an Am-ha-aretz. The Pharisees could only teach the Halachah to those who were willing to learn it, and they could not enforce it upon anyone. The theoretical discussion and definition of Halachah was confined to the assemblies of the Rabbis, as appears on every page of the Mishnah.

Now it is no doubt true that very much of what is recorded as Halachah in the Mishnah is of later date than the time of Jesus; that in his time the amount of defined Halachah was much less than in the time of Rabbi (135–219 C.E.), and that there are differences between the old Halachah and the new. Nevertheless, and this is the only point that matters at present, there *was* some amount of defined Halachah in the time of Jesus, and the principle of it was derived from the Sopherim, if not from Ezra himself. Unless, therefore, a man stood within the Pharisaic circle he could have no means of knowing what they meant by Halachah or even what exactly they taught. He would be an outsider, with no means of forming a correct judgment upon what he saw, and at the mercy of rumour as to what he believed in regard to Halachah. This would be the position of anyone not a Pharisee or an adherent of Pharisaism, and it would be especially so of Jesus. For that intensity of spiritual force which I have pre-supposed in him would tend towards concentration upon his own conception of religion and not at all towards comprehension of, still less sympathy with, any other conception. This explains why the question of the Pharisees drew forth from him that sudden and explosive retort. If the figure may be allowed, it was as if they had touched a live wire, when they encountered a personality so highly charged with energy. But the incident indicates (if it be truly reported) that Jesus really was ignorant of Pharisaic Halachic teaching, and showed it by the example he gave to prove his case. The Gospels naturally do not record any Pharisaic reply to the charge hurled at them, but it would have been a damaging one.

If the above explanation be not accepted, then the only alternative is to suppose that the record of the incident rests on a misunderstood tradition, written down by men who knew nothing about Halachah, and sharing the anti-Jewish feelings of the early Church. But, in that case, the whole force is taken away from what was meant to be an effective retort by Jesus to the challenge of the Pharisees, and the incident is left without meaning or importance. This seems to me a very lame conclusion, and I adopt the first alternative as being in every way reasonable and probable.

If the case were so, how would it appear from the Pharisees' point of view? All idea of what Christians have come to see in Jesus must of course be ruled out, since the Pharisees could not by any possibility have known then what the followers of Jesus would think about him. They would see before them a man who evidently had great power over the people, intensely in earnest, ready to fire up in a moment if he were challenged, a preacher of religion whose ideas were not theirs, and who denounced the Halachah with none the less fierceness because he knew little or nothing about it. Religion, for the Pharisees, was unimaginable without the Halachah, as the main and dominating element in the Torah. They believed in it, and taught their followers to believe in it, as " the Way, the Truth and the Life," as for them it really was. Necessarily, therefore, they looked upon Jesus as a source of serious danger, a revolutionary teacher whose influence threatened to destroy what to them was of life and death importance. They must resist him or be false to their own convictions. The only alternative was to capitulate and own that they and their forerunners had all been mistaken. But why should they capitulate ? Their opponent had not attempted to show them " a more excellent way " ; he had only lashed out at them, with a fierceness which would not tend to make them yield to him. To ask which was right and which was wrong in this opposition is a useless question. For the matter of that, both were right. But the significance of the incident is that it shows clearly the nature of the collision between Pharisaism and Jesus as the mutual impact of two irreconcilable conceptions of religion. What is more, there was never any attempt at a reconciliation, not the slightest approach of the one side to the other, with a view to an understanding of the other's position. No such attempt is mentioned in the Gospels, in connection with any of the numerous encounters between Jesus and the Pharisees. It is true that Jesus commended one Scribe (Mark xii. 34) for saying only what any Scribe would have assented to ; as Jesus would have known if he had ever asked them. The only attitude of both parties throughout the short career of Jesus was that of distrust and fear on the one side, and indignant denunciation on the other ; an attitude perfectly intelligible, yet one which no follower on either side ought to contemplate without regret. Such an

opposition gave plenty of occasion for the lower passions
of hatred and jealousy and malice and slander ; and if
the Pharisees, when Jesus died on the cross, " stood by
consenting to his death," though it was not their doing,
the followers of Jesus have amply, if very humanly,
revenged themselves during all the centuries since. But
that belongs to a later stage.

In the incident reviewed above may be seen what may
be called the declaration of war between the Pharisees
and Jesus ; and the other encounters recorded in the
Gospels are so many battles in that war. Being recorded
in the Gospels, the victory is always assigned to Jesus.
But in truth there was no victory, for one party or the
other. Various questions were raised and each side
approached them from a standpoint totally different
from that of the opponent. The details differed as
between one encounter and another ; now it was the
question of healing on the Sabbath (Mark iii. 1-6), now
the question of divorce (Matt. xix. 3-12), now the giving
of tribute to Cæsar (Matt. xxii. 15-22). But they all
serve to illustrate, by reference to the several points
raised, the sharpness of the conflict between Jesus and
his opponents. It is not necessary, for the purpose of the
present chapter, to deal with them all seriatim. But
something must be said of the great denunciation in
Matthew xxiii (cp. Luke xi. 42-54), which, whatever may
be thought of it, certainly forms an essential part of the
representation of Pharisaism in the New Testament.
Whether that famous passage contains the *ipsissima
verba* of Jesus, or represents the mind and utters the
voice of the early Church, does not greatly matter so
far as the Pharisees are concerned. Nothing can soften
the hostility expressed in it ; and, whatever its origin,
it sums up and focuses in burning indignation the
antagonism between the Pharisees and Jesus as felt on
his side. I find no difficulty in believing that Jesus himself
said what is there recorded, because it is quite intelligible
that a man, driven to bay by his opponents, should turn
and rend them. His attitude at the end is only the

natural outcome of his attitude all through. The various ' woes ' hurled at the Pharisees exceed in their cumulative force all that he had said previously ; but in detail they do not add anything to the knowledge of the real nature of the controversy. Neither do they throw any fresh light, or any light at all, upon the true character of Pharisaism. As far as that goes, the Pharisees would have had an answer from their point of view to all the charges hurled at them. An answer which would have been as powerless to persuade as the attack was. But there is nothing to be learned from the attack as to the real nature and meaning of the system attacked, though there is much to be learned as to the state of mind and point of view of the assailant. From his point of view, shared of course by his followers ever since, what he expressed was righteous indignation, denunciation of a system which he believed to be corrupt and false. If Pharisaism had been, in its true intent and real effect, anything like what he supposed, then of course his denunciation would have been well deserved. But he only saw its outward appearance, he did not know it from within, nor apparently ever try to understand it. That there were hypocritical Pharisees is admitted by all, and by none more explicitly than the Pharisees themselves, but whatever features of Pharisaism might tend to provoke attack, they would not be withdrawn or modified as the result of attack. In other words, the constant denunciation of their system would not tend to conciliate the Pharisees, but would arouse in them the lower passions of hatred and malice and calumny from which human nature is not exempt, either in Pharisees or Christians. That the Pharisees were roused to such feelings against Jesus cannot be denied. That they had great provocation can also not be denied, except by those who know only one side of the case. And even they, believing that Jesus justly regarded the Pharisees as his enemies, might sometimes wonder what had become of the earlier precept (Matt. v. 44) : " Love your enemies and pray for them that persecute you." If the Pharisees were as he supposed, were they not in even greater need of healing than the sinners and the outcasts ? If they were blind, deaf and spiritually dead, had he no mission to heal them, no pity and no sympathy for those lost souls ? The more the alleged spiritual depravity of the Pharisees be emphasised, the more striking is the absence of any slightest attempt to lead them into a better way on the part of one who " came to seek and save that which is lost " (Luke xix. 10). The note throughout all the Gospel record is (apart from individual cases) that of hostility, denunciation and defiance on the part of Jesus towards the Pharisees, and of growing anger, fear, yes, and hatred, on their part towards him. That he was put to death was primarily the work of the Sadducees, they being the party of the chief priests, with whom the Pharisees had little to do. But the Pharisees could not but see in his fate the overthrow of a dangerous enemy, and they would know of no reason why they should express any disapproval.

It is useless to speculate on what might have been, if the opposite parties in this controversy could have come to some understanding of each other. It is true that there could have been no compromise, the conceptions of religion, for which each stood, were in principle irreconcilable, but yet each might have learned something from the other. Jesus was not just a Rabbi, saying only what other Rabbis had said. That he was a profound and original genius in religion needs no showing, in view of the immense religious movement which had its origin in him. Pharisaism was no " organised hypocrisy," no dead corpse of a once living religion. It was very much alive, and is alive still. These two great spiritual powers, the greatest that were then in the world, might have learned something from each other, might even have strengthened each other in that service of God to which each was consecrated. Instead, a fierce controversy, ended for the moment by the death of one opponent, and leaving behind it a legacy of mutual hostility to the adherents of both. So far as Jesus was concerned, the

Pharisees went their way and thought but little more of him. Their own literature contains only a few references to him,[1] and those merely contemptuous or scurrilous, showing no recognition of the greatness of their opponent. Pharisaism, to all appearance, remained unchanged by the denunciation of Jesus. Its own adherents upheld it with undiminished zeal; and its opponents, the followers of Jesus, gradually becoming the Christian Church, condemned it with increasing severity. The presentation of the Pharisees in the rest of the New Testament differs in some important respects from that in the Synoptic Gospels, but not in the direction of greater mildness or greater fairness. To the study of this further development I now proceed.

The controversy between Jesus and the Pharisees was fought out on Jewish ground. Whatever was implicit in the ideas of Jesus of a significance of the Gospel for Gentiles, it does not appear that he ever looked on himself as being other than a Jew. Certainly his first followers continued their observance of Jewish usage after he was gone, with as much or as little strictness as before. Peter and John " went up to the Temple at the hour of prayer " (Acts iii. 1). Apparently the only difference between a converted and an unconverted Jew was that the former did and the latter did not believe that Jesus was the Messiah. But when, with the adhesion of Gentiles, the Christian Church began to realise that its religion was fundamentally different from Judaism, and accordingly drew apart from close association with it, the natural result was that in the later literature of the New Testament the term Pharisee tended to be merged in the general term Jew. Thus Paul, in his elaborate argument about the failure of the Law, in the Epistle to the Romans, was really attacking the Pharisaic conception of the Torah, but he only speaks of Jews, and of Israel as a whole. So, too, the Diaspora Jews, from whom he encountered so much opposition (e.g. at Thessalonica,

[1] See my *Christianity in Talmud and Midrash*, where the passages are collected and discussed.

Acts xvii. 5), may not have been, strictly speaking, Pharisees, and might therefore be left out from an attempt to show how Pharisaism is represented in the Acts and Epistles. But no stress can be laid on this, for the opposition, after all, was between Christianity on the one side and a Judaism on the other, of which Pharisaism was the strongest and most highly organised element. The Pharisees, alone amongst Jews, had a carefully thought-out conception of religion, firmly held and unflinchingly practised. Whatever, therefore, is said in the New Testament by way of condemnation of the Jews finds its mark in the Pharisees. If there had been no Pharisees, the Church would have met with little or no opposition.

The attitude of the Church towards the Jews, as represented in the New Testament, was one of increasing hostility as the breach became wider. The breach did not indeed disclose itself all at once, but it was inevitable. By no possibility could Judaism, let alone Pharisaism, be brought into accord with Christianity. From the point of view of the Church, therefore, the Jews were very naturally regarded as the enemy, the people who had rejected Christ and were themselves rejected of God. Although Paul tried to make out some sort of a case for the Jews as a people to whom God had given much, and whom He had not finally cast off (Rom. iii. 1 ff.; xi. 1 ff.), the author of the Fourth Gospel made Jesus say to the Jews : " Ye are of your father the devil " (John viii. 44).

Denunciation of this kind was of course not based on a careful and critical study of the views of those who were denounced. It was rather the expression of a side already chosen, a view already held ; or, if such phrases be thought too weak, it expressed the detestation on the part of men who felt that they had been won to a glorious and sacred cause towards those who tried to defeat that cause, who refused to own its leader, who had indeed rejected and killed him. Such denunciation only gained its significance from the magnitude of the forces arrayed against each other. Its form, the terms of abuse, it derived from the human nature which was quite as strong in the Christian as in the Jew. The New Testament shows the controversy from one side only, as indeed is but natural ; and nothing can be learned from its pages which directly throws fresh light upon the essential meaning of Judaism. But much is to be learned, indirectly, from the study of the controversy, as to why there was a controversy at all, let alone why it was so fierce and unsparing. The conflict between the Pharisees and Jesus had been, in its essence, a conflict between two types of religion, each valid on its own premises, and each having a right to exist, but such that neither could be assimilated to the other. The religion of the Pharisees was expressed in terms of Torah ; its central feature was an Idea, an intellectual as well as moral conception, by means of which it defined and represented the relation of the human soul to God. The religion of Jesus was not expressed in terms of Torah, and did not centre on an Idea. It was the outcome of his own immediate consciousness of God, apart from all forms of thought, apart from all traditional authority.

Now the conflict between Judaism and Christianity was inevitable for much the same reason as before, but it took on a different form because, while Judaism remained as before, the religion of the followers of Jesus was not the same as his own. Their religion was definitely centred in a Person, not in an Idea, and he was that person. The fundamental difference, felt perhaps rather than perceived while Jesus was the antagonist, became at once apparent when belief in him defined the essence of the new religion. The earliest disciples may have supposed that they were still Jews ; but in professing their belief in Christ, they had, whether they knew it or not, changed, so to speak, the centre of gravity of their religion. The ineffectiveness and gradual decline of the Jewish-Christian element in the early Church is a proof of the inherent inconsistency of their attitude. They had to choose, and they thought they could compromise. The Church, as a whole, chose, and never dreamed of compromise. Accordingly, even if the Church had been able to recognise the true meaning of Judaism as a type of religion, it must still have gone its own way and sought its ideal by its own methods. It could never have been a mere modification of Judaism, and if the earliest disciples of Jesus supposed that it could, experience very soon proved that they were mistaken.

The religion which the Church set out to teach was then necessarily a religion founded on Christ ; he was its revealer and teacher. But he was much more than this. He was the Saviour and Redeemer, and the Gospel was not so much the record of what he had said as the " glad tidings " of what he had done. The Christian watch-word from a very early period, perhaps from the beginning, was " Believe on the Lord Jesus, and thou shalt be saved " (Acts xvi. 31, and cp. Acts ii. 38). The fact that Christianity was centred on Christ and not on the Torah, involved the inference that it was in no way confined to the community of Israel, but could be offered to the Gentiles ; and not only could but ought to be so offered. The idea of the mission to the Gentiles was implicit in the teaching of Jesus, though he may not have expressly recognised that it was the natural outcome of what he taught.[1] But very soon after he was gone, the idea of preaching the Gospel to the Gentiles came into the minds of some of his followers (see Acts xi. 20), who at once put it into practice. Paul was not the first to do this, but beyond all comparison he was the greatest. He cut the Church loose from Judaism, and rendered futile the Jewish-Christian compromise. If others before him had made a beginning of preaching

---

[1] The command in Matthew xxviii. 19, "Go ye therefore and make disciples of all the nations " is attributed to Jesus only after the resurrection. If the Evangelist had known of a precept to that effect uttered by Jesus before his death, presumably he would have recorded it. But he showed a true instinct in ascribing that command to Christ, since it necessarily followed from the ground principle of his religion.

the Gospel to the Gentiles, he was the first to grasp the full significance of that new departure ; and he became virtually the founder of the Christian Church, no longer Jewish but universal. We are here concerned only with his attitude towards Judaism, a subject on which his own letters give definite and emphatic testimony. What he says about Judaism is the most detailed presentation of that religion to be found in the New Testament, and calls for careful study accordingly. Whereas Jesus denounced the Pharisees in practice, for various vices and defects, Paul condemned Pharisaism in theory, as being intrinsically harmful because its right of existence was gone. It had fulfilled its function (Gal. iii. 24) and no longer served any useful purpose. It was superseded by the Gospel. Paul's strictures on Judaism have been accepted by Christians ever since as being justified by the facts of the case. Jews, who alone have been in a position to say what were the facts of the case, i.e. in regard to the nature of Judaism, have protested, though in vain, against what they deem a grave misrepresentation of their religion.

The fullest exposition of Paul's theory of Judaism is found in the Epistle to the Romans, where it forms an essential part of the argument which fills up nearly the whole of that Epistle. But it is only a part of the argument. Paul did not set out to explain, to any who might be interested, what Judaism was. His purpose was to interpret the person and work of Christ in relation to the human race as a whole, and the great design of God in relation thereto. Judaism only came in because, until Christ had appeared, the Jews had been the representatives and agents in carrying out the divine purpose. To the Jews were given the oracles of God (Rom. iii. 2). Moreover, Jesus and his first followers, to say nothing of Paul himself, had been Jews ; and, whether Judaism were right or wrong, it had to be reckoned with and in some way disposed of, before the Christian Church could go freely out into the world with the message of the Gospel.

The theory which Paul worked out, and which may be gathered from the Epistle to the Romans supplemented from the other Epistles, had its origin in his own relation to Christ. For him Christ had become the centre of his religion—the risen Lord who had claimed him for his own, who had entered and taken possession of him. " It is no longer I that live, but Christ that liveth in me " (Gal. ii. 20). Christ became to him the clue by which all the dealings of God with the human race were to be interpreted. His appearance on earth meant far more than the life and death of a man of Nazareth ; it marked the end of an old order and the beginning of a new one, in the design which God had intended from the Creation. It was especially " Christ crucified " who, in Paul's thought, had this immense significance. And we shall not perhaps be far wrong if we connect this thought of Christ in Paul's mind with his horror at the state of the Gentile world as he saw it—blind, ignorant and morally vile, as is briefly but vividly suggested in Romans i. 18–32. How could the human race have come into that appalling condition, and what hope was there of delivering them out of it ? Others before Paul had made a beginning of preaching Christ to the Gentiles ; but he was the first to realise what it really meant to do so, that here was the opening of a door of hope, the fulfilling of the divine purpose hitherto undiscerned. The world lay in the grip of sin because the Gentiles, though once they had known God, had turned away from him and given themselves up to idolatry and vile practices (*loc. cit.*). And the Jews also, to whom the ' Law ' had been given, had disobeyed the Law and were thenceforward helpless to save themselves (Rom. iii. 19–20). The very Law itself was given " to cause the trespass to abound " (Rom. v. 20), so that all alike, Jew and Gentile, were shut up under sin (Gal. iii. 22). From this state of bondage deliverance came through Christ, for he died for all (Rom. v. 6) and by his death broke the power of sin over man. The saving power of Christ was apprehended by the sinner through faith in him. A man is justified by faith, not by anything he could do for himself (for he could do nothing to save himself), but by what Christ had done for him, as an act of redeeming love, a free gift of grace, not the recognition of any merit (Rom. v. 12–21).

This was the Gospel which Paul went forth to preach to the Gentile world ; with what results the whole Christian Church is his witness. But he preached it to Jews also and first of all, and the Jews would have none of it. Mainly for two reasons : first, because it was based upon premisses which they did not admit, and secondly because it chose to represent Judaism as something far other than what they knew it to be. From their point of view Paul's theory was fundamentally wrong and definitely unjust ; and while it might offer to Gentiles very much that would be of benefit to them, it offered to Jews nothing that was better than what they had already.

The premisses on which Paul based his whole theory were, of course, the supremacy of Christ as the heaven-sent instrument or agent of God, and the consequent recognition of him as Lord and Master. If he were owned as the final revealer of God, then the Torah was dethroned. The Jew could not accept Christ without disowning the Torah. But why should the Jew abandon the Torah ? He could not do so until he had felt that it was insufficient ; and this he did not feel, nor ever has felt down to the present day, individual cases of conversion apart.

Paul's theory depended on the premiss of the unique significance of Christ. If that were not admitted there could be no acceptance of the theory. But even if that premiss were admitted, the particular conclusion which Paul drew from it, and worked out in his theory, did not necessarily follow from it. Christ might be supreme in spiritual things and yet not have had the special function which Paul's theory assigned to him. It was one thing for Paul to affirm, on the witness of his own experience of communion with the risen Christ, that " Christ was all in all " ; it was quite another thing to affirm that the past history of the human race had been such that the appearance of Christ had the particular significance

which he assigned to it. No inward experience could
establish the truth of that ; it was pure speculation, which
the actual facts of history might confirm or might con-
tradict.

Now the facts of history as they were known to Paul,
the history not of the distant past but of the time in
which he was living, did not by any means fit in with
his theory. He had got all the human race in bondage
under sin, and Christ had come, " in the fulness of time,"
to bring deliverance, to offer salvation through faith.
But the plan did not work as a divinely appointed plan
might be expected to work. The Jews rejected Christ,
and consequently the deliverance in their case was not
effected. The divine plan was held up ; and unless Paul
could find some way of accounting for this apparent
breakdown of the intended arrangement, his whole theory
would go to pieces. It could only be saved, as a theory,
if it could be shown that Judaism was such as to make
the intervention of Christ necessary, and if the Jews
were only prevented from seeing this by their own
blindness and hardness of heart. Judaism, accordingly,
was depicted by him as a religion exclusively of Law,
in which commands were given but no power to fulfil
them, in which failure in respect of even one commandment involved a breach with God which could never
be closed, a system in which the accumulation of precepts
became a heavy burden to the will and the consciousness
of guilt a terror to the conscience (see Rom. x, xi). The
hardening of the Jews, shown in their rejection of Christ,
was the opportunity of the Gentiles ; and though God
had not cast off His people (Rom. xi. 1) they would have
to wait for their salvation " until the fulness of the Gentiles
be come in " (Rom. xi. 25).

Now, if Judaism had really been at all like what Paul
described, it would have become extinct long before
Christ appeared. No people could ever have survived
with such an intolerable religion ; clearly not, because
until Christ came there was under the Law (according
to the theory) no means whatever of deliverance from the

burden of sin. Israel would have been a prey to religious mania. In actual fact, Israel was nothing of the kind; and, also in actual fact, Judaism was widely different from the misshapen phantom conjured up by Paul. He could only evolve that by leaving out essential elements of Judaism, in particular the conscious personal relation of the soul to God through which came strength to do the divine will, and forgiveness for repentance after sin. Paul presented a mere travesty of Judaism, and nothing can ever make his picture of it anything else. To defend it as being possibly true of some obscure school of Pharisees would be futile even if it could be shown that there was such a school. His theory required a judgment upon Judaism as a whole, for it was Judaism as a whole which, according to him, stood in the way of the realisation of the divine plan. Paul's theory did not fit the facts; and, whether by conscious intention or not, the facts had to be distorted to fit the theory. He was not writing as an historian, describing this or that type of religion, this or that development of history. He was expounding a great and overwhelming idea of divine providence, to whose inner meaning the clue was found in Christ. And it is quite conceivable that, being possessed with this idea, he saw not only human history (so far as he knew it), but that Judaism in which he had once lived but which now he had left behind, not as they really were, but as they appeared in the light of his great idea. Judaism, as the religion of Torah to one who believed in Torah, could not appear the same to one who no longer believed in Torah but did passionately believe in Christ. If Paul could have recognised that while the two conceptions were incommensurable yet both were valid, he could still have had a Gospel to preach to the Gentiles, even a Gospel of faith in Christ. As it was, and however he came to do it, he did but set the one conception against the other, and by the light of Christ saw only black shadows in the religion of Torah; with the result that from his day to the present, Judaism has suffered under a cruel injustice, which no protestations on the part of

Paul that " his heart's desire was for Israel that they
might be saved " (Rom. x. 1) have ever in the slightest
degree removed. The Christian Church, as was only
likely, has followed Paul, and even gone beyond him,
as will be shown presently, in condemnation of Judaism ;
and it has maintained that wrong through nineteen
centuries.

Such was the way in which Paul tried to account for
the fact that the Jews rejected Christ, and would not
listen to the Gospel as it was preached to them. That
the Pharisees rejected Christ is not wonderful, considering
that even as he saw them only from the outside so they
saw him only from the outside. Neither came into any
sort of contact with the other through mutual understanding and sympathy. That the Jews would have none
of Paul's gospel is still less wonderful. Paul offered them
a salvation of which they felt no need, recommended
by a theory whose premises they denied, and involving
a conception of their own religion which they repudiated.
They had their own ideas about the dealings of God with
the human race ; and they found ample room within those
ideas for a firm belief in the righteousness of God and
His saving mercy towards that human race which He
had created. They saw the moral corruption of the
Gentile world as clearly as Paul did, but they had no
reason to adopt his theory with respect to it. That
whole theory was nothing but a speculation of his own ;
the offered deliverance was as unreal as the alleged
universal bondage under sin. Paul's theory was only
his reading of facts which were patent to them as well
as to him, and which they read in a wholly different
way   He might have something to say to Gentiles, and
Jews have always admitted that the work of Christianity
in the Gentile world has been a powerful means of
spreading the knowledge of God, and bringing light into
the dark places of the earth ; but Christianity, whether
preached by Paul or the Church since his day, had not,
and has not, anything to offer to Judaism of which
Judaism stands in vital need. That each would be vastly

the better by learning to appreciate the good in the other is true ; but they can never be reconciled except as equals, and the age-long attempt of Christians to convert the Jews only shows that Christians have not the slightest understanding of the real nature of the case.

There remains to be considered the consequences of the injustice of the Christian view of Judaism as felt by the Jews. Whether or not the Church adopted Paul's theory in all its details, it did take up the attitude of definite hostility to the Jews. But the Church was faced by this difficulty, that its own position depended largely on the witness of Scripture, and according to that Scripture the Jews had been the chosen people of God. That Scripture was the only sacred book which the Church at the first possessed, the only writing to which the Christian missionary could appeal when trying to convince the Gentile. How could the Jews be wrong when they were only doing what in that Scripture they were commanded to do ? Yet the Jews were wrong, according to the Christian view, wrong now whatever they might have been before Christ came. The Church solved this problem by an act of sheer usurpation, boldly declaring that Christians and no longer Jews were the true Israel, that the Scriptures belonged of right to the Christians and not to the Jews, and that Christians alone were competent to interpret them, that the real meaning of those Scriptures was a foreshadowing of Christ and the Church, while the Jewish dispensation had been only a temporary order now definitely overthrown. This attitude of the Church does not appear fully defined in the New Testament, but there is plenty of evidence there which points to that result. Paul had distinguished between Israel after the flesh and Israel according to the promise (Rom. ix. 8). The truth which underlay that distinction did not need that Israel should be brought in at all ; it was not an historical but a theological distinction, and only served to contrast active faith with passive prerogative as a ground of religious certitude. It had nothing to do with Israel, and the application of it to Israel was wholly unjustifiable.

So also Paul had used the Scriptures in what may be called a Christian sense, interpreting them to mean something very different from what Jewish teachers read in them. He may not have arrived at the position that only Christians had the right to the Scriptures, but he was far on the way to it. The Church was not slow to follow his lead, and to deny to Israel the possession of her own Scriptures—the right to hold any longer the position which those Scriptures had declared to be hers.

This policy may have been, or may have seemed to be, right in the eyes of those who were out to preach the Gospel to the Gentile world. It may have appeared to be justified by the alleged failure of Judaism and the wicked obstinacy of the Jews. Yet one might have hoped that the Christian conscience, presumably enlightened by the Gospel, would have refused to countenance that policy. Or had the Church already forgotten the injunction : " Do unto others as ye would that they should do unto you " ?

But if this act of usurpation could seem to be warranted on Christian premisses, those premisses had no validity for Jews. They could only regard the policy of the Church as a violent outrage, perpetrated against their religion and themselves who professed that religion. Paul refers in his epistles to the opposition of the Jews to his preaching (2 Cor. xi. 25-6, and cp. Acts xiv. 19, xvii. 5, xviii. 12). Is it wonderful that the Jews should oppose a man who preached as Paul did, against all that to them was sacred ? Were they not right to defend it against insult and injury ? What ground had they, or could they have, for admitting the superiority of a religion which was commended to them by such methods ? Were they likely to be persuaded to own the supremacy of one whose followers proclaimed the failure of the Jewish religion wherever they came, and who himself had set them the example ? The Jews were only human after all ; and if they showed a good deal less than saintly forbearance under severe provocation, it is not for the Christian Church, which inflicted on them that provocation, to hold up its hands in horror and be shocked at the violence of the Jews against its holy apostles.

All this, shameful story as it is, belongs to the subject of the presentation of Judaism in the New Testament, and is necessary in order that those who read only the New Testament may know something of the other side of the picture. It all goes to confirm what was said at the beginning of this chapter, that Judaism and Christianity are two incommensurable types of religion, of which neither starts from the premises of the other, uses its terms or reaches its conclusion. There need be no opposition between them ; but, if there is to be opposition, it can never be ended by the conquest or suppression of one by the other. Their adherents may argue for ever against each other, but neither will ever convince the other. They may persecute each other, though Christians alone have been in a position to use this method, but they will never succeed. How many millions of Jews have been slaughtered by Christian hands, harried and afflicted by Christian rulers, and yet the Jews remain, unconquered and unconquerable !

CHAPTER IX

CONCLUSION

In the foregoing chapters I have described, to the best
of my ability, the origin, the main principles and the
leading conceptions of Pharisaism, and have shown how
it was distinguished from the special type of Judaism
represented in the Apocalyptic and other Apocryphal
writings, also how it was related to the earliest form of
Christianity. If I have succeeded to any extent in what
I have tried to do, then the reader ought to have acquired
some fair knowledge of who the Pharisees were, what
their religion meant to them, and how they expressed it.

In this concluding chapter I shall take the general
conception arrived at by the lines of study already
followed, and try to form some estimate of the significance
of Pharisaism as a factor in the religious development of
the human race. In this estimate I include Rabbinism
along with that which bore the name of Pharisaism, since,
as has been shown, there was no difference of principle
between them. If a distinction be drawn it would only
be that Pharisaism was the forerunner, or better, the
parent, of Rabbinism ; the latter only developed the
principles of the former, and arrived at results greater
in amount but not different in kind from those reached
by the Pharisees. Rabbinism was implicit in Pharisaism.
Given Ezra and the Sopherim, and the Talmud was
bound to come, sooner or later.

That Pharisaism had a significance as an element in
the religious development of mankind is not denied by
anyone. For if Judaism was a preparation for Chris-

tianity, as is generally assumed, then that preparation depended largely, though not wholly, upon Pharisaism. It is true that Christianity rejected what was especially distinctive of the Pharisees, namely the Halachah, and expressed its disapproval of them and their ways in terms of remarkable severity. It owed much more to the Apocalyptic type of Judaism than to the Pharisaic, so far as immediate influence was concerned. But it was the Pharisees who developed the Synagogue ; and beyond any question Christianity owed a great deal to the Synagogue as an institution whereby religion was fostered on lines of personal piety, without priest and without ritual. It was the Pharisees, or more particularly the Scribes, who collected and arranged the Hebrew Scriptures, without which Christianity would have lacked its chief means of proving to the Gentiles the truth of its message. And the general ethical teaching taken over by Christianity was certainly Pharisaic, though not exclusively so. The Judaism out of which Christianity arose was by no means entirely Pharisaic, and Christianity was doubtless influenced by all the various types of Judaism which it found in existence. Nevertheless, Pharisaism was the one which had most of self-supporting vitality, and could therefore exercise the most powerful influence, directly or indirectly, upon Christianity. It was a living Judaism which gave birth to Christianity, and its life was strongest in Pharisaism.

Now if the significance of Pharisaism were really confined to its having enabled Judaism to prepare the way for Christianity, it would necessarily follow that with the rise of Christianity Pharisaism would disappear, or at least lose its vitality and worth as a religion. This is indeed the usual opinion held by Christians ; and, from the Christian point of view, such an opinion is very natural. Paul, as we have seen, tried to provide for the fact of a continued existence of Judaism by his theory that a hardening in part had befallen Israel, which would last until the fulness of the Gentiles had come in (Rom. xi. 25). After all, even Paul could not quite forget what he had felt

and believed about the religion which had once been his
and the people to whom he had once belonged. But the
Church did not adopt his view, and instead took the
line that the day of Judaism was over, and its inheritance given to another. Christ had annulled the authority of the Law, and those who might still cling to the
Law were clinging to a mere phantom. The Jews had
rejected Christ, and that was the end of them ; the loss
of their Temple and the ruin of their land were the evident
signs that God had done with them.

This theory is conclusively shown to be wrong by the
undeniable fact that Judaism, and more particularly
Pharisaism, did not die out either then or since. And
what is more, the rise of Christianity did not injure its
vitality or weaken its validity in the eyes of its adherents.
The terrible suffering inflicted by the two great wars,
those against Vespasian and Hadrian, tried to the utter-
most the faith and endurance of the Jewish people ; but
it did not break their spirit nor awaken any misgiving
as to the validity of that religion which helped them to
stand fast in the evil day. Such misgiving found expression in IV Ezra, and perhaps in other quarters on the
outer fringe of Pharisaism ; but it did not utter the real
mind of the Pharisees. And the proof of that is the fact
that after the Hadrianic persecution, the Rabbis took up
their old task of maintaining and developing the religious
life of their people, with undiminished belief in their
task and trust in God who had appointed it for them.
From that time onward the Jews were for the most part
a people with a burden of sorrowful remembrance ; but
they were also a people of undying hope and unconquerable faith. Such they have continued to be down
to the present day, in spite of all that Christians could
do to convert them, to crush them, to ignore them.
Throughout the whole course of Christian history the
Jews have been present, looked on as unwelcome
intruders on the scene, the obstinate factor which
resisted all attempts to bring it into the Church's scheme
of unity, the stubborn dissenters from her teaching, the

witnesses to testify that there was another side to what
she would have to be a *chose jugée*. They lived on,
whether the Church would or no ; and they lived on
because their religion was to them as true, as real, as
living as it had ever been. Neither Christ nor Paul nor
anyone else had cancelled or destroyed it, whatever
Christians might say. And so it has remained.

Evidently, therefore, the usual answer that Judaism
was the preparation for Christianity and that its work
was done when Christ had appeared, cannot be accepted,
at all events as usually understood. Judaism, Rabbinical
Judaism, is as deeply rooted in the hearts and souls of
its adherents as Christianity in those of Christians. And
that is the only impartial test which can be applied.
Mere assertion of the part of one against the other can
carry no weight. The Christian denial of the validity of
Judaism rests only on Christian premises and, as an
absolute judgment, is worthless. Jews have never denied,
or attempted to deny, the validity of the Christian
religion.[1]

Yet the view that Judaism was a preparation for
Christianity is capable of another meaning beside the
one which has been usually assigned to it. A meaning,
moreover, which takes in both Christianity and the
Judaism which has kept even pace with it, as being both
parts in one great whole, each having there a necessary
place, and neither being the rival of the other or implying
the supersession of the other.

Christianity, in the course of its history, took up and
assimilated many Gentile, and especially Greek, ideas.
To what extent it was influenced by the mystery religions
is uncertain ; but the presence of mystery as an element
in the Christian conception of religion was not derived
from Judaism, except in so far as there is an element of

---

[1] For Jewish views on Christianity see *J.E.* iv. 56–7, and the
references there given. The passage in Maimonides' *Hilc. Melachim*,
xi. 4, must be read in an uncensored text. The British Museum
copy of the *Editio princeps*, *Soncino* 1490 has the passage, but heavily
censored and partly torn away.

mystery in all religion. If it were not original, it was
developed by influences from Gentile, not from Jewish
thought. The sacrificial and sacerdotal elements in
Christianity were no doubt developed from the use made
of the Old Testament by the Church ; but they would
not have been developed at all, unless they had satisfied
Gentile needs, and harmonised with previous Gentile
usage. The Judaism which gave birth to Christianity
regarded priesthood and sacrifice solely as adjuncts of
the Temple, having no place or function in the religion
of the common life. Pharisaism was never at any time
a priestly and sacrificial religion. Christian theology was
almost entirely shaped by applying Greek, and afterwards
Latin, thought to its original concepts. To such Gentile
elements Christianity no doubt owes much of its value
as a means of developing a real world-religion. The
rapidity with which it expanded, and the completeness
of its final triumph over Paganism show how well it
fitted itself for its great task, and with what success it
discharged it, so far as it has yet gone. To have rooted
out Paganism and replaced it by a religion of infinite
spiritual possibilities was an achievement than which no
greater has been seen on earth. Paul saw only the
beginning of it, indeed himself made the first real beginning of it ; but in idea he saw the whole of it, and saw
it as part of the design of God for the redemption of the
human race. No one who believed in God at all would
question the truth of Paul's prophetic interpretation.

It was part, and a necessary part, of the function of
the missionaries of the Church to take the Gospel right
out into the Gentile world, preach it there and defend it
there, expose it to all the risks of adverse influences
which might corrupt its purity or confuse its thought.
They went forth trusting in the inherent power of the
Gospel they preached to maintain itself and prevail over
such evil influences, being under no delusion as to the
character of the Gentile world which they sought to
redeem. They learned to build up the Church out of the
best that the Gentile world had to offer ; and only so

could they make it able to fulfil its purpose. This is not the place to dwell upon the defects and failures of the Church in the course of its long history. Whatever Christianity has done, and whatever it is now, is the expression of the whole movement summed up in the conception of the Church.

Now it is evident that the introduction of Christianity into the Gentile world was an extremely dangerous operation. I do not mean personally dangerous to its advocates, though, of course, it was that. I mean dangerous to the Gospel itself, from contact with, and possible corruption by, the influence of religion and morality of a lower order than itself. Christianity boldly assimilated much that it found in Gentile thought and practice, and turned it to higher use. But it also refused much and condemned much. And while it variously modified or abandoned some of its original Jewish conceptions, and though it definitely dissociated itself from Judaism, it never wholly cut the roots of its Jewish origin. Christianity began as a spiritual monotheism, and it has never lost that character, though it has introduced qualifications into its idea of monotheism for which Judaism is not responsible. Moreover, Christianity took over as its sacred book the Hebrew Scriptures; and though it interpreted these in a Christian sense and applied their teaching in non-Jewish ways, still those Scriptures formed the basis of the Church's teaching and they remained for Christians the Word of God. The Church never dreamed of disowning them; and however much might be taken up of Gentile contributions to Christian thought and practice, it never sufficed to overcome the regulating and restraining influence of the Hebrew Scriptures. If that restraining and regulating influence had been absent, if the Church had cut herself off from Judaism as completely as she wished to do and thought she had done, it is at least conceivable that she would have amalgamated completely with the religions of the Gentile world. In that case, it is safe to say that Christianity would have stood on a much lower level in the scale of absolute religion than it does now, and would hardly, if at all, have been able to claim the rank of a world-religion. Apart from the original creative impulse, which was neither Jewish nor Gentile, but individual and personal to its Founder, it can hardly be denied that the Jewish inheritance which the Church took over has been of immense importance in guarding Christianity from the danger of its immersion in the Gentile world.

All this is admissible on the usual theory that Judaism was a preparation for Christianity. The Scriptures were part of that preparation. I go on to a further development of the thought which I believe to be no less true, and no less important, but which cannot be reconciled with the usual theory. Christianity is a religion based upon faith in a Person, and the main theme of its message is the offer of salvation through faith in Christ. It placed, and places, faith before everything else. This is shown, if it needs to be shown, by the fact that the condition of membership in the Church was a confession of faith, which at a very early period took the form of a series of articles of belief, in short a Creed. The Creed became the bond of unity which held the Church together. It is, of course, perfectly true that the Church always taught a pure morality, a holy life. But she did not insist on this with the same vigour with which she insisted on right belief. No one was ever burnt at the stake for being an evil liver. In other words, the doing of the will of God took the second place and not the first amongst the objects to which the Church directed her efforts. This is a perfectly valid theory, and the Church was entirely consistent in the way in which she worked it out. Judged by its results it has been the means of incalculable benefit to mankind.

Now Judaism in general, and Pharisaism in particular, was a religion which put the doing of God's will in the first place, and faith in the second place ; faith, moreover, not in a Person but in God Himself. Faith, therefore, in Judaism kept its original meaning and never became such that any creed could express it. Judaism has never had a creed, though Maimonides tried to devise one. But Judaism, since the Pharisees came on the scene, has had the Halachah, which was the definition of the will of God. The Halachah is the analogue of the Creed. Whether its authors succeeded in fully defining the divine will is not now the question. The point is that for them the doing of the divine will was the first and foremost essential of religion, whatever else might come after it. Pharisaism and Rabbinism accordingly took on a form peculiar to itself, and widely different from that assumed by Christianity. It was an interpretation of the same spiritual realities as those which were present to Christian minds, but it reasoned from different premises and stated its conclusions in different terms. It was a different religion, and not capable of being harmonised with Christianity, but it was in every way just as valid, had just as good a right to exist. As in fact it has existed, and does still exist.

It has been admitted that Christianity was better qualified to bring good to the Gentile world than Judaism was. That Gentile world being what it was, a religion with the peculiar adaptive power of Christianity was the best type of religion for the purpose. Presumably that was why Christianity appeared at all, and developed on the lines which it actually followed. But that is not to say that the truth for which Judaism stood became untrue when Christianity appeared, nor that as an independent type of religion it lost what value it had previously possessed. In fact it did neither. And, what is more, it has kept its vitality alongside of Christianity as a continual reminder that no one religion, and not that particular religion, exhausted all the possibilities of revelation, summed up the whole of the divine purpose towards mankind. Christianity held up one ideal, Judaism held up another ; and both ideals were visions of what God had shown to human souls. If we may with reverence speak of the divine intention as shown in the religious training of mankind, may we not say that that intention needed for its fulfilment *both* these religions

and not one only ? This contention is not met by saying
that Christianity adopted the best in the Jewish religion
and combined it with the best in Gentile religion, becoming
thereby the one supreme world religion. My point is
that Christianity, having taken over what it did from
both these sources and becoming thereby what it is seen
to be in history, still needed Judaism as its correlative
term, because Judaism represented religious elements
which were not represented in Christianity, and which
were incompatible with Christianity. Whatever part
Christianity was intended to play in the divine design
for mankind, that part could only be played if there
were present also a living Judaism, partly to guard Christianity from complete assimilation to Gentile religion,
and partly to maintain and represent other aspects of
revelation beside those which Christianity offered. If
Judaism had died out, or had succumbed to Christianity,
the whole effect of its continued presence in the world
would obviously have been lost. Christianity itself would
necessarily have failed to do what it was appointed to
do, if its appearance in the world had any meaning, any
relation to the divine plan. Christian efforts to convert
the Jews or destroy Judaism were in reality attempts
against her own life, since they were efforts to suppress
a form of religion other than her own and equally necessary with her own if her own task were to be fulfilled.
The Church regarded a living Judaism as a continual
danger. A dead Judaism would have been a fatal
disaster.

Still speaking in terms of the divine plan, we may say
that both Judaism and Christianity were necessary for
the work of raising and spiritualising the religion of the
human race ; Christianity as the immediate agent in that
work, and Judaism as safeguarding elements in religion
of which Christianity could not for her immediate purpose make use, but which would find their application,
" When the fulness of the Gentiles had come in "; in other
words, when the world was ready for them. Judaism
waited, and still waits, not because of any " hardening

in part " which has befallen her, but because the best she has to give will only find acceptance when the preparation of Christianity has done its work, and the world is ready for a religion which will at last unite the imperishable elements of both its forerunners. This is what I mean by the larger whole in which both Judaism and Christianity are taken up, and in which each has its necessary part to play.

Judaism is a reasoned attempt to discern and interpret the fundamental spiritual realities, and it stated its results in terms of Torah. Christianity is another reasoned attempt to discern and interpret those same spiritual realities, and it stated its results in terms of Christ. As the standards were of a wholly different order, in the one case an Idea and in the other case a Person, so the terms in which the results were stated in the one case differed widely from those in which the results were stated in the other. But both were contemplating the same spiritual realities ; and each saw what the other saw, though it did not describe that in the same way, nor draw from it the same conclusions. Each, therefore, has an independent right of existence ; and while the adherents of each may, as they naturally would, find more satisfaction for their own spiritual needs in their own type of religion, neither is entitled to deny the validity of the other.[1] Neither the one nor the other can establish a claim to be the absolute religion. Perhaps an absolute religion is not possible, but the claim of any existing religion to be absolute is not proved merely by its own assertion. If the claim be put forward by or on behalf of Christianity, it is met by the question which, out of all the varying types of Christianity, is the true one ? If one of these be the absolute religion, it must establish its claim against all the rest, who have not so far admitted it. And even while the Church was

[1] On this whole idea, see an essay by the present writer already referred to, in the *Hibbert Journal* for January 1923, entitled " The Fundamentals of Religion as Interpreted by Christianity and Rabbinical Judaism."

undivided, and could still claim with some justification to represent Christianity as a whole, its principle of *nulla salus extra ecclesiam* was only valid for itself, except in a sense which it did not intend. For, as the Church understood *salus*, there certainly was no *salus*, and no desire for it, *extra ecclesiam*. As an argument against the validity of Judaism, or any other non-Christian religion, it is merely futile.

Judaism has continued to exist from the days of Paul to the present time as a religion by which Jews have lived and for which they have died. It has been to them as true, real and effective a means of expressing their relation with God as Christianity has been to Christians. It has afforded them all that a living religion could afford. It has done this by its own intrinsic power, felt and owned in Jewish hearts, steadfastly maintained there in spite of all the temptations to apostasy presented by persecution, and the varied ill-treatment dealt out by an unfriendly world. Christians had their experience of persecution under Decius and Diocletian, and very bitter they found it. Yet all that is but a trifle in comparison with what they have inflicted on Jews. The Christian Church lived through the fiery trial under Diocletian and found safety under Constantine. She did so through the heroism of faith, for which she rightly honoured her martyrs and confessors. The Jews have had centuries of Diocletian and have not yet, except here and there, found their Constantine. But they, too, have endured through the heroism of faith, for which they also honour their martyrs and confessors. What is true in the one case is true in the other. If Christianity is vindicated as a living religion, a true revelation to the human soul of divine realities and a true interpretation of those realities to human thought and apprehension, so in like manner Judaism is vindicated as another true revelation of those same divine realities, another true interpretation of them to human thought and apprehension. To object that there cannot be two revelations differing in form and contents yet equally valid is to beg the question. Here are these two ; and the same criterion by which alone the validity of the one can be established, viz. the test of experience in life and thought, will establish the validity of the other.

That Rabbinical Judaism and Christianity are fundamentally irreconcilable, differing both in their standard of reference and in the terms by which their contents are described, is a fact plain to be seen by any competent and impartial student of both religions. But the meaning of that fact only comes into view when brought into relation with such a conception of the divine plan as has been suggested above. The fulfilment of that design required the presence and influence of *two* types of religion, not one only. It would have failed if the one religion could have been superseded by the other. Therefore the two types had to be mutually incommensurable, though not necessarily antagonistic. The hostility arose only through human inability on each side to read the deeper meaning of the relation between the two contrasted opposites. But it was surely no accident which produced these two types of religion, of which neither could be changed into the other, and neither could convert or destroy the other. Both were necessary and both in due time appeared in the world. Judaism was long anterior to Christianity ; and Pharisaism, with which alone we are at present concerned, had been in existence, in principle if not in name, for several centuries before Christianity arose. In the course of those centuries Judaism, under the influence of the Pharisees, was being moulded into the form which would make it best able to discharge the function assigned to it in the divine plan. It was developed into a religion which would be able to maintain its vitality and individual character when it should be called on to meet the difficulties and dangers of co-existence with Christianity. Pharisaism, therefore, developed to the fullest extent the principle of faithfulness to the divine will, and took the Torah as its supreme revelation. The Pharisees were the forerunners of the Rabbis, and it was the Rabbis, as contemporary with Christians through the centuries, who had to meet the difficulties and dangers of the co-presence of the two religions. Theirs was the supremely hard task of keeping Judaism a living religion, true to its own vision of divine reality, in spite of all the efforts of a scornful or hostile world and a persecuting Church. Their defence against being borne down in the struggle was partly the fact itself that their religion was of a fundamentally different type from Christianity. The younger religion had nothing to offer them better or truer than what their own religion already possessed. From a worldly point of view they had everything to gain from accepting Christianity; from the spiritual point of view they had nothing to gain. It was so even in the earliest days of the Church; and, as the centuries passed by, and the Church went further and further along the path of being " all things to all men," she had less and less that could induce a Jew to prefer her religion to his own.

But the defence of Judaism against the disintegrating influence of Christianity was not only in the inherent difference of its character as a religion. The whole system of the Halachah acted both as a bond to keep the Jewish community together, and also as an external protective covering, within which the spirit of Judaism could maintain its strength and vitality. Without the Halachah it is hardly conceivable that Judaism should have survived through all the strain and stress of persecution which fill the centuries of its history in Christian times. The Halachah was thus an indispensable part of the equipment of Judaism for its task, the " armour of God whereby it should be able to stand fast in the evil day; and having done all, to stand." That has certainly been its effect.

Now the Halachah was especially the creation of the Pharisees. They laid down the principles on which it was formed; and while it is perfectly true that the amount of defined Halachah in the Mishnah and the Talmud is far greater than what was already in existence in the time of Jesus, yet there is no difference of principle between them. The Rabbis worked out more fully what the Pharisees had begun. What they both did was to build up a strong wall of protection within which Judaism might be safe, fearing no danger that might threaten it from any quarter. That they were conscious of the deeper meaning of what they did I by no means maintain. They had their own conception of religion, and they developed it consistently and faithfully. But, looking back, that deeper meaning can be plainly seen, and it is this: that the creation and elaboration of the Halachah denote the special preparation of Judaism for the hard and dangerous task which was awaiting it in the future. That is the meaning of what is usually described as the degradation of Judaism, at the hands of the Pharisees, into a barren formalism, the descent from prophetic freedom to organised hypocrisy. A greater misreading of history it is scarcely possible to imagine. Pharisaism was the application of prophetic teaching to life, and such the Pharisees understood it to be. But, beyond and above what they consciously understood, was the deeper meaning of their work as making ready their religion to endure its age-long martyrdom in the coming time. They had their faults—who has not ? Their system was not perfect ; they themselves knew well the moral and spiritual dangers to which its adherents were exposed, and they were not always successful in averting those dangers. But they did their work in their day, in spite of the sneers and ill-will of the Gentiles ; the Rabbis carried on what the Pharisees had begun and, through the labours of both, Judaism was carried safely down the ages.

What form its task may assume in ages yet to come, it is vain to speculate. But when the time shall come when Christianity shall have done all it can do, under the forms and conditions which it has hitherto adopted, there will then be a Judaism able and ready to offer its imperishable treasure, kept safe through the ages, to a world which will no longer scorn. And at last the two great religions, which will have each accomplished that for which God made them two and not one, will join in His service, and side by side utter the prayers and praises and inspire the lives of His children.

To have begun the preparation for that " far-off divine event " is the true significance of Pharisaism.

INDICES

I. GENERAL INDEX.

Abelson, J., 150 n.
Akabja b. Mahalalel, 108 n.
Akiba, 45, 52, 73, 84, 85, 124,
179, 189.
Alexandra (Salampsio), 46 n, 97.
Alkimus, 25.
Am-ha-aretz, 31, 32, 34, 35,
119
Antigonos of Socho, 23.
Antiochus III, 24.
Antiochus Epiphanes, 28, 49.
Apocalyptic literature, 180–1,
182–5, 190–3.
Attributes, the divine, 154.

Bacher, W., 78 n, 85 n.
Baḥya, 34, 157.
Bousset, W., 12.
Büchler, A., 51 n, 155 n, 164.

Charles, Canon, 180, 186, 193.
Church, the, its attitude towards
Judaism, 195, 209, 213, 221,
222–4.
Cocheba (Simeon) Bar, 45, 52,
82, 159, 179, 187, 189.
Conscience, under the Halachah,
120–2.
Corban, 205.
Creed, the Christian, 231.
Chwolson, D., 12 n, 13 n, 47 n.

Daniel, book of, 182–3.
Derenbourg, J., 46 n.

Dogma, the analogue of Halachah, 105–6, 232.

Eerdmans, 14 n.
Eliezer b. Horkenos, 108 n, 109.
Essenes, the, 51.
Evil, the problem of, 163–9.
Ewald, H., 13.
Excommunication, 108 n.
Ezra, 18, 19, 20, 21, 55–9, 102.

Gamliel I, 72 n.
Gamliel II, 122.
Geiger, A., 15.
Gemara, 84.
Gezeroth, 61.
God, Pharisaic conception of,
151–4.
Grätz, H., 15, 26 n, 36 n.

Ḥaberim, 31, 33.
Haggadah, 71, 78–82.
Halachah, 71, 72 n, 73–8, 80, 83,
84, 85, 86, 87, 105, 106, 107,
107–14, 116–23, 131, 138,
144, 145, 162, 185, 186, 193,
194, 195, 196, 205, 206, 207,
208, 226, 232, 237, 238.
Halevy, I, 36 n.
Hasidim, 27, 28, 33, 35, 51, 193.
Hellenism, 23, 25, 28, 36, 49.
Herod, 45, 49–51.
Hilgenfeld, A., 13.
Hillel, 72 n, 84, 109.
Hypocrisy, 116–19.

242

II. RABBINICAL PASSAGES CITED.

III. OLD TESTAMENT PASSAGES CITED.

IV. NEW TESTAMENT PASSAGES CITED.